A CULTURAL HISTORY OF MARRIAGE

VOLUME 1

A Cultural History of Marriage
General Editor: Joanne M. Ferraro

Volume 1
A Cultural History of Marriage in Antiquity
Edited by Karen Klaiber Hersch

Volume 2
A Cultural History of Marriage in the Medieval Age
Edited by Joanne M. Ferraro and Frederik Pedersen

Volume 3
A Cultural History of Marriage in the Renaissance and Early Modern Age
Edited by Joanne M. Ferraro

Volume 4
A Cultural History of Marriage in the Age of Enlightenment
Edited by Edward Behrend-Martínez

Volume 5
A Cultural History of Marriage in the Age of Empires
Edited by Paul Puschmann

Volume 6
A Cultural History of Marriage in the Modern Age
Edited by Christina Simmons

A CULTURAL HISTORY OF MARRIAGE

IN ANTIQUITY

Edited by Karen Klaiber Hersch

BLOOMSBURY ACADEMIC
LONDON • NEW YORK • OXFORD • NEW DELHI • SYDNEY

BLOOMSBURY ACADEMIC
Bloomsbury Publishing Plc
50 Bedford Square, London, WC1B 3DP, UK
1385 Broadway, New York, NY 10018, USA

BLOOMSBURY, BLOOMSBURY ACADEMIC and the Diana logo are trademarks
of Bloomsbury Publishing Plc

First published in Great Britain 2020

Copyright © Bloomsbury Publishing, 2020

Karen Klaiber Hersch has asserted her right under the Copyright, Designs and
Patents Act, 1988, to be identified as Editor of this work.

Cover image © Coin of Ptolemy I and Berenice I, Ptolemaic kingdom of Egypt,
3rd century BC © The Print Collector/Alamy Stock Photo

All rights reserved. No part of this publication may be reproduced or transmitted
in any form or by any means, electronic or mechanical, including photocopying,
recording, or any information storage or retrieval system, without prior
permission in writing from the publishers.

Bloomsbury Publishing Plc does not have any control over, or responsibility for,
any third-party websites referred to or in this book. All internet addresses given
in this book were correct at the time of going to press. The author and publisher
regret any inconvenience caused if addresses have changed or sites have ceased
to exist, but can accept no responsibility for any such changes.

A catalogue record for this book is available from the British Library.

A catalog record for this book is available from the Library of Congress.

ISBN: HB: 978-1-3500-0180-0
       Set: 978-1-3500-0191-6

Series: The Cultural Histories Series

Typeset by Integra Software Services Pvt. Ltd.
Printed and bound in Great Britain

To find out more about our authors and books visit www.bloomsbury.com
and sign up for our newsletters.

CONTENTS

LIST OF FIGURES vi
CONTRIBUTORS ix
GENERAL EDITOR'S PREFACE *Joanne M. Ferraro* xi

Introduction
Karen Klaiber Hersch 1

1 Courtship and Ritual
 Katherine Wasdin 23

2 Religion: The Gods and Rituals of Greek and Roman Weddings
 Matthew P. J. Dillon 37

3 State and Law
 Matthew J. Perry 59

4 The Ties That Bind
 Katariina Mustakallio 77

5 The Family Economy: Consent and Consensuality in Ancient Greek and Roman Marriage
 Judith P. Hallett 89

6 Love, Sex, and Sexuality: Marriage: The Myth of Intimate Strangers
 Vered Lev Kenaan 97

7 Breaking Vows
 Eva Cantarella 113

8 Representation
 Noelle Zeiner-Carmichael 125

NOTES 147
BIBLIOGRAPHY 178
INDEX 194

FIGURES

INTRODUCTION

I.1   Scene with Andromache, Astyanax, and Hector, Apulian red-figure column-crater, 370–360 BCE. Museo Nazionale of the Palazzo Jatta. Wikimedia Commons.   4

I.2   *Odysseus and Penelope*, 1802, Johann Heinrich Wilhelm Tischbein (1751–1829). Private collection. Wikimedia Commons.   5

I.3   *Penelope and the Suitors*, 1912, John William Waterhouse (1849–1917). Aberdeen Art Gallery and Museums. Wikimedia Commons.   6

I.4   Scene of Medea killing her child, Campanian red-figure amphora, Ixion Painter, 330 BCE. Louvre Museum. Wikimedia Commons.   8

I.5   *The Anger of Achilles*, 1819, Jacques-Louis David (1748–1845). Kimbell Art Museum, Fort Worth. Wikimedia Commons.   9

I.6   *Dido and Aeneas* (Venus and Mars), fresco from House of the Citharist, Pompeii, first century CE. National Archaeological Museum of Naples (inv. 112282). Wikimedia Commons.   12

I.7   Sardonyx cameo depicting Livia with the bust of the deified Augustus, first century CE. Kunsthistorisches Museum, Vienna. Wikipedia.   17

I.8   Roman bas relief of Claudius and Agrippina, Sebasteion of Claudius, first century CE. Aphrodisias Archaeological Museum, Caria, Turkey. Alamy Stock Photo.   18

I.9   *The Gemma Claudia*, depicting (left) Emperor Claudius and Agrippina the Younger, and (right) Germanicus and Agrippina the Elder. Roman, first century CE. Kunsthistorisches Museum, Vienna. Wikimedia Commons.   19

I.10   Cameo showing Nero flanked by Augustus and Livia, first century CE. Hermitage Museum. Wikimedia Commons.   19

I.11   Fragment from the front of a sarcophagus, married couple with Concordia, Roman, second CE. British Museum. Wikimedia Commons.   21

COURTSHIP AND RITUAL

1.1   Detail from a terracotta *lebes gamikos* attributed to the Wedding Painter, *c.* 430–420 BCE. De Agostini / G. Dagli Orti via Getty Images.   27

FIGURES   vii

1.2   Terracotta lekythos (oil flask) attributed to the Amasis Painter, *c*. 550–530
      BCE. Dea Picture Library/De Agostini via Getty Images.   29

1.3   Fragment of a *loutrophoros* depicting the preparations of a bride, Phiale
      Painter, 430–425 BCE. Julia Bradford Huntington James Fund and Museum
      purchase with funds donated by contribution, Museum of Fine Arts Boston,
      10.223. Photo: © 2018 Museum of Fine Arts, Boston, Massachusetts.   30

1.4   Detail from the Aldobrandini Wedding, from Rome, Esquiline Hill,
      27 BCE–14 CE, detached fresco. Biblioteca Apostolica Vaticana,
      Vatican Museums, Rome, Italy, Cat. 79631. Photo: Alberto Pizzoli/AFP/
      Getty Images.   32

1.5   Wedding scene (*dextrarum iunctio*), detail from a Roman sarcophagus,
      second century CE. Museo Nazionale Romano Palazzo Massimo Alle
      Terme, Rome, Italy. Photo: DeAgostini/Getty Images.   34

1.6   Fresco from the Villa of the Mysteries, detail of young woman in bridal
      yellow arranging her hair, while a cupid holds the mirror, second half of
      first century BCE. Pompeii, Italy. Photo: Werner Forman/Universal Images
      Group/Getty Images.   36

RELIGION

2.1   Athenian red-figure *loutrophoros* showing details of wedding rituals. Boston
      Museum of Fine Arts, 03.802.   46

2.2   Roman marble sarcophagus, *c*. 180 CE, showing a goddess between the
      couple being married, with a small flaming altar in front. The "Belvedere
      sarcophagus." Vatican Museum, Belvedere Court 38. Alamy Stock Photo.   49

STATE AND LAW

3.1   Scarab commemorating the marriage of Egyptian King Amenhotep III
      and Queen Tiye, *c*. 1390–1352 BCE. Metropolitan Museum of Art,
      10.130.1643. Public Domain, CC0.   61

3.2   Law Code of Babylonian King Hammurabi, *c*. 1792–1750 BCE. Louvre.
      Public Domain, CC0 3.0.   63

3.3   Marriage contract from late period Egypt, *c*. 380–343 BCE. Metropolitan
      Museum of Art, 35.4.1a, b. Public Domain, CC0.   64

3.4   Marriage contract from Hellenistic Egypt, 285–247 BCE. Metropolitan
      Museum of Art, 27.254a, b. Public Domain, CC0.   69

3.5   Military diploma granted to Roman soldier upon his discharge (confirming
      the veteran's Roman citizenship, including the right of *conubium*), *c*. 149
      CE. Metropolitan Museum of Art, 23.160.32a, b. Public Domain, CC0.   71

LOVE, SEX, AND SEXUALITY

6.1 The birth of Aphrodite from a shell. Eros or Himeros flutters by her side. A detail from an Attic red-figure pelike, fourth century BCE. The Archeological Museum of Thessaloniki. Alamy Stock Photo.   98

6.2 *Apollo and Daphne*, 1908, John William Waterhouse (1849–1917). Private Collection. Wikimedia Commons.   106

6.3 The abduction of Persephone by Hades, detail from Amphipolis mosaic, Macedonia, fourth century BCE. Alamy Stock Photo.   107

6.4 *The Abduction of the Sabine Women*, 1634–1635, Nicolas Poussin (1594–1665). Metropolitan Museum of Art. Wikimedia Commons.   108

6.5 The birth/creation of Pandora, Attic red-figure krater, fifth century BCE. Ashmolean Museum. Alamy Stock Photo.   110

REPRESENTATION

8.1 Black-figure hydria depicting a wedding procession, Lysippides-Andokides Group, Greek, *c.* 520 BCE. Walters Art Museum. Wikimedia Commons.   128

8.2 Detail from an Attic red-figure pyxis, Marlay Painter, 440–430 BCE. British Museum. Wikimedia Commons.   129

8.3 Woman spinning, detail from an Attic white-ground oinochoe, Byrgos Painter, *c.* 490 BCE. British Museum. Wikimedia Commons.   136

8.4 *Admetus and Alcestis*, Roman painting, first century CE. Pompeii, Naples National Archaeological Museum. Wikimedia Commons.   139

8.5 *Arria and Paetus*, Pierre Lepautre (1659–1744). Louvre. Wikimedia Commons.   140

8.6 *Laudatio Turiae*, marble, late first century BCE. Epigraphic Museum of the Baths of Diocletian, Rome. Wikimedia Commons.   142

8.7 Scene of a *dextrarum iunctio, Sarcophagus of the Brothers, c.* 250 CE. Naples National Archaeological Museum. Wikimedia Commons.   145

8.8 Sestertius showing betrothal of Marcus Aurelius to Faustina the Younger, 139 CE.   145

CONTRIBUTORS

Eva Cantarella has been Professor of Roman Law and Ancient Greek Law in the Law School of the University of Milan. She has taught as a visiting professor in the Global Law School Program of the Law School of the University of New York and in other American and European universities. She is the author of twenty-six books, including *Secondo natura. La bisessualità nel mondo antico* (1995; published in English as *Bisexuality in the Ancient World*, 1992); co-author with Andrew Lear of *Images of Greek Pederasty: Boys were their Gods* (2008); *Non sei più mio padre, Il conflitto tra genitori e figli nel mondo antico* (2016); and *Come uccidere il padre, Genitori e figli da Roma a oggi* (2017).

Matthew Dillon (PhD, University of New England, Australia, 1993) is Professor of Classics and Ancient History at the University of New England, Australia. He is the author of *Pilgrims and Pilgrimage in Ancient Greece* (1997; translated as PROSKYNHTES KAI IERA PROSKYNHMATA STHN ARXAIA ELLADA, 2001); *Girls and Women in Classical Greek Religion* (2002); *The Ancient Greeks in their Own Words* (2002); *Omens and Oracles: Divination in Classical Greece* (2017); co-author with Lynda Garland of *Ancient Greece* (2010; third edition, *The Ancient Greeks*, 2012); *Ancient Rome* (2015, second edition).

Judith P. Hallett is Professor of Classics and Distinguished Scholar-Teacher at the University of Maryland, College Park, holds a BA in Latin from Wellesley College, and an AM and PhD in Classical Philology from Harvard University. She has published widely in the areas of Latin language and literature; women, the family, and sexuality in Greco-Roman antiquity; and the study and reception of classics in the Anglophone world. A former Blegen Visiting Scholar in the Department of Classics at Vassar College and Suzanne Deal Booth Resident Scholar at the Center for Intercollegiate Studies in Rome, she has also held fellowships from the Mellon Foundation and the National Endowment for the Humanities. A 2013 collection of essays—*Domina Illustris: Latin Literature, Gender and Reception*, edited by Donald Lateiner, Barbara Gold, and Judith Perkins—celebrates her academic career.

Karen Klaiber Hersch (PhD, Rutgers University, 2002) is Associate Professor in the Department of Greek and Roman Classics at Temple University and was the recipient of an Arthur Ross Pre-Doctoral Fellowship from the American Academy in Rome (2000–2001). Her research interests include all aspects of Roman religion, history, women, and imperial literature. She is the author of *The Roman Wedding: Ritual and Meaning in Antiquity* (2010); "Violentilla Victa," *Arethusa* 40, no. 2 (2007): 197–205; "Ethnicity and the Costume of the Roman Bride," *British Archeological Review* (2009): 135–141;

"The Woolworker Bride," in Lena Larsson Lovén and Agneta Strömberg, eds., *Ancient Marriage in Myth and Reality* (2010); "Introduction to the Roman Wedding: Two Case Studies," *Classical Journal* 109, no. 2 (2013): 223–233; "Violence and Submission in Wedding Ritual: Greek and Roman Sources," in Jeffrey Beneker and Georgia Tsouvala, eds., *The Discourse of Marriage in the 1st Century CE* (2018).

Vered Lev Kenaan (PhD, Yale University, 1995) is an Associate Professor of Classical Studies and Comparative Literature at the University of Haifa, Israel. Her work focuses on the relationship between ancient textuality and gender, ancient psychology, myth and its reception. In addition to many articles in these fields she is the author of *Pandora's Senses: The Feminine Character of the Ancient Text* (2008). She is co-editor of *The Voice and The Gaze* (2002) and *Odysseus' Scar: Childhood Memories and Identity* (2018; in Hebrew). Her recent book, *The Ancient Unconscious*, is forthcoming.

Katariina Mustakallio (PhD, University of Helsinki, 1994) was the Director of the Institutum Romanum Finlandiae in Rome from 2009 to 2013, is Senior Lecturer at the University of Tampere, and concentrates her studies on Roman religion, gender, family, and lifespan. She is a co-editor of several volumes concerning childhood and lifespan, including *On Old Age, Approaching Death in Antiquity and the Middle Ages* (2010), *Agents and Objects: Children in Pre-Modern Europe* (2015), *Children and Family in Late Antiquity: Life, Death and Interaction* (2015), and *Infirmity in Antiquity and the Middle Ages: Social and Cultural Approaches to Health, Weakness and Care* (2016).

Matthew Perry (PhD, University of Chicago, 2007) is an associate professor of History at the John Jay College of Criminal Justice, in the City University of New York. He is the author of *Gender, Manumission, and the Roman Freedwoman* (2014); "Sexual Damage to Slaves in Roman Law," *Journal of Ancient History* 3, no. 1 (2015): 55–75; and "Quintus Haterius and the 'Dutiful' Freedman: The Consideration of Sexual Conduct between Patrons and Freedpersons in Roman Law," *Ancient History Bulletin* 25, no. 3–4 (2011): 133–148.

Katherine Wasdin (PhD, Yale University, 2009) is Assistant Professor of Classical Studies at the George Washington University. She is the author of *Eros at Dusk: Ancient Wedding and Love Poetry* (2018), "Honorius Triumphant: Poetry and Politics in Claudian's Wedding Poems," *Classical Philology* 109, no. 1 (2014): 48–65, "The Undead Past in Kathy Acker's Blood and Guts in High School," *Classical Receptions Journal* 9, no. 2 (2017): 268–286, and "Weaving Time: Ariadne and the Argo in Catullus 64," *Helios* 44, no. 2 (2017): 181–199.

Noelle Zeiner-Carmichael (PhD, Indiana University, Bloomington, 2002) is Professor of Classics at the College of Charleston, South Carolina. Her research specialties include the literature and material culture of the Roman Empire with a particular emphasis on topics concerning gender and self-identity. She has authored two books, *Nothing Ordinary Here: Statius as Creator of Distinction in the* Silvae (2005) and *Roman Letters: An Anthology* (2014). Her current projects focus on epistolarity in the correspondence of Fronto.

GENERAL EDITOR'S PREFACE

JOANNE M. FERRARO

The six-volume Bloomsbury Academic Cultural History of Marriage series is designed for both students and scholars of history, gender and cultural studies, anthropology, sociology, and related disciplines. Its chronological boundaries and periodization are in accordance with the various other Bloomsbury Academic history series. While the volumes are implicitly Western and European in chronological perspective, the contributors have made strenuous efforts to make world comparisons where appropriate; to be mindful of religious differences where possible; and to reach across the disciplines. Together they offer a set of peer-reviewed original works of synthesis and interpretation that engage recent scholarship and use representative primary sources.

With a uniform set of themes in mind, each of the six volumes contains the same chapter titles so that readers can explore a particular topic across the entire series. Each chapter offers an overview of a theme as well as a wide range of case material derived from original research. There are eight common areas of investigation. The volumes open with a chapter on the preludes to marriage in the way of courtship and rites. Two chapters follow, covering the evolution of law and practice in both the religious and secular spheres, respectively; examining how authorities made marital consent binding; and exploring the ways in which clerics and secular officials attempted to regulate the behavior of wives and husbands. The fourth chapter, "The Ties that Bind," encompasses a broad spectrum of behavior, situating marital unions within the context of kinship groups and social networks as well as amidst alliances of property and power. Marriage as an economic contract and unit of production and reproduction is the general theme of the fifth chapter, "The Family Economy," and includes the subjects of dowry and estate management as well as the role of wives and husbands in income-producing activities and child rearing. While marriage legitimized sexual relations, whether or not it included love in times past continues to be the subject of vigorous debate, particularly for the period preceding the eighteenth century. In the sixth chapter, "Love, Sex, and Sexuality," historians tread cautiously, examining the quality of marriage and sexual relations on a case by case basis as well as reviewing expected, albeit ideal, norms in contrast to practice. Extramarital sex is also treated under this rubric and connects well with the theme of the seventh chapter, "Breaking Vows" through separation and divorce. Finally, the eighth chapter explores the myriad ways in which marriage was represented in art, material culture, theatre, and literature.

The contributors have availed themselves of a wide array of both prescriptive and descriptive sources. Among the former are biblical, classical, and religious texts; legal treatises and legislation; and an assortment of mythological, literary, and artistic works. These documents and visual materials often represent the ideal templates of an age, such as the cloistered maiden, the faithful wife, or the successful husband. Among the descriptive sources are letters and diaries as well as court testimonies from archival repositories; ledgers and account books; ecclesiastical records of marriage and marital litigation; and for the modern age, film as well as digital media. Their descriptions often transcend the ideal templates offered in prescriptive writings and afford insights into the realities of social experience. They shed light on human behavior and the ways in which women and men negotiated and contested the enforcement of formal laws and parental authority. It is important to note, however, that there are fewer such sources for the classical period, wherein scholars often must rely more heavily on artifacts, while the number of available textual sources steadily increases over time.

In tracing the evolution of marriage over the long term, the series highlights no less than sweeping changes in its significance to religious and secular institutions, to family status and estate management, and to the affective desires of women and men. Marriage was not available to everyone; opportunities were heavily dependent on financial means. Further, gender and social class were important determinants of marital experience and thus are important categories of analysis throughout the series. In principle men enjoyed more freedom within the conjugal bond than women, and free people had more flexibility than slaves or serfs. Yet it remains important to nuance such generalities by devoting close attention to regional differences as well as to the social and political status of individuals. Contributors in Volume 1, covering Antiquity, for example, have found that in contrast to Greece or Rome slaves in Ptolemaic Egypt could marry. These scholars have also determined that consent to marry was important in the Greco-Roman world, but nonetheless elite men as well as elite women were obliged to respect the priorities of their families and given little choice in the selection of spouses. Their marriages were arranged without a period of courtship, an experience that might possibly evolve within the union over time. It was not a sacrament but, rather, a legal transaction that provided for the transfer of property and the reproduction of the male line. Beyond family interests, marriage was of central importance to both community and state; the primary means of creating new households and citizens. It was fundamentally a patriarchal institution. However, scholars in Volume 1 suggest that the happiest marriages were in feminine hands.

The period between 500 and 1450, termed broadly the Medieval Age in Volume 2, witnessed a dramatic change in perceptions of the institution of marriage in Christian communities. The transformation was in large part a product of the growth of the Christian Church both as an institution and as a primary organizing principle for European society. Between roughly the sixth and eleventh centuries prelates gradually converted the pagan tribes of the West to Christianity. Irish monks, with reinforcement from the Franks, fostered and defended the spread of the new creed in the face of non-Christian invaders, making it the majority religion. Religious men preserved classical scholarship and oversaw the administration of secular government. Importantly, they were the dominant sponsors of cultural advancement in art, philosophy, and political ideology, all infused with Christian themes. In the social sphere they slowly but persistently regulated marital life, insisting on free will, even for serfs, and that a valid marriage require the mutual consent of the couple. The philosophical, theological, and legal developments that unfolded between the twelfth and fifteenth centuries solidified the church's position as a dominant force in social life, influencing sexual norms, family economy, relations between the state and the individual and transforming both liturgy and iconography. Insofar as marriage was concerned several developments stand out: the establishment of incest restrictions that set the kinship boundaries for marriage; the insistence on free will; and the declaration that marriage was a sacrament, where the consent of the couple, rendered it legally and spiritually binding before God. The twelfth and thirteenth centuries in particular witnessed changes in theologians' understanding of canon law and with them the conjugal union became central to discussions about salvation. Marriage was both a spiritual and physical state of mind. Spiritually it was to reflect Christ's loving relationship with the church, something that both the various members of the clergy and the laity could experience. However, while the clergy were bound by vows of celibacy, the laity were taught that monogamous marriage was the only place for sexual activity, and its sole purpose was for procreation. In the West a further proviso was established that veered away from the Gospels and the teachings of St. Paul: marriage could not be dissolved. This remained in stark contrast to both Greek Orthodox, Judaic, and Muslim traditions.

The economic, intellectual, and religious reorganization of Western European society that took place between 1450 and 1650, described generally in Volume 3 as the Renaissance and Early Modern Age, brought the parameters of marriage instituted by the medieval church under scrutiny. The period witnessed a commercial revolution that gave rise to a more literate and secular-minded professional class in Europe's urban centers; the expansion of Europe to the Americas, Africa, and Asia; and a new approach to education termed humanism that, together with the scientific revolution, challenged medieval scholastic epistemology. With the rise of secularism both materially and intellectually, theologians and jurists debated over whether marriage was a sacrament or a contract. For many families it was a means of guarding or improving their social and political positions as well as their financial status. Thus parental control over the choice of their children's spouses was tantamount, making notarial contracts essential. This more secular model of marriage challenged the church's jurisdictional claims of primacy and conflicted with the religious mandate that only the verbal consent of bride and groom was required in order to make the union valid. For young couples, privileging the contract over the sacrament exacerbated the conflict over free choice and parental control. These tensions were particularly high among the classes of economic substance, such as the nobility or the commercial and juridical elites.

The Protestant Reformation introduced a second challenge to the medieval parameters of marriage: the possibility of divorce. The practice was largely limited during the sixteenth and seventeenth centuries but nonetheless a dramatic conceptual break with the medieval past. Divorce in Protestant areas of Europe recognized the possibility of failed marriage. It was not necessarily under the sole jurisdiction of the ecclesiastical courts. In some places secular consistories also heard petitions to dissolve marital unions. In Catholic areas, on the other hand, ecclesiastical tribunals sometimes granted a separation of bed and board, but the institution of marriage remained permanent in the eyes of God. Ecclesiastical courts also judged whether marital unions were legally valid and binding. Betrothals, promises to marry, and the marriage rite itself had unfolded throughout the Middle Ages in a variety of ways, reflecting both regional and confessional differences but also the urgency in some cases to have sexual relations prior to wedlock. When one partner, generally the man, reneged on the promise the litigation reached the ecclesiastical court. The flood of breech of promise suits and general confusion over whether couples were in a binding relationship led Catholic theologians to regularize the form of marriage at the Council of Trent in 1563. Prelates laid down some basic requirements: publication of the banns three times in the parish where the marriage would take place; the presence of a prelate and witnesses at the service; and the couple's verbal expression of mutual consent.

The marriage also had to be consummated and registered. Ironically, the regularization of marriage rites also led to a proliferation of petitions to annul unions, ostensibly because couples had not followed the prescribed form.

The conflict between religious and secular models of marriage and between free will and parental control remained unresolved throughout the Renaissance and Early Modern Age and continued into the Age of Enlightenment, 1650–1800. The main issue, treated in detail in Volume 4, became whether marriage could be an affective bond and the fruit of love rather than an arranged match. Historians of that period are still debating whether marriage was a cold, business affair or filled with love and affection. Obviously no one model applies. However, the contributors in Volume 4 find that by the late eighteenth century there was greater emphasis on marrying for love, a trend that intertwined with historic economic developments and new Enlightenment ideals. Europe was expanding both economically and territorially, and there was a growing trend to allow free choice away from paternal authority. This did not break the religious stranglehold on marriage but it did attenuate it in some areas of the European continent.

The Age of Empires, 1800–1900, also witnessed several changes in the domain of marriage. Generally, government and secular law took on greater influence in the regulation of conjugal unions than in the past. The introduction of civil marriage made registration by the state compulsory, a development that encouraged the practice of civil ceremonies. In some areas, however, common-law marriage prevailed over unions concluded under government supervision, while in others the influence of religion and religious rites remained substantial. The idea of romantic love, introduced in earlier times, featured prominently during this "Age of Romanticism," particularly in literature and theatre. Novel plots where lovers played a leading role more often than not ended happily. Nonetheless, in some parts of the world marriage was still arranged by the parents of the couple, keeping in mind the exchange and extension of wealth and labor power as well as the future of the family lines. The opportunities for premarital sex varied from place to place. Where individuals married young there was no room for romance or sexuality prior to the wedding. Southeast Asia, Japan, Polynesia and parts of Africa, North American and Europe afforded some ritualized opportunities for sexual experience before marriage in the form of "night courting." Peers of the unmarried couple would supervise the activities in hopes of preventing unwanted pregnancies. In Western societies experiencing greater rural-to-urban migration and urbanization, the incidence of out of wedlock fertility rose, reaching its peak in the latter half of the nineteenth century with the introduction of birth control. The stigma of such pregnancies, however, prevailed and contributed to the spread of sexually repressive codes both in Europe and its colonies. The later nineteenth century also witnessed an increase in divorce, signaling a weakening of marriage as an institution and presaging what was to come in the twentieth century.

Perhaps the most sweeping change in the institution of marriage during the twentieth and twenty-first centuries, featured in the scholarship of Volume 6, The Modern Age, is that it was no longer the central organizing principle of social life. With the increasing autonomy of individuals, many people have chosen not to marry, living life as singles or simply cohabiting with a partner. It is not uncommon for individuals to have multiple sexual relationships over their life cycles or for childbearing to take place outside of marriage. A variety of factors have undermined both marriage and close connections with kin. Among them, globalization, improved means of long-distance transportation, and shifting labor opportunities, developments that have resulted in people leaving their natal villages, towns, and cities to settle in other far-off places, where family bonds are less accessible and there is less social pressure to conform to tradition. In this context kinship groups have become less cohesive, and the extended family has given way to nuclear units or individual autonomy. Increasing opportunities for women in the labor force, especially during the twenty-first century, have also contributed to changes in the nature or necessity of marriage. Women are less dependent on having husbands and are more reluctant to subscribe to the rigid gender roles of times past. The second-wave feminist movement of the late twentieth century has been critical in challenging patriarchal authority and in defining new roles for women in family and society. More women are obtaining advanced degrees and participating in the labor force. Finally, the twentieth and twenty-first centuries have also witnessed no less than a revolution in the recognition of the complexities of human sexuality. The LGBTQ movements have liberated individuals to have sexual relationships and bear children with preferred partners, and in many countries same-sex marriage has become legal. These dramatic changes have not come without turmoil, and religious leaders, politicians, civic authorities, the media, communities, and individuals continue to question the origins and meaning of marriage and to attempt to define its parameters and purpose. Thus Bloomsbury Academic's Cultural History of Marriage constitutes a timely and important body of scholarship addressing the ongoing debates of a broad segment of society today.

Introduction

KAREN KLAIBER HERSCH

In her brilliant *Pride and Prejudice,* Jane Austen details the dismaying, grim determination with which Charlotte Lucas (best friend of the novel's heroine Elizabeth Bennett) enters into matrimony.[1] Austen reveals Charlotte's interior debate, lamenting that:

> Mr. Collins, to be sure, was neither sensible nor agreeable; his society was irksome, and his attachment to her must be imaginary. But still he would be her husband. Without thinking highly either of men or matrimony, marriage had always been her object; it was the only provision for well-educated young women of small fortune, and however uncertain of giving happiness, must be their pleasantest preservative from want.

At the end of the novel, the reader rejoices along with Elizabeth, who has had the good luck to avoid Charlotte's fate, as she writes of her own impending nuptials, "I am the happiest creature in the world. Perhaps other people have said so before, but not one with such justice. I am happier even than Jane; she only smiles, I laugh."[2] Which scenario best describes marriage among the elite of nineteenth-century England: the first, detailing the lengths to which a woman will sink to gain merely the status of marriage itself, or the second, showing true love and intellectual compatibility paving the way for a lifetime of happiness? The answer must be that as many as there are marriages, so there are opinions on them.

Modern scholarship on Greek and Roman marriage suggests that the ancients could no more decide than modern people if marriage was a blessing or a curse.[3] Few marriages in antiquity were perfectly happy, and a number of Greek and Roman authors remarked that marriage was, at best, no more than a necessary evil for both men and women. Moreover what these primarily male authors claimed about marriage—and therefore what we think we know about the daily experience of marriage in antiquity—must be approached with caution, for the evidence is scattered and varied. For example, the ancients claimed that many of the gods they worshipped were bound in wedlock. Yet they asserted too that a number of their gods lived fully realized divine lives in the blessed freedom of perpetual virginity. Still other gods, both male and female, had many sexual partners, human and divine, male and female, and we know that the king and queen of the gods each bore children without the other.[4] In the mortal realm, things were different but no less varied. While marriage was represented as the raison d'être of an Athenian woman's life, Athenian married men lived with wives but could at the same time commit themselves extramaritally to any number of male and female partnerships. Romans held up the ideal of the *univira* (a woman married only once), but we know that divorce in the Roman world, if not rife, was commonplace. At least we may say with some degree of accuracy that sexual fidelity in marriage was an ideal that only human women were expected to aim for.[5] Then too, some never married and were lauded for their unmarried states. Long before the rise of asceticism in the early Christian period, Romans recognized and celebrated the unique sacrality of the virginity and celibacy of the women who served the most chaste goddess Vesta, the famed Vestal Virgins.

Opinions on marriage—what constitutes a marriage, whether it is a blessing or a curse, who may have the right to enter into one—have always varied throughout human history, from culture to culture. We could easily get a different account of the meaning of marriage from each person living in any time period. We might attempt today to satisfy our curiosity about what a majority of people believes about marriage in any one place by taking a broad sample of public opinion, but any satisfaction we could derive from such a poll would be short lived. Such a survey cannot give us an accurate detailed picture, and in any case such opinions and statistics change almost daily.

Given the importance so many of the world's cultures have placed on marriage— often defined, as the Greeks and Romans did, as a lifelong partnership of a woman and a man leading to the production of legitimate children, sometimes sanctioned by a religious body—it remains a topic of perennial interest.[6] In every country today, books and articles broadcasting marital triumphs and tragedies are published hourly, but these accounts may reflect beliefs about matrimony, or the lived marital experience, of any modern person no more than, for example, tales of the marriage of Odysseus and Penelope or the wedding of Nero and Sporus reflect the beliefs held by any Greek or Roman person. Of course, in studying ancient peoples our challenges in handling the evidence are doubled or trebled. Our informants have been dead for thousands of years, and our comparatively slender but wide-ranging written evidence (for example, law, poetry, history, theatre) is in the main the product of elite male minds. In addition we may have doubts about the actual words of the ancient texts themselves, for our texts have often been copied and re-copied, then edited and re-edited, and finally we cannot always be certain of authorship. Moreover, while the ancient authors we examine in this volume were eyewitnesses to antiquity, almost all of their writings are highly polished literary works and give us no more a glimpse of the average Greek or Roman's opinion than they tell us the inner thoughts of the author himself (or rarely, herself). Archaeological, epigraphic and papyrological finds supply us with ever-changing evidence, but this evidence too must be quite literally sifted through, analyzed and interpreted before it reaches the hands of the average scholar. Material goods, such as written works, may reflect popular styles of the period and thus may be modernizing or archaizing, and have little relationship to any core beliefs of the makers or owners. We assign motivation and belief systems to any living artist at our peril, and this caveat must be doubly applied to the study of the long dead.

If we remember to keep a firm grasp on the deficiencies and flaws in our sources and our own scholarly limitations, we can however presume to make some cautious generalizations. Marriage from antiquity to today, and its attendant pleasures and pains, has been the perennial favorite subject of story and song, not least because, as we have noted, marriage among many peoples worldwide is a union that is meant to last a lifetime. Consequently the embarkation on such a lifetime journey carries no little weight. Cross-culturally, the seemingly most private union of matrimony usually begins in the most public fashion imaginable, with a wedding ceremony,[7] for many if not most cultures deem their community's sanction of the marital union indispensable. As with other rites of passage around the world, the beginning of a marriage must be seen to be believed,[8] and such rites of passage are marked by a clear division from everyday routines, and are likely to include arcane rituals and costumes and a rare combination of solemnity and celebration with prayers to deities. Moreover, we may surmise from the evidence we have that around the world marriage is viewed as an achievement, or at least a necessity, an advancement in status that may signal the entry of one or both spouses into adult society, regardless of how joyful or dismal its daily realities. A lasting and happy marriage may be portrayed as chief among blessings for humans, while the dissolution of the marital union, at least putatively meant to last a lifetime, may be treated as a failure, as a death.[9]

In one very real sense, the history of marriage in Greek and Roman antiquity is a history of wives. The evidence we have suggests that men's status did not change as significantly as women's did upon marriage.[10] Literary descriptions of Greek and Roman weddings focused squarely on brides: their joys and fears, their beauty and modesty. In art, too, we can see the same focus on the feminine: a well-known motif on Greek vases, for example, is the bridal preparation scene, in which a bride is beautified by attendants, and often by divinities.[11] No analogies exist for grooms; to my knowledge, a "groom's beautifying scene" in Greek or Roman art has yet to be discovered.[12] Attentively examining the rites of Greek and Roman weddings is crucial, for in the focus on women we see in these ceremonies a highlighting of ideas about the proper functioning of wife, marriage, and home. While of course husbands had duties and responsibilities, and we may catch a glimpse of these tasks enumerated in texts as far separated as Xenophon's *Oikonomikos* from the fourth century BCE and Plutarch's *Advice to the Bride and Groom* written the second century CE, we may say with some degree of certainty that ancient men's duties were believed to lie primarily outside the home, and that the happiness of any marriage, home, and family was the concern of women. We note that the Greeks and Romans elected a woman to be the divine overseer of marriage, and this goddess, Hera or Juno, had a notoriously difficult marriage with an ever-wandering, sexually insatiable and violent spouse, the very king of the gods.[13]

Taking the widest view possible, we may say that the history of Greek and Roman marriage was not unique in that, like the history of marriage across cultures and time periods, it is a history of impossible standards, a jumble of cultural expectations that were, in all likelihood, rarely met by men and women in real life. But it seems fair to say that most of the expectations for the success of marriage were heaped on women. One common theme we encounter in both Greek and Roman literature is that the happiness of any given marital home is predicated on the wife's ability to stay cloistered within it, working wool. Therefore portrayals of happy marriages in Greek and Roman literature often appear as hopeful dreams concocted by men that highlight women's obedience. Marriage as a subject seems to have been of interest to elite male writers when cultural expectations are disrupted for both glory and ruin.[14] As we will see, the wives who earned a space in ancient writing gained notoriety for breaking rules to aid or harm their spouses.

But legal marriage was not the only committed union enjoyed, or endured, by adults in antiquity. We know from literary and epigraphic sources the wide variety of extralegal and often extramarital unions that far better characterize, or just as well capture, our modern concepts of marriage for love. Many nonmarital unions achieved the aims of ancient Greek and Roman marriage: "a union for all time."[15]

Thus one concrete, universal opinion on marriage from Greek and Roman antiquity is as impossible to uncover as it would be today. Not surprisingly, even the sources we have do not always agree: the history of marriage is characterized by example and counter example. It is then the aim of this introduction to give a selection of depictions of marriages spanning the centuries of classical antiquity. The limitations of space demand the briefest examinations of only a few texts, but it is hoped that these examples will give the fullest picture possible of the challenges facing any scholar studying ancient marriage. The essays that follow in this volume will serve to enlarge upon the themes I explore here and put my wide, but not exhaustive, sample of evidence into context.

GREEK MARRIAGES

Herodotus famously noted that Homer and Hesiod gave the Greeks their gods,[16] but it is equally true that these authors give us glimpses of early Greek conceptions of marriage. What we know of Greek marriage, both human and divine, begins primarily with Homer's *Iliad*, recounting the end of the war between Greeks and Trojans, and the *Odyssey*, the tale of one Greek warrior's painful peregrinations after that war. These texts, the oldest literature we possess from the ancient Greek world, have at their core stories of marriages, both happy and troubled. The war that comprises the narrative of the *Iliad* is the lamentable aftermath of the attempted destruction of but one royal marriage, that of Helen and Menelaus. In the *Iliad* we are witnesses to the suffering of men drawn (willingly or unwillingly) into combat by the Trojan prince Paris's illicit love affair with the married Helen. All the while, Homer uses their notorious adultery as a foil for the domestic bliss of Paris's brother Hector and his wife Andromache.[17] The *Iliad*

FIGURE I.1 Scene with Andromache, Astyanax, and Hector, Apulian red-figure column-crater, 370–360 BCE. Museo Nazionale of the Palazzo Jatta. Wikimedia Commons.

leaves us with the dreadful impression that good marriages cannot last; the only happy marriage given any attention in the *Iliad* is destroyed.[18] There is no satisfactory moral to the story where marriage is concerned. At the end of the *Iliad*, the miscreants Helen and Paris, if not exactly flourishing, are alive and well, while the just suffer or perish: Hector is cruelly slain and his body abused by Achilles, and Andromache is left a desolate widow. Later sources tell us that Andromache's fate is perhaps even more brutal than Hector's: her baby son will be killed, and she will become the slave of Achilles's son.[19]

In the *Odyssey*, we learn that Helen is safely back from her sexual tourism, at the home of her husband Menelaus in Sparta and duly ashamed of her actions.[20] The wives featured in the *Odyssey*, including Helen and her spouse-killing sister Klytemnestra, are presented in implied, or open, comparison to the faithful Penelope.[21] While the chaste Penelope refuses contact with men for the twenty years of Odysseus's absence, busily weaving to stave off the advances of boorish suitors who have invaded her home, Odysseus manages both to endure the perils of land and sea, and manages too to engage in sexual relationships with the divine Circe and Calypso. But the very first lines of the *Odyssey* assure us that these extramarital relationships are mere distractions, for Odysseus never stops longing for home *and* wife.[22]

The *Iliad* and the *Odyssey* make clear that a man's sexual or intellectual relationships outside of marriage for the most part may be assumed; a man could have multiple sexual partners, and these relationships had no bearing on the putative success of his marriages.[23] When the *Iliad* commences, we learn that the Greek army is in disarray because of an argument among its leaders over captive female sexual partners. So the first words of

FIGURE I.2 *Odysseus and Penelope*, 1802, Johann Heinrich Wilhelm Tischbein (1751–1829). Private collection. Wikimedia Commons.

FIGURE I.3 *Penelope and the Suitors*, 1912, John William Waterhouse (1849–1917). Aberdeen Art Gallery and Museums. Wikimedia Commons.

Greek literature let us know that for most if not all of the Greek men fighting in Troy, longing for wife and home (if it even exists) can be assuaged or wiped out entirely in the arms of sex slaves. It is more than telling that the Greek term *alochos* in Homeric epic is applied to both sex slave and wedded wife.[24] Yet while Homer's epics show us a variety of marital outcomes, we cannot escape another conclusion: that the depictions of Hector and Andromache, Penelope and Odysseus represent marital ideals.[25]

The didactic epics of Hesiod, chronologically speaking, follow closely on the heels of Homer's works.[26] But while Homer's epics show us an incredible array of marriages, and leave us to decide on conjugal sinners and saints, Hesiod's *Works and Days* leaves us with the uneasy notion that marriage is, for mortal man, at best a dubious good. The story of the first woman, Pandora, leads to Hesiod's declaration that even if a man is fortunate in his choice of wife, marriage is always a struggle. He only concedes that dying alone is worse.[27] Pandora herself is a creature of great mystery and nuance, but Hesiod leaves us in no doubt that she is a beautiful evil devised by Zeus to torture men.[28]

Lyric poetry, emerging in the so-called Archaic period following Hesiod, is characterized by shorter poems on individual topics that span the human experience. One poet known to most readers is Sappho, whose inimitable reflections on love and longing are still beloved. Sappho's poems celebrate erotic love of both women and men, yet they also celebrate marriage. Significantly, while Sappho's erotic poems to women have encouraged many to make reasonable claims about Sappho's sexual preferences, fragments of Sappho's epithalamia (poems in celebration of weddings), for example, show that she was as deft at tackling heteronormative subjects as her male contemporaries, however we might define *their* sexualities.²⁹ Sappho's epithalamic fragments contain *topoi* that would become standard in Greek and later Roman epithalamia in the following centuries: praise for the bride and groom and praise of the joys of marriage are prominently featured.³⁰ That a poet as great as Sappho would turn her hand to the writing of epithalamia suggests to us the great value Greeks placed on weddings and therefore marriage itself; the poems themselves give us an indication of Greek ideals and societal expectations for grooms (tall and handsome) and brides (chaste and beautiful).³¹

Significant for our purposes here are poems from the same period which we might call anti-epithalamia, that is, epigrams mourning youths and maidens who died before they could marry. In these poems we may glimpse the value Greek society placed on marriage as they lament the young person's "marriage to death" instead of the intended spouse.³² Notably, a fragment of a poem by Pindar³³ records the death of Hymenaeus, a youth who died on his wedding night, and references to the god Hymenaeus and a chant for him surface in Roman literature.³⁴ Young people dying just before marriage—because, of all tragic fates, it seems to have been considered the most pitiable—proved to be a popular *topos* throughout both Greek and Roman literature. A deep cultural expectation was clearly expressed herein: whether it is a blessing or a curse, marriage is a necessity.

Marriage lies at the very heart of the myths that inspired so many of the famed tragedies and comedies of the golden age of Athens of the fifth century BCE. Both tragedy and comedy, fascinatingly, steer us to the conclusion that men acknowledged the impossible demands Greek marriage placed upon both men and women (but especially on women). Consider the surviving works of the three great tragedians spanning the fifth century. The curse on the house of Atreus, which we begin to understand in the pages of Homer, that centers in fact on adultery, is the focus of Aeschylus's trilogy the *Oresteia*.³⁵ His play *Agamemnon* recounts the triumphant return from war and the slaying of Agamemnon and his captive Cassandra at the hands of his wife Klytemnestra (taking revenge on her husband for his slaying of their daughter Iphigenia) and her lover Aegisthus. The adulterous pair is in turn slain by Klytemnestra's son Orestes in the *Choephoroi*, and the curse on the house of Atreus seems finally resolved with Athena's help in Orestes's trial and release in the final play, *Eumenides*. Later, Sophocles' retelling of the myth of the horrific destiny of Oedipus explores the nightmare of his fated, incestuous marriage and its terrible aftermath. Even the children of this tragic union are not spared: after her brothers die, the eponymous heroine of the *Antigone*, instead of enjoying her wedding, marries death in a cave by hanging herself. These terrible outcomes notwithstanding, Sophocles explores tremendous love in these plays as well: Oedipus and Jocasta, we understand, have lived happily with their children, reigning supreme over their contented citizenry before the devastating discovery of their incest. Then too Antigone's fiancé Haimon faces the wrath of his intractable father in trying desperately to save Antigone's life.

The prize for the most scathing account of marriage's toll on women must surely be awarded to Euripides' *Medea*, written near the end of the fifth century. Euripides puts into the mouth of a woman³⁶ a speech of incredible force, wit, and pathos on the lot of wives in a world ruled by men. Medea's sad fate is to have loved and to have been discarded by the hero Jason, but her bitter tirade on wife- and motherhood may indeed reflect the experience of many Greek women living at the time of the play's production. If I may be forgiven for summarizing her immortal lines, Medea declares that women are the most unfortunate creatures because they must spend so much money (their dowries) just to buy a man, who may turn out to be worthless; they must travel to a potentially hostile new home, and be a prisoner there forever, as they are allowed no other companion but their husbands.

She ends her morose musings on marriage by noting that multiple forays on the battlefield are easier to bear than the pains of having one child.³⁷ Medea's speech seems a perfectly crafted rebuttal to the argument offered in the pages of Hesiod (above): that the dangers of marriage are all borne by men. Alas, the tables will again be turned at the end of the play, when Medea shows herself the most dangerous wife and mother in the history of women.

But Medea's speech is not Euripides' last word on marriage, of course. While Medea speaks of women's sacrifice in marriage, the maiden Iphigenia actually becomes a sacrifice

FIGURE I.4 Scene of Medea killing her child, Campanian red-figure amphora, Ixion Painter, 330 BCE. Louvre Museum. Wikimedia Commons.

herself. Euripides' *Iphigenia in Aulis* draws us into the beautiful dream of Iphigenia's wedding to Achilles; in fact the wedding is a ruse, engineered by her father to get her to Aulis so that he may slay her as an offering to Artemis. Her death of course leads to the famous slaying of Agamemnon in turn. Other Euripidean masterpieces give us multifarious marital horrors and delights. The doomed Hippolytus, for example, is the anti-Medea, giving in his great speech a man's-eye view on marriage, beginning with a reference to Pandora, the world's first woman, then spitting out his disgust for all women and the poor fools who marry them.[38] But Hippolytus will be proved the fool, for while there are many cautionary tales interwoven in the *Hippolytus*, chief among them is the danger of remaining unwed: we know from the first lines of the play that the goddess Aphrodite wishes to destroy Hippolytus for his willful celibacy and concomitant neglect of her worship.[39] The wrath of the god Dionysus moves the action of Euripides' *Bacchae*, a play that gives its audience an apocalyptic view of what can happen when wives leave their husbands and homes and head for the hills. Taking revenge on their too-proud king Pentheus, Dionysus drives the Theban women to the forest to worship him in their bloody feasts; the leader of this band is Agave, the king's mother. The community is destroyed from the top down, and when the dust settles, the bloodstained women are quite literally left with a gory mess on their hands, both psychological and physical. Yet Euripides' genius provides us too the tale of a happy marriage in his tragicomedy *Alcestis*, in which the eponymous heroine gives her life to save her husband, the rather uncourageous Admetus. Alcestis is plucked from the jaws of death by Heracles, and all ends satisfactorily.

FIGURE I.5 *The Anger of Achilles*, 1819, Jacques-Louis David (1748–1845). Kimbell Art Museum, Fort Worth. Wikimedia Commons.

Marriage is likewise held up for ridicule and praise in the comedies of the fifth century. For example Aristophanes' masterwork *Lysistrata* (whose eponymous heroine's name, "disbander of armies," identifies her role in the play) details the heroism of both Athenian and (enemy) Spartan wives as they successfully craft a rebellion to the Peloponnesian War in the form of a sex-strike. Their menfolk capitulate, and the war is stopped. Anyone might argue that *Lysistrata* is a comedy, a mere fantasy, pure entertainment with no ties to reality. But for such a play to be successful with its audience, its humor must speak to some societally acknowledged truisms or stereotypes. That the entire premise of the play rests on the idea that men cannot live happily without wifely intimacy is surely significant and suggests, if it cannot prove, that at least some Greek men and women were happily monogamous. Moreover, one pivotal moment in the play comes as Lysistrata, having extolled wool work as perfectly good training for running a city, envelops a male magistrate with the symbols of a wife—her veil and woodworking implements—thereby making him an "honorary woman."[40] As I have begun to hint and the essays in this volume will show, we know from a plethora of both Greek and Roman sources that wool work was a powerful indicator of a woman's industry and fidelity. Therefore, can we hazard a guess that Aristophanes' portrayal of men's love for their wives is as accurate a reflection of cultural truisms or norms as his discourse on wifely wool work?

We have seen that the Greeks we know best from literature are, in the main, Athenian. Sparta left us few literary works, and Thucydides' prediction that the remains of Sparta would not impress later generations came true. Yet Plutarch, writing six centuries after Sparta vanquished Athens, left us an account of the Spartans' marriage customs of yore. Plutarch claims in his *Life of Lycurgus* (15.3–5) that Spartan wedding customs arose from the need to aid Spartan men, enjoying only the company of other men since boyhood, in their journey through marriage into the unknown territory of women. Therefore to soothe their grooms, Spartan brides cut off their hair, dressed in men's clothes, and awaited their new grooms in the dark. Husbands would visit wives but not live with them. How many Spartans endured such a wedding and lonesome marriage? We cannot know, and such vivid, imaginative accounts of such anomalous rites will always remain suspect until further evidence arises.

ROMAN MARRIAGES

Roman culture is not an exact replica of Greek, but Romans were burdened with confronting the triumphs of the Greeks at every turn, and in rejecting or vying with their predecessors, Romans were in an important sense perpetually paying homage to all aspects of Greek culture. However, while we will see in Roman accounts of marriage re-imaginings of much of the Greek art and themes we have just begun to examine above, I am not suggesting that Romans spent their days in abject attempts to follow Greek blueprints.

The evidence Romans left us on marriage is all the more fascinating for the consistency of its sheer inconsistency. Romans defined marriage as a "union for all time" and necessary for the production of legitimate children,[41] the second element crucial for determining inheritance. But for all the Roman elites' interest in marriage as the transmitter of power, wealth, and status, for which we have ample evidence from a host of sources,[42] Romans seem to have been quite comfortable with the idea that, legally speaking, their legendary founders were bastards. No legal wedding or marriage produced the great heroes Aeneas, the founder of the Roman race, nor Romulus, the founder of the Eternal City, Rome.

And yet the public and private spaces of Italy were replete with images of these two illegitimate men whose divine parents flouted the idea of lifetime togetherness. And so we are left to ponder the greater and lesser ironies of any culture's claims about marriage. The greatest of these ironies may be that in the first century CE, in Rome itself, a temple to Marital Harmony erected by Rome's first empress Livia[43] to commemorate her happy marriage with Augustus, the hopeful ameliorator of Roman morals, stood nearby the temple her husband erected to Mars, the rapist of Romulus's mother.

We begin with the legendary founder of the Roman people and the world-famous retelling of his story. A Trojan warrior-prince briefly mentioned in Homer's *Iliad*, Aeneas and his travails were set in literary stone by the master poet Vergil in his epic the *Aeneid* composed in the first century CE. Vergil tells us that Aeneas fled the destruction of Troy, leading his weary fellow survivors on a perilous, miserable journey around the Mediterranean to find a home. Landing in Italy, his armies vanquish those of the indigenous people and Aeneas establishes a new civilization sprung from the mixed blood of Trojans and Italians.

Keen readers have noted the convoluted messages given about marriage in Vergil's tale. Aeneas is the product of the mésalliance of the already-married, philandering goddess Venus and her mortal lover—decidedly not husband—Anchises.[44] The curious absence of anything resembling a happy, lasting marriage looms large in the *Aeneid* and is perhaps to be viewed as part and parcel of the palpable sadness with which Vergil shrouds the glories of Aeneas's labors.[45] Vergil seems to go out of his way to drive home the point that wives can be replaced. Aeneas's wife Creusa perishes in the fall of Troy, but, a helpmeet even in death, her ghost urges him on to a better fate. Creusa's death, of course, neatly provides the opportunity for Aeneas to unite later with the beautiful young Italian princess Lavinia (after he pitilessly executes her fiancé in the last, ultraviolent act of the *Aeneid*).

Two episodes must suffice to illustrate the sad state of marriage in the *Aeneid*. Surely one of the stranger lines from the stylus of Vergil comes in the third book of the *Aeneid*, at the end of Aeneas's mournful encounter with Hector's widow Andromache, whom he finds busily tending the cenotaph she has erected for Hector in a town on the Greek coast depressingly modeled on the now-destroyed Troy. Aeneas listens to Andromache's tearful recitation of the horrors she endured since last they met[46] and then receives a direful prophecy of his labors to come from her newest husband Helenus (a fellow exile, Trojan slave, Priam's son, and Hector's brother). In their final moment together, as Andromache gives Aeneas's son Ascanius parting gifts, mournfully recalling her own dead child, Aeneas extricates himself by responding with the immortal lines: "Live happy, whose destiny is complete!" It may be that these lines were carefully crafted to highlight Aeneas's singularity of purpose: Aeneas views the brokenhearted inhabitants of this literal ghost town as happy, because they are fortunate to at least have a home (and a new spouse). Marriage, spouse, and child, it seems, are necessary but replaceable items in the life of man on a mission like Aeneas's. It may be too that Aeneas's seemingly callous response reflects a peculiarly Vergilian, stoic impatience with grieving over the tragedies of war, perhaps shared by many Romans, characterized by an upper lip so stiff it is almost paralyzed. Aeneas seems to wish away his own grief and that of others: survivors should grieve briefly what they have lost and move on; he himself has people to lead and no time to abandon himself to the luxury of grief. Humans live and die, but empire lasts forever. But Aeneas's abrupt utterance still shocks today, and leaves a deep feeling of unease about the place of marriage in the life of a man Vergil grants the epithets *pius* (pious), *magnanimus* (great-hearted), and even the *pater* (father) of his people, an unease that will reach a culmination in Aeneas's interactions with Dido.

FIGURE I.6 *Dido and Aeneas* (Venus and Mars), fresco from House of the Citharist, Pompeii, first century CE. National Archaeological Museum of Naples (inv. 112282). Wikimedia Commons.

Of Aeneas's treatment of queen Dido in Book Four much has been written. Dido is driven to near-madness by the machinations of Venus and Juno who poison her with love for Aeneas, himself driven to the shores of her queendom in North Africa. She is torn by conflicting desires: on the one hand, she has vowed to live in perpetual celibacy to honor her dead first husband Sychaeus, on the other, she is overcome by her passionate love of Aeneas. In the midst of Aeneas's sojourn with the Carthaginian queen, they meet alone in a cave during a storm, attended by divinities. Since the *Aeneid* was published, this meeting has been the subject of lively debate: did this assignation make them husband and wife?[47] In their last meeting, as Aeneas prepares to leave, the agonized Dido furiously berates Aeneas for what she believes is cruel infidelity, while Aeneas calmly insists that they were never married and that he takes his orders not from her but from a much higher authority, the king of the gods himself, who demands that he move on.[48] Dido commits suicide as the Trojan contingent sails away, and Aeneas pursues his destiny, finding land for his people in Italy and a new wife for himself.

Importantly, Aeneas is an anti-Odysseus,[49] sailing away from the people and place he loves to find a faceless wife in an unknown land rather than toward a known and beloved wife and home. Aeneas expresses little interest in marriage save for dynastic purposes—admirably, to think of his people first—which may perhaps help explain why he is pursued by the goddess Juno, whose worship he neglects throughout the work.[50] Juno, enflamed with rage at the beginning, middle, and end of the epic, has to negotiate with and quite literally be pacified by Jupiter:[51] little marital concord can be found in this divine union.

Rape and abduction were the alpha and the omega of the founding of the city of Rome. Romulus, founder of the Eternal City, was himself the product of the rape[52] of the Vestal Rhea Silvia by the war-god Mars. In turn Romulus and the denizens of his new city, denied wives by the neighboring communities who despised the low status of his citizen-refugees, engineered the mass abduction (the so-called Rape of the Sabines) of the daughters of these arrogant neighbors. In Livy's account, after the capture, Romulus explains to the captive herd the boons of *matrimonium*; Livy says too that when their captors claimed to have acted out of love, the girls quickly adjusted to their lot. Importantly, we note that a sanctifying, or legitimizing, wedding is never mentioned: their abduction alone seems to have made them married.[53]

Romulus's act represents well the complexity of ancient views on marriage. Again, ancient opinions were divided. Plutarch named this episode the "first marriage of the Romans," and he and other ancient writers attributed a number of the queerest Roman wedding customs to the event.[54] Yet the poet Ovid used the abduction of the maidens as a negative (if toadying) *exemplum*, contrasting Romulus's barbarism with Augustus's levelheaded rule, saying "Romulus, you rape, while he (Augustus) commands wives be chaste."[55] And so, while the abduction of the Sabines was commemorated at every turn in the Roman wedding, we can clearly see that this "first marriage of the Romans" lacked any of the elements that characterized the formation of a Roman marriage in Roman literary sources: family status and connection, the consent of the brides' families[56] and of the spouses themselves, an engagement, and a wedding ceremony before the community, even dowry. The varied opinions of Romans on this foundational marriage makes us question what, for elite Romans, comprised courtship, legality, consent, family ties, and concord in marriage. The answers are not straightforward, as the essays in this volume will show.

Of the marriages of the Regal period (753–509 BCE) for which we have extended descriptions, those of the two Tarquins (Tarquinius Priscus and Tarquinius Superbus[57]), were happy but marred by violence. Livy claims that their wives were the driving force behind their husbands' political successes. Tanaquil the Etruscan aristocrat urged her husband Lucumo to abandon Etruria and make his fortune in Rome. There he became L. Tarquinius Priscus, the fifth king of Rome and enjoyed a long and successful reign advised at critical junctures by Tanaquil,[58] until he was cut down by assassins' axes. The daughter of the sixth king Servius, Tullia, unhappily married to one Tarquinius brother, whom she considered weak and powerless, set about wooing his ruthless, power-hungry brother, already married to her own sister. Tullia's proposal of marriage to Tarquinius is no more than a list of murders that stand in the way of their mutual happiness and success: their spouses and her father, the reigning king. With their spouses out of the way, King Servius is killed by Tarquinius, and the evil pair rules happily until the family is driven from the throne.

In fact the death of a matron and the end of a marriage ushered in an entirely new form of government: the Republic. The matron Lucretia's heroic suicide roused the Roman people to expel the evil Tarquin family and made her world famous.[59] When her husband makes the innocent but fatal mistake of opening the doors of his home to the inspection of his male friends, they find Lucretia dutifully spinning by lamplight surrounded by female servants. The wives of the other men, presumably the ladies of the court, in contrast, party late into the night. The son of Tarquinius Superbus, Sextus, returns later to Collatinus's home and rapes the modest Lucretia, who carries out her self-imposed death sentence in the presence of her horrified husband and father. We are told little about Lucretia save that she exemplified a number of feminine ideals: beautiful, industrious, and chaste, she could not live with her own dishonor.

In my view, one critical central message in all of these stories about arguably the most famous marriages of legendary Rome, from Aeneas to Lucretia, are the missing children. This absence is significant, for we know that, as we have noted above, marriage is defined by a number of Roman authors as a union "for the production of legitimate children."[60] Yet legitimate children of the kings are hard to find, and when we do find them, they are murderers. We may note that Aeneas's own son Ascanius occupies a minimal role in Roman history. While Romulus was said to have issued a decree concerning offspring (that Romans were responsible for raising all of their male children, but their first daughters only),[61] no great deeds are ascribed to any of Romulus's progeny. Indeed there was debate even in antiquity about their very existence.[62] King Numa may have been married to a nymph, or claimed he was; Numa's children, like Romulus's, are effectively unknown.[63] The disgruntled sons of the previous king, Ancus Marcius, plant an axe in Tarquinius Priscus's skull;[64] his wife Tanaquil puts the son of a household slave, Servius Tullius, on the throne instead of her natural children, perhaps because her talents as a seer clued her in to the fact that her own progeny would prove to possess questionable virtues. King Servius Tullius dies at the hand of Tarquinius Superbus (Tarquinius Priscus's son or grandson) at the urging of his own (Servius's) daughter Tullia, who subsequently desecrates his corpse. They eagerly gain and retain the throne, and only lose it years later when their son Sextus rapes Lucretia and the people revolt. In sum, the fruits of the marriages of the kings were as far as we can tell legitimate and were at best almost forgotten and at worst thoroughly rotten.

Anyone might reasonably object that literary accounts of Aeneas and the kings had little or no meaning to most Romans, illiterate as many probably were. Stories of the

Regal period reflected what authors of the early empire wanted to write about them,[65] and these stories of ancestors had little connection to the lives of their audience, an audience that presumably was meant to cheer with one voice the downfall of the monarchy. But fairy tales, as scholars have shown,[66] transmit in their repetition shared cultural values. And Roman sources, literary and material, assert that the kings and their accomplishments were commemorated at every turn in prominent sites in the city of Rome itself: priesthoods said to have been created by the kings still served the Roman people, and festivals attached to them were celebrated every year. Perhaps not every Roman knew that the temple of Jupiter Optimus Maximus was said to have been built by Etruscan kings, but presumably any citizen living in ancient Rome could direct visitors to the Regia (literally the "kingly place," and legendary home of the second king, Numa) in the Forum Romanum or describe the Lupercalia (a festival connected to the saviour of Romulus). It seems that Romans lived happily with mixed feelings of pride in the kings' deeds but apparent loathing for monarchy as an institution, and believed that marriage as an institution, too, could not run smoothly under kingly rule.

Following the Regal period, a number of extraordinary wives emerged in the Republic. All of these heroic wives devoted their lives to husband and family or both, and two towering figures were Cornelia and the so-called "Turia" of inscriptional fame. Multiple legends, all concerning her husband and sons, surrounded Cornelia (c. 190–102 BCE), the daughter of the hero of the Second Punic War, P. Cornelius Scipio Africanus. Gaining fame in her title the "Mother of the Gracchi" (two great reformers of late Republican politics slain in the prime of life), Cornelia was rumored to have been exceptionally fertile, bearing twelve children of alternating sexes, and to have inspired the love of her husband Tiberius to such a degree that he bore the brunt of an evil omen to ensure that he would die before her.[67] How many "average Romans" knew of the deeds of Cornelia? Quite a few, if Pliny the Elder was correct; he claims that in his lifetime Cornelia's statue stood in the *porticus Octaviae*.[68] Cornelia, like the kings, would have been in the public eye presumably for centuries—unlike the kings, of course, her image would have stood as a symbol of marital felicity coupled with her stalwart courage in facing the losses of husband and children.

Impressive in both size and scope, the inscription known as the "Praise of Turia"[69] (*Laudatio Turiae*) was dedicated to a woman of rare courage and spirit by her grieving husband. It stands as a remarkable testimony to events spanning the late Republic to early empire, and is important for us here because it recounts acts by both wife and husband that defy the gender norms we have been discussing. "Turia" was compelled by the difficult circumstances of her life to provide money for her impoverished relations, regain her rightful inheritance, and even suffer injury as she was dragged away in the act of publicly begging for her husband's life in a time of state crisis. She begged her husband to divorce her when she found that she could not bear children, and he notes in his eulogy that he refused to do so, in a rage. The *Laudatio Turiae* forces us to re-evaluate the image of the ideal Roman wife, present in other funerary inscriptions, on which many wives are commemorated with the brief phrase *lanam fecit, domum servavit* (she worked wool, she kept house).[70] Moreover, we are urged too to re-evaluate the role of husband, as Turia's husband seems hardly the stereotypical grim Roman lord and master, an autocratic *paterfamilias* with the power of life and death over his family, in whose household a wife is treated as a child, and whose only concern is the birth of a son who would inherit his name and fortune.

To balance out the happy marriages of the Republic, we have sensational divorces. Turia's husband's refusal to divorce her, as we saw above, is all the more moving when we learn that the first divorce in the Republican period was initiated by Sp. Carvilius Ruga, who put aside his own (unnamed) wife due to her putative barrenness.[71] Three other memorable divorces, lauded by Valerius Maximus who claimed such divorces acted as deterrents to female misbehavior in the olden days, were meted out as punishment to three unnamed, unlucky wives who had the audacity to appear in public with an uncovered head, speak in private with a freed slave, and attend games, respectively.[72] But again, Valerius is writing of a far distant past (if it ever occurred) and doing so in the Augustan Age.

In contrast the many marriages of Julius Caesar, adoptive father of Augustus, show how common remarriage was by the late Republic for which we have better records. Married to Cornelia until her death, he then married Pompeia, sister of the great Pompey, whom he divorced because she presided over a religious rite that ended in a scandal. When asked why he divorced the likely innocent Pompeia, haughty Caesar reputedly replied that he believed his wife should be above suspicion.[73] He then married Calpurnia, with whom he remained until his death. His last marriage, however, did not prevent him from having a significant extramarital relationship with Cleopatra, queen of Egypt. Given the very public nature of their relationship, and the resulting child, we can easily guess that Caesar might have enjoyed other, unrecorded affairs that escaped the pages of history. But of course no ancient author would condemn a man for enjoying many sexual partners or divorcing often. To my knowledge there is no masculine equivalent of the Latin adjective *univira* (a term used to describe a woman married only once); a Roman man, at least, certainly would not routinely gain fame for being labeled *uxorius*. As long as a Roman man stayed within the prescribed boundaries, steering clear of virgins headed for illustrious marriages and already-married women,[74] it seems that he could enjoy a lifetime of relative sexual freedom.

The first of the emperors, Augustus, attempted to control Romans' private lives, centering on marriage, with a string of laws known as the *Leges Iuliae*, to which a number of authors in this volume allude or discuss at length. Augustus's laws, in brief, aimed to discourage adultery and bachelorhood as well as marriages between those considered of low and high birth; conversely the laws aimed too at increasing the birth rate of aristocratic families by offering perks for elite families with more than three children and freedwomen who bore four or more. The ironies, hypocrisies and failures of Augustus's attempt to legislate these "elite values" are too many to record here, but we would do well to bear in mind that Augustus himself divorced his first wife Scribonia to marry the pregnant Livia, who also divorced her first husband. Did Augustus, later the despiser of adultery, lay a hand on Livia before their wedding night? Was her second baby, Drusus, Augustus's true son? The world may never know. But fascinatingly, as was the case of the kings discussed earlier, with all of our sources on marriage highlighting the supremacy of the imperative to have legitimate children, none of the biological children of the Julio-Claudian emperors ascended the throne of Rome. Later, Augustus would banish (among many others) his only child Julia from Rome for adultery as well as the poet Ovid, who celebrated adultery in a series of famous poems. And so we see the wide divergence in the evidence: distinctly Roman *univirae* populate some sources and adultery and divorce abound in others.

A quick glance at the historical sources would make us believe that marriage to one woman was a deed accomplished by few prominent men in the early empire. I exaggerate here for emphasis, yet no emperor managed a lifetime of monogamy until Emperor Galba, who reigned for seven months after Nero's death in 68 CE, and in any case he was said to prefer the company of men.[75] Tiberius divorced his first wife (with whom he had one son), Vipsania, to marry Augustus's daughter Julia. Caligula was imputed to have committed

FIGURE I.7 Sardonyx cameo depicting Livia with the bust of the deified Augustus, first century CE. Kunsthistorisches Museum, Vienna. Wikipedia.

incest with one or more of his three sisters, and had already been married three times when, at the age of only twenty-eight, he was murdered along with his fourth wife and young daughter. Even Caligula's relatively sane successor Claudius had four wives; his third wife Messalina was implicated in a plot to overthrow him and summarily executed, and the emperor himself may have been killed by his last wife, his brother's daughter Agrippina the Younger, whose son Nero Claudius adopted in 50 CE. Nero's marriages were many: he divorced his first wife Octavia (Claudius's daughter) to marry Poppaea Sabina, and when she died, Statilia Messalina. Moreover, Nero raised hackles by celebrating weddings with three men, Sporus, Pythagoras, and Doryphorus with the trimmings Romans would have recognized as crucial to the weddings of a man and a woman.[76]

FIGURE I.8 Roman bas relief of Claudius and Agrippina, Sebasteion of Claudius, first century CE. Aphrodisias Archaeological Museum, Caria, Turkey. Alamy Stock Photo.

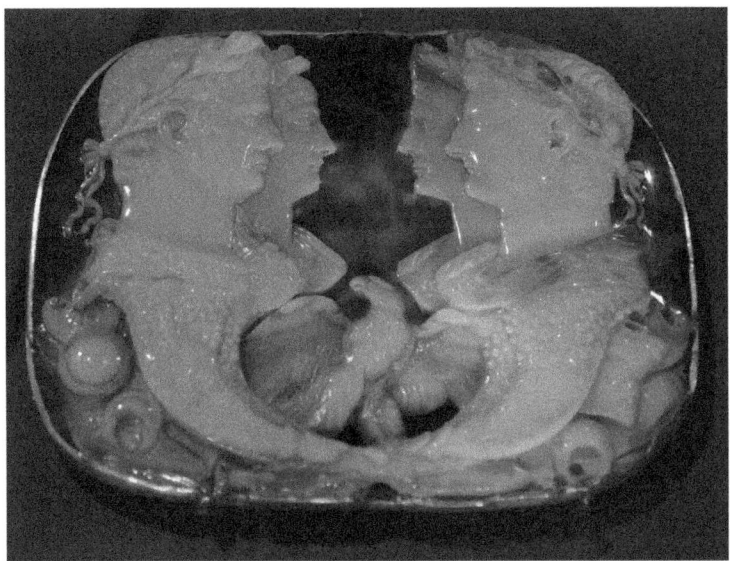

FIGURE I.9 *The Gemma Claudia*, depicting (left) Emperor Claudius and Agrippina the Younger, and (right) Germanicus and Agrippina the Elder. Roman, first century CE. Kunsthistorisches Museum, Vienna. Wikimedia Commons.

FIGURE I.10 Cameo showing Nero flanked by Augustus and Livia, first century CE. Hermitage Museum. Wikimedia Commons.

Marriages of the Julio-Claudian emperors may not have been "unions for all time," but the early empire was not without its heroic wives and husbands whose virtues Roman writers placed firmly in opposition to the often badly behaved, superrich royals. Pliny the Younger records the deeds of non-royals as he immortalizes two great women in one letter, as he writes to his friend of the heroic Arria.[77] Pliny relates how her famous suicide overshadowed her even greater deeds: while nursing her ailing son and husband, the child tragically died, and Arria bravely concealed her child's death from her husband Caecina Paetus, staying cheerful to aid his recovery. We learn that Paetus had joined a rebellion abroad against the emperor Claudius and was taken prisoner, so Arria followed him at great danger to herself. Arriving in Rome, she openly condemned the wife of Paetus's co-conspirator, blaming her for staying alive after her husband's death. When her own Paetus was similarly condemned to death, Arria snatched the sword, stabbed herself, drew the bloody sword from her breast, and held it out to her husband, uttering as she died, "It doesn't hurt, Paetus." Arria's own daughter, Arria the Younger, married to an outspoken opponent of Nero, and her daughter Fannia (living in Pliny's own lifetime) were possessed of the same heroic courage and adamantine resolve as their ancestor Arria.[78]

Tacitus in the *Annals* expresses disdain for the marital peccadilloes of the Julio-Claudian royal family, and his portrait of marriage among the "noble savages" in his *Germania* sheds light on his, and perhaps many Romans', disgust at the marital follies of their louche, many-times-divorced elite compatriots of the first century CE. Tacitus holds up the marriages of the monogamous Germans as estates to which Romans should aspire, emphasizing the almost superhuman courage and chastity of German wives. These simple red-haired barbarians may live in squalid huts but they have something to teach Romans about lifelong commitments.[79]

Tacitus gives his (again, probably exclusively elite) readers a glimpse of marital love amid the filth of the provinces that few Romans would have the chance to observe, but a slightly earlier writer, Petronius, gives his (also probably elite) readers another, and perhaps as equally imaginary, glimpse of marital love amid the squalor right next door in Neronian Rome. In a famous episode preserved from his *Satyrica*, "Trimalchio's dinner," Petronius mocks the gaucherie of monied, ostentatious freed slaves, the seedy underbelly of Roman society, but he shows us too that wives are beloved companions. One diner at the feast remarks that their host, Trimalchio, is hopelessly devoted to his wife Fortunata, who in harder times was so dirty "one would not take bread from her hand."[80]

It is perhaps well to end our discussion here, with a brief look at some startling evidence from the period following Nero. Following the Julio-Claudian dynasty, the Roman Empire evolved and changed ever more rapidly. The title of emperor was held by no fewer than nine men between the years 68 to 100 CE, and by the end of the first century, the empire experienced a surge in new forms of religious worship, many arising outside the Italian peninsula.[81] Roman art, too, evolved to accommodate new trends. One innovation was especially significant for us here.

Marriage alliances of the wealthy and powerful had long been celebrated and publicized, especially in coinage (one outstanding example graces the cover of this book, the coin of Ptolemy and Berenice from the Hellenistic period). In Rome, marriages of Romans of all statuses were commemorated[82] on a variety of funeral monuments, from simple busts adorning *loculi* covers to full-length portraits on elaborate sarcophagi. By the end of the first century, we may observe a rise in depictions of married couples clasping hands on urns and sarcophagi.[83] One common type, found on so-called "biographical" sarcophagus, features three consecutive panels highlighting the virtues of the deceased man within. The leftmost panel shows him in his role of triumphant military leader granting clemency to conquered enemies, the center panel boasts of his piety as he offers sacrifice to the gods, and the rightmost shows him clasping hands with his modestly draped wife. The presence of a goddess embracing the couple, once widely believed to be Juno Pronuba but nowadays identified as Concordia, lends to many of these scenes a divine aura. Scholars disagree about whether this tableau indicates a wedding or lifetime marital harmony;[84] all, however, agree that the gesture represents a married couple comprising a man and woman. Photographic reproductions of funerary monuments featuring this handclasp may be found in almost every handbook of Roman art and culture to provide readers with a snapshot of Roman marriage. Such monuments seem to us windows into deeply cherished Roman beliefs and values; on them we see clear, indisputable expressions of Roman military strength, piety, and married love that anyone can understand without being able to read or write.

FIGURE I.11 Fragment from the front of a sarcophagus, married couple with Concordia, Roman, second CE. British Museum. Wikimedia Commons.

But archaeology has a surprise in store for us, and makes us question what we claim of any graven images from antiquity, for in fact we may possess a startling counter-example to all I have written above concerning visual depictions of marriage. In Rome today in the epigraphic collections of the Terme museum complex resides a cinerary urn from the very period I have been discussing, adorned with a man and woman, putative spouses with their faces half-turned to the viewer, fixed in an eternal handclasp. Yet the inscription above these spouses reads, "To the divine shades. (For) Gaius Iulius Hermes[85] who lived 34 years, 5 months and 3 days, Gaius Iulius Andronicus his fellow freedman set this up for the well-deserving (one) from his own funds." Why does a generic portrayal of a man and woman joined in marital concord decorate an ash-urn dedicated to one man by another? Were such urns so expensive that our dedicator Andronicus bought it on sale, caring not for its depiction of married love? Or did he choose it as a generic depiction of friendship? Was it a mistake of the urn's carver, or a reuse of an urn without the purchaser's knowledge? Or perhaps no mistake at all but so common an artistic trope that it confirms all we have examined above?[86] While the urn's inscription says nothing about marriage, could this urn represent a rare example of a dedication made by a man to his beloved deceased partner, declaring his love in death with a scene borrowed from "heteronormative" practices? We may never have an answer for this particular urn, but its existence surely hints that many of our pronouncements about the valence of the *dextrarum iunctio*, and about marriage itself, among Romans needs constant re-evaluation and reassessment.

I would like therefore to end, as one must, by noting that if we are observant students of antiquity, we will always be left with more questions than answers. What answers we do have I trust will be found in the pages written by my colleagues that follow.

CHAPTER ONE

Courtship and Ritual

KATHERINE WASDIN

Greco-Roman wedding rituals served many purposes, such as uniting families, marking the bride's transition from daughter to wife, and inaugurating a marriage that would hopefully result in heirs. This chapter will explain the wedding ritual and the preliminary arrangements for marriage in the Greco-Roman world, such as the selection of partners and betrothal.[1] Evidence for these social customs comes from a variety of sources. Lexicographers, both Greek and Roman, provide much of our information about precise terminology and ritual details, while literary works such as wedding songs, plays, and novels demonstrate the assumed emotional and social resonances of the wedding rite.[2] Legal and epigraphic sources offer other glimpses of daily life. Visual evidence allows us to observe the central characters of the ritual, including their garments and physical gestures.[3] Greeks and Romans shared similar traditions, particularly in the selection of partners, and I will discuss both cultures together in the section on preliminaries to the wedding. We will then observe two stereotypical weddings, one in classical Athens and one in Rome, to witness how the wedding commemorates the start of the marriage with elements of romance and fertility. I will show that the courting or persuasion of the bride was generally understood as part of the wedding. Finally, the chapter will close by mentioning other ways that marriages could begin. As a public event that marked a private union, the wedding ritual was central to the foundation of communities and to the personal lives of its participants.

CHOOSING A PARTNER AND MAKING AN ENGAGEMENT

Leucippe and Clitophon, a second-century CE Greek novel by Achilles Tatius, demonstrates some potential considerations for selection of a spouse.[4] Although dating from the Second Sophistic period when the Greek world was controlled by Rome, the novel's characters maintain standards of elite marriage established much earlier. The protagonist, Clitophon, was first engaged by his father to his half-sister, with whom he shared a father but not a mother. This engagement was presumably made with his agreement but was designed to preserve the family's wealth, not to validate the sexual or romantic desires of the bride or groom. Such pragmatic motivations and parental influence were the most common factors for forming unions in the ancient world.[5] Despite these careful plans, Clitophon falls in love with his cousin Leucippe and they elope after being caught *in flagrante delicto* by her mother. His passion for a cousin, instead of an unrelated stranger, results in part from the relative sequestration of elite women in ancient Greece, especially Athens.[6] After Leucippe is captured by bandits and presumed dead, Clitophon agrees to marry Melite, a rich widow who is desperately in love with him. As a widow, Melite has greater freedom in choosing her next husband. In the end, both Melite's missing first husband and Leucippe reappear, and Clitophon wins Leucippe's hand in marriage from her father after proving that they remained physically chaste during their travels. Clitophon thus makes a legitimate and endogamous marriage with parental support, despite brief detours through other types of engagement.

A normative first marriage, particularly among the elite classes for whom we have the most ample evidence, would be based on family connections, finances, and social status as well as more intangible factors such as physical attraction and the personality of potential partners. It was assumed that all citizen women would marry, and few women remained single throughout their lives before the rise of Christianity.[7] Men, on the other hand, could choose whether or not to marry, but most did so.[8] Partners did not often select each other but followed the guidance of their elders and sometimes professional matchmakers.[9] A potential groom would seek out the father of the bride rather than the bride herself. Romantic love may have played a role in some unions, but such an idealized romanticism is expressed only in certain generic contexts, particularly comedy and the novel, such as that of Achilles Tatius discussed above.[10] Brides ideally agreed or acquiesced to the wishes of their fathers, and women marrying for the first time were seldom allowed much say in the choice of groom.[11] Grooms might also marry brides chosen by their fathers, as in the union arranged for Clitophon by his father. Roman men whose fathers were alive still fell under their legal control, and some jurists debated how much agency they could have in their own marriages.[12]

Since the primary purpose of marriage was the production of legitimate citizen heirs, typically to continue the father's lineage, it was paramount that the partners have appropriate citizenship status.[13] In Athens, at least after the marriage legislation of Pericles in 451/450 BCE, only fathers and mothers from citizen families could produce citizen offspring; previously only citizen fathers were required.[14] In Rome, intermarriage between inhabitants of Rome and those of other cities (the right of *conubium*) was permitted in an increasingly wide range. Indeed, the foundational myths of Roman marriage are cases of intermarriage with other communities.[15] By the time of Caracalla in 212 CE, all free persons in the Roman Empire were legally citizens. The same rights were not extended to unfree populations. Slaves were not permitted to marry and produce heirs but in Rome could enter into partnerships that were otherwise equivalent to marriage, called *contubernium*, often at the discretion of their owners.[16]

For a parent or guardian, socioeconomic class was an essential consideration in the choice of their child's future spouse, and marriages were normally made between families of a similar income. In fact, humorous texts throughout antiquity mock men who marry into families wealthier than their own as being unavoidably subservient to their elite wives. A character in Menander (fr. 802 K-A) says that the husband of a rich wife "gives himself in marriage instead of taking her," thus reversing the ideal gender hierarchy.[17] Respect for differences in social status could be legally mandated. Thus the Roman emperor Augustus placed restrictions on marriage between people of unequal status in the *Lex Julia de maritandis ordinibus* of 18 BCE.[18] According to this law, those of the senatorial class could not marry freedpersons or those involved in disreputable professions, and freeborn people could not marry adulterers or those connected to prostitution. In the sixth century CE, long after Christianity became the official state religion, these provisions were reversed, allowing for marriages between any partners.[19]

Brides were often much younger than their grooms, although the gap could be larger or smaller and even reversed in some rare situations.[20] Greek girls were married fairly close to the onset of menstruation, around fourteen to eighteen years old, but men more often married after maturity and once they had completed all coming-of-age rituals, around the age of thirty.[21] In Rome, marriage occurred generally when women were in their late teens, although perhaps earlier for elite women and men.[22] The minimum age for legal marriage was twelve for women and fourteen for men. Early age at first marriage was a way to guarantee the bride's chastity, not necessarily to ensure that she maximized her childbearing years. In fact, some writers recommend that families wait until the bride was several years past menarche before marriage and pregnancy, since childbirth was understood to be risky for younger women.[23]

Finally, the partners could not be too closely related. Incest norms differed in various ancient communities. Marriage between cousins or half-siblings was permitted in most Greek communities, as we saw above in the tale of Clitophon and Leucippe, although full siblings could not marry.[24] Some such endogamic unions were mandatory, as in the case of the Athenian *epiklerate*.[25] An *epikleros* was a female survivor of a father who had no direct male heirs. Since women could not inherit in their own right, the *epikleros* had to marry her closest male relative, such as an uncle, in order to produce an heir and keep her father's property within the family line. In Rome, neither half-siblings nor cousins were allowed to marry each other. In Egypt, on the other hand, it appears that full siblings could, and did, marry. This custom was infamously practiced by the Ptolemies, the Macedonian Greek rulers of Egypt, as well as others who inhabited the area during the Greco-Roman period.[26]

Second marriages, following a divorce or the death of a spouse, could involve more agency on the part of the bride.[27] The adventures of Clitophon illustrate this well, since the rich widow Melite eventually browbeats the protagonist into marrying her. Our most detailed historical example of a previously married bride choosing her next husband is Cicero's daughter Tullia, who arranged her own engagement to Dolabella with the input of her mother but not her father. Letters between Cicero and his family describe the process. It appears that the two women decided on the candidate without first clearing him with Cicero, who seems to have had some reservations about the groom.[28] A first-century CE wedding poem by Statius describes the marriage of a widow, Violentilla, without mentioning her parents at all.[29] Widows and divorced women were presumably older and better equipped to express their own preferences, whether or not they were under the legal control of parents or guardians.

As these sources show, the choice of partner was based on social and economic considerations; marriage served to provide heirs and to connect two families. Other factors may be mentioned but are not commonly given prominent attention. A letter of Pliny the Younger (*Ep.* 5.16) praises Minicia, who died right before her marriage, as an ideal bride. The young woman is described as lovable, chaste, and reliable.[30] Romantic elements could of course be considered: a character in Menander's *Dyscolus* (788–790) claims that marriage is more pleasant when the groom feels *eros* at the beginning of a marriage. But the more normal approach is probably illustrated by another fragment of Menander, in which a character chides his fellow citizens for caring more about the pedigree than the personality of their brides (fr. 804 K-A).

Once the partners had been selected, the next step was their engagement (*engye* in Greek; *sponsalia* in Latin).[31] In both Greece and Rome, a betrothal was an agreement between the future husband and the bride's father or guardian to transfer the bride from her birth home to her husband's dwelling for the production of male heirs. Unlike the wedding, which required the presence of the bride, the engagement was an agreement between men and could be made without her.[32] With her would usually come her dowry, wealth that passed to the temporary control of the groom but which could be returned in the case of divorce. The length of engagement could vary widely, as could the amount of contact between fiancée and fiancé. In Athens, interaction would have been limited unless the future spouses were family. In Rome, they may have had extensive contact, perhaps even including cohabitation.[33]

Greek traditions record the symbolic importance of the betrothal. Menander provides an Athenian engagement formula, not found elsewhere, in which the father of the bride states "I pledge my daughter to you, young man, for the plowing of legitimate children and I give as dowry three talents."[34] While his plays are driven by the emotional connections between characters, the formula reminds the audience of the legal and financial elements of the marriage: it ensured legitimate heirs and was accompanied by the transfer of property along with the bride.[35] Furthermore, the metaphor of plowing speaks to the larger cultural equation of agricultural and human reproduction. According to Gloria Ferrari, the etymology of *engye* shows that it preserved the bride like a treasure, hiding her until she is revealed to her husband at the wedding (*ekdosis*).[36] The procedures for betrothal in Rome are similar. Again, comedy seems to preserve a betrothal formula. In two plays by Plautus, a groom asks his father-in-law "Do you promise her?" and receives in reply the response "I do promise her."[37] The engagement might be marked by the gift of a ring from groom to bride.[38] Several Roman rings that show clasped hands may be markers of such a ceremony or could represent harmonious relations between husband and wife. Latin authors attest to parties celebrating engagements thrown by the father of the bride called *sponsalia*.[39] Official documentation was common, as attested by the many marriage contracts found on papyri, but was not required.[40] In both Greece and Rome, engagement was conducted between men and concerned the transferal of a woman from one household to another. The actual transferal of the bride occurred in the wedding rite.

RITES

Athens

Let us imagine the wedding of a typical Athenian bride, as seen in Greek textual and visual sources.[41] For the sake of convenience, we will call our bride (*nymphe*) Timarete, the name of the maiden from the epigram quoted below, and assume that she marries in the latter part of the fifth century in Athens.[42] A young woman from a family of some means, she has spent most of her time at home and has met few men from outside her own family. Her wedding will separate her from her familiar home and send her to a new household (*oikos*) to live with her groom, Eratosthenes. Like many brides, our nymphe will marry in the winter month *Gamelion*, which takes its name from the *gamos* (marriage) between Hera and Zeus.[43]

Ancient sources mention three separate days for celebration: *proaulia, gamos*, and *epaulia*.[44] For the *proaulia*, Timarete will prepare herself. She takes a bath using special water from a sacred spring, the Enneakrounos or Callirhoe.[45] The sacred water would be brought to her in a commemorative vase with an elongated neck called a *loutrophoros* (see Figure 1.1).[46] Many red-figure wedding vases show the adornment of the bride as a secluded and romantic occasion.[47] In these scenes, she is assisted by groups of women, at

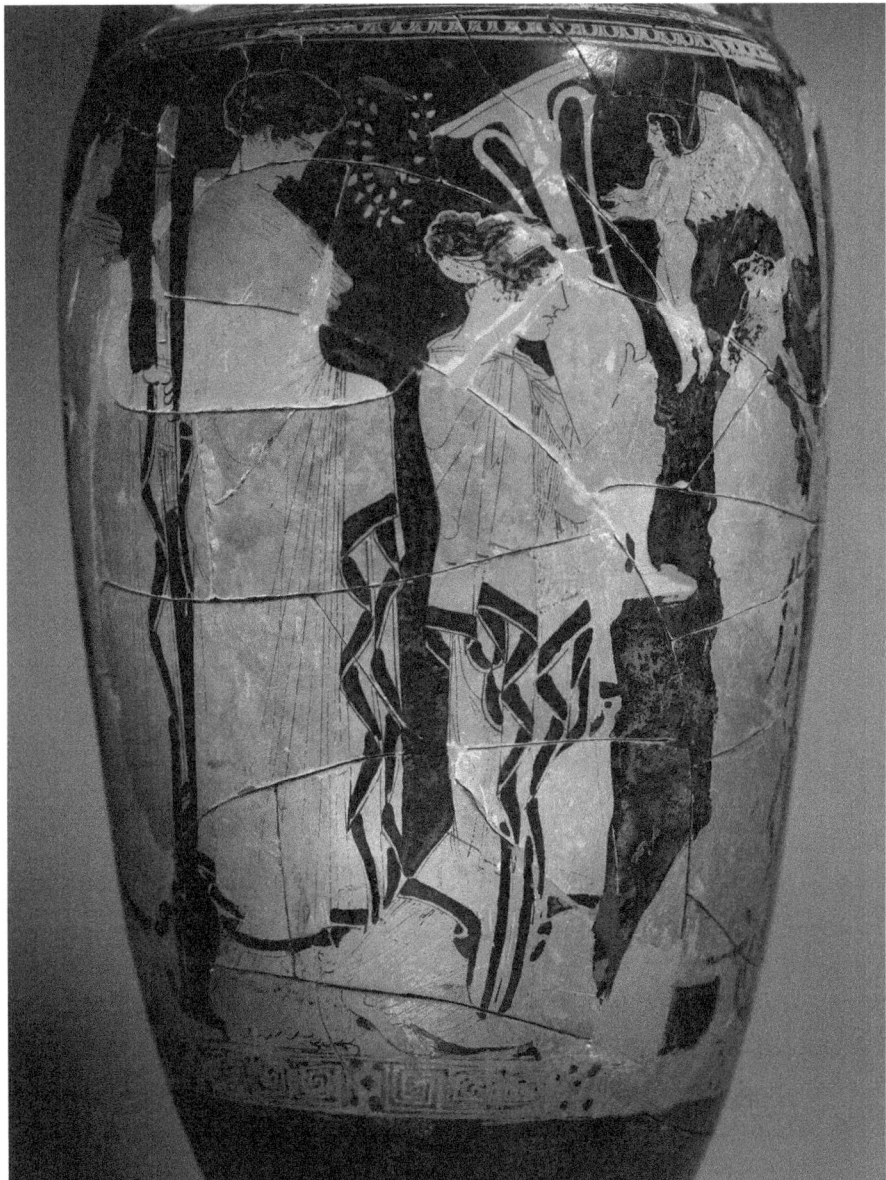

FIGURE 1.1 Detail from a terracotta *lebes gamikos* attributed to the Wedding Painter, c. 430–420 BCE. De Agostini / G. Dagli Orti via Getty Images.

times joined by Eros or even Aphrodite. Eratosthenes also prepares for the wedding, but the dressing of the groom was less significant and seldom described or represented. This day might also see offerings and sacrifices called *proteleia* to Artemis or other goddesses associated with the wedding and marriage, such as Aphrodite or Hera.[48] An anonymous epigram (*AP* 6.280) commemorates such an offering:

Before her wedding, Timarete dedicated her tambourine, her lovely ball, the headdress that protected her hair, and her dolls, as is fitting, gifts from a girl to you, also a girl, Artemis Limnatis, as well as her dolls' clothes. Daughter of Leto, may you place your hand over the daughter of Timaretus, and purely preserve her as pure.

Timarete hopes for the goddess' protection as she leaves behind her status as maiden (*parthenos*) and looks toward her future pregnancy and delivery, which were believed to be the concern of Artemis.

The day of the wedding was given many names by antiquarian sources. In addition to the rather generic term *gamos*, it could be called the *ekdosis* (handing over). Timarete is the focal point of the ceremony, as it is she who will be handed over and revealed to her groom. For the wedding, a bridal assistant called the *nympheutria* helps her dress in costly fabrics. She wears a veil, which covers her face completely, a tiara, and special shoes.[49] The importance of the veil can be seen in another term for the day, the *anakalypteria* (unveiling).[50] Some scholars, such as Oakley and Sinos (1993: 25–26) presume specific moments of unveiling. Ferrari (2003), on the other hand, argues that the unveiling does not refer to a specific point in the ritual. In her reading, the day of the wedding feast and procession would be the day that Timarete is presented to the community as a chaste and veiled bride who reveals herself to her husband alone. The day of the *anakalypteria* gave its name also to the gifts received by the bride, such as boxes of perfumes, clothing, and vases. These, or other additional presents, would be brought to her the next day during the *epaulia*.[51]

Wedding songs for specific points in the ceremony express the general atmosphere and presentation of the couple.[52] Groups of men and women of the same age as Timarete and her husband perform songs as part of the ceremony, addressing the couple with the ritual cry of *hymen,* and greeting them with *chairete,* a common salutation which literally translates as "rejoice!" or "fare well!"[53] Songs praise the divine beauty of Timarete and trumpet her groom's good luck in marrying her with the *makarismos* (blessing).[54] Extant wedding songs also show the importance of mythical analogues. Wedding poetry praises brides and grooms as divine or heroic in beauty and birth, temporarily elevating them beyond their normal existence.[55]

Timarete's father hosts a lavish feast at his house, featuring many rich and expensive foods as well as celebratory sesame cakes.[56] Both men and women come to witness the wedding and enjoy the banquet, but they dine at separate tables and do not mingle with each other.[57] Timarete sits surrounded by the women and closely veiled, perhaps revealing herself to the groom. She is both hidden and shown, and part of the wedding display is an exhibition of her seclusion.[58] Certain rituals connected with fertility may have occurred during the feast, with the aid of a *pais amphithales,* a child with both parents still living who embodies the couple's hope for a future heir. Some sources claim that such a child recited "I have fled evil; I have found something better" and carried a *liknon* (grain basket).[59] This act may symbolize the fertility of the bride and continue the agricultural metaphor seen in the Menandrian betrothal formula.[60]

The most public point in the wedding was a procession (*nymphagogia*), which brought the bride to the groom's residence when the Evening Star appeared at dusk (see Figure 1.2).[61] Timarete and Eratosthenes ride in a cart through the streets, along with one of his friends as guard.[62] This groomsman is present in part to ensure the safety of the procession and prevent anyone from attempting to abduct Timarete.[63] Those in the wedding party wave torches to light their path.[64] A fragment from the Archaic poet Sappho (fr. 44 V.) describes the wedding celebrations for a mythical couple, but the jubilant scene would have been familiar to almost all Greek weddings:

FIGURE 1.2 Terracotta lekythos (oil flask) attributed to the Amasis Painter, *c.* 550–530 BCE. Dea Picture Library/De Agostini via Getty Images.

> And the flute singing sweetly was mixed …
> along with the noise of the castanets … and the maidens
> sang a sacred song and the divine noise rose to the sky
> and there was everywhere in the roads …
> mixing bowls and libation cups …
> myrrh and cassia and frankincense were mingled together
> and all the older women cried out piercingly
> and all the men loudly sang a delightful high-pitched strain
> calling on Paean the far-shooter with his lovely lyre,
> and they celebrated Hector and Andromache, similar to the gods.

As Timarete passes through the streets, she is accompanied by torchlight, dancing, music, and singing. All those living along the route would be aware of her wedding. The procession is the literal manifestation of one of the common verbs for marrying, *ago* (to take or lead), and on some vases the groom even takes the bride by the wrist.[65] Like her veil, the procession toys with displaying the bride by revealing her to the community but in a way that emphasizes her concealment from full view.

The procession is accompanied by rituals that mark the bride's departure from one *oikos* and integration into another. Timarete's mother proudly holds a torch as she bids farewell to her daughter.[66] The bride's mother plays a pivotal role, and the ceremony includes the melancholy parting of the bride from her mother.[67] In Euripides' *Iphigenia at Aulis* (691–741), the putative bride's mother Clytemnestra insists on performing her duties in arranging the ceremony, waving torches, and attending a special banquet for women. While Timarete maintains emotional and legal ties to her father and mother, she will dwell with her groom, help manage his domestic life, and provide him with children. After the procession, she must be incorporated into her groom's household, and her mother-in-law greets her arrival with torches. Inside the household, she and Eratosthenes are showered with fruits and nuts in a ritual called the *katachusmata* (see Figure 1.3).[68] The couple are finally led to a decorated bridal chamber, where Timarete eats a slice of quince to sweeten her breath.[69] These fruit-based rituals encourage the fruitfulness of the couple, joining other hints at the bride's future role in the household.[70]

FIGURE 1.3 Fragment of a *loutrophoros* depicting the preparations of a bride, Phiale Painter, 430–425 BCE. Julia Bradford Huntington James Fund and Museum purchase with funds donated by contribution, Museum of Fine Arts Boston, 10.223. Photo: © 2018 Museum of Fine Arts, Boston, Massachusetts.

The celebration continues without the couple through the night, with songs performed outside the bedroom door.[71] Her friends might call out to Timarete, but the *nymphagogos* prevents them from interfering with the couple's first night together.[72] In the morning, waking songs (*exergetika*) greet the married couple. On this day, gifts are brought to the bride, and the day and the gifts share the name *epaulia*. The wedding ritual is now at an end, but Timarete retains her status as *nymphe* until she gives birth to her first child. Later, Eratosthenes will offer a sacrifice and feast called a *gamelia* in honor of his marriage to members of his civic clan, the *phratry*.[73] This ceremony would ensure group awareness of the union and establish the legitimacy of the couple's heirs. Throughout the wedding itself, however, the bride is the center of attention. Her ideological centrality to the Greek wedding is demonstrated by the fact that her appearance is the focal point in the procession scenes common in black-figure representations of the wedding as well as the interior adornment scenes more common in red-figure vases.[74]

Rome

The Roman wedding ritual, like the Greek one, centers on the movements of the bride.[75] Our ideal Roman bride is called Cornelia, and we will assume that her wedding takes place in the early years of the first century CE. She is seventeen years old, and her father has arranged for her marriage to Gaius Claudius Rufus, who is twenty-six. The two have met several times, and she proudly wears the ring marking her engagement to him.[76] Even after her wedding she will remain in the legal control of her father, since she will marry *sine manu*. Older wedding rituals, seldom practiced in her day, had transferred the bride to the legal control (*manus*) of her husband. These ceremonies, called *coemptio* and *confarreatio*, took place only sporadically in the late Republican and Imperial periods, and were maintained because certain priesthoods required them.[77] The *coemptio* seems to have involved the "sale" of the bride to the groom. The more archaic and restricted *confarreatio* was named after a sacrificial cake made of spelt (*far*). It required the presence of the important priests, such as the *Flamen Dialis* and the *Pontifex Maximus*.[78] Brides could also pass into their husband's *manus* automatically, by spending a year living together, but this could be avoided by having the bride spend three nights a year elsewhere.

Cornelia marries in the second half of June.[79] Before the wedding she offers objects from her childhood to the gods and dedicates her doll to the household protectors, the *Lares*.[80] Unlike her groom, who formally put aside the trappings of youth in puberty, at around fifteen or sixteen, Cornelia has had no coming-of-age ceremonies until her wedding and is still considered a child. In preparing for her wedding and during the ceremony, she is assisted by a *pronuba*, who leads her through the ritual.[81] As a devoted wife who has had only one husband, the *pronuba* models the Roman ideal of the *univira*. In literary works, such as Stat. *Silv.* 1.2, the role is often filled by the goddess Venus, which demonstrates the sensual elements in her guidance. Before the wedding, Cornelia must sit patiently while her hair is arranged by being divided into six strands and piled on top of her head in an intricate hairstyle called the *sex crines* or *seni crines*.[82] Unusual implements are employed, including a spear, the *hasta caelibaris*, with which Cornelia's hair is parted.[83] She and her attendants may discuss the different meanings of the spear, recalling the original wedding of Rome, the rape of the Sabine women, and Cornelia's upcoming submission to her husband.[84]

The bride's unique costume identifies her as the center of the ceremony and would have been instantly recognizable to any ancient Roman. On the day of her wedding Cornelia wears a *tunica recta* (upright tunic), tied with a special belt (*cingulum*) and covered with a large yellow-orange veil (*flammeum*).⁸⁵ This veil is one of the most important features of the Roman wedding, frequently used as a metonymy for the ceremony as a whole.⁸⁶ It gets its name from its flame-like tone and is also described as *luteus* (yellow).⁸⁷ The veil covers part of Cornelia's face, rendering her mostly unrecognizable, and runs down her back to cover much of her body as well.⁸⁸ As appropriate for such a festive occasion, both she and the groom wear crowns of flowers and perfume. Figure 1.4 may show a woman in a bridal costume with yellow-orange shoes and a *flammeum* on the bed beside her. She is joined by a semi-nude Venus.⁸⁹

Cornelia's wedding begins in her father's house, as she prepares to leave it behind. A traditional part of Roman weddings was the taking of the *auspices*, a practice by which a religious official determined whether the gods were in favor of the day's activities by observing the flight of birds. Cicero tells us that in his day, the presence of an *augur* (a religious specialist) at a wedding was standard, albeit primarily ceremonial.⁹⁰ On the day of Cornelia's wedding, an *augur* pronounces that the gods support the day's ritual. Cornelia and Claudius then sign the wedding documents before witnesses. While they could be married without such procedures, it was standard for the parties to strictly delineate the dowry and their own property.⁹¹ Cornelia's departure from her family home is marked by her public separation from her mother. She is manifestly afraid to lose her virginity on the wedding night and longs to stay close to her beloved mother. She might even cling to her and in a ritualized abduction be ostensibly stolen away from her lap.⁹²

Cornelia will now at last move from her father's house to her new home in a procession (the *pompa* or *domum deductio*). The groom and others beseech her to leave what had until now been her home.⁹³ Reluctantly, Cornelia emerges from the door, covered in the

FIGURE 1.4 Detail from the Aldobrandini Wedding, from Rome, Esquiline Hill, 27 BCE–14 CE, detached fresco. Biblioteca Apostolica Vaticana, Vatican Museums, Rome, Italy, Cat. 79631. Photo: Alberto Pizzoli/AFP/Getty Images.

flammeum. As she moves through Rome, she is accompanied by exuberant celebration, featuring the ritual cry *talasio*.[94] Even this cry was thought by some to have originated in the capture of the Sabine women, a reminder of the forceful removal of the bride from her family. During the procession, there is explicit mockery, mostly teasing the groom in crude songs called the Fescennines. Such songs created a jovial atmosphere and may have served to avert the evil eye.[95] As they sing the Fescennines, members of the wedding party playfully throw nuts.[96] Even if the wedding takes place during the daylight, Cornelia's path is illuminated with torches carried by a boy as well as perhaps the groom.[97] Like the veil, the torches can represent the marriage rite as a whole, so central were they to public perception of the celebration. The procession was a necessary element of the ritual, and legal texts suggest that leading the bride to the groom's house could successfully mark the start of a valid marriage even if the groom himself happened to be absent.[98] As in the Greek rite, the revelation of the bride is at the center of the wedding. Cornelia has been hidden in her father's house and is now shown to the community as she passes from one household to another, covered with the brightly colored *flammeum*.

Upon reaching the house, Cornelia takes part in rituals of incorporation. As she is led inside, she pronounces the ritual phrase "Where and when you are Gaius, there and then I am Gaia."[99] With this, she perhaps hopes to emulate the ideal wife, Gaia Caecilia or Tanaquil.[100] Finally, Cornelia garlands the doorframe with oil and wool, and cautiously crosses the threshold.[101] To stumble at such a moment would be a terrible omen, so she takes great care as she enters and is assisted by the *pronuba*.[102] Once inside, Claudius offers her fire and water, symbols of civilization and acceptance.[103] It is at this point that she begins to be considered a married woman.[104] Inside the house, Cornelia finds a feast.[105] The *pronuba* leads her to a special couch, the *lectus genialis*, on which she dines together with the groom.[106] The name of the couch indicates its connections to the guardian spirit of the groom's household, the *Genius*, and the couch may have remained in the courtyard of the house as a prominent reminder of the wedding. At the end of the evening, Cornelia is led to the wedding chamber and joined there by Claudius. There, in the darkness, they spend their first night together as husband and wife.

Behind much of the Roman ritual lies the mythical first wedding of Rome, known today as the Rape of the Sabine Women.[107] In this story, popularized during the Augustan era and recounted in Livy and others, the Romans were not granted treaties of intermarriage with neighboring towns and thus lacked a way to reproduce and continue the city. They decided to trick the other communities by inviting them to a festival as a pretense for abducting their marriageable women. According to Livy, they flattered the women by claiming they had stolen them out of love to make them more amenable to their new lives (1.9). The men, including the Sabines, waged war against the Romans to retrieve their kinswomen. In the end, the war ceased when the women threw themselves and their newborn children between the two sides, unwilling to watch a battle between their natal families and their new husbands. Many rituals (the *hasta caelibaris*, the cry of *talasio*, taking the bride from her mother) are ascribed to this original marriage by capture, which foregrounds the ongoing tension in ancient society between natal and marital bonds, and presents marriage as both forceful abduction and seductive persuasion.

The conclusion of the myth of the Sabine women in the foundation of Rome marks the agreement (*concordia*) between different communities and between husband and wife. Marital *concordia* is inaugurated at the wedding, and many sarcophagi from the high Roman Empire show the personified goddess Concordia uniting husband and wife, sometimes with other wedding iconography. The couple demonstrate their union with the

FIGURE 1.5 Wedding scene (*dextrarum iunctio*), detail from a Roman sarcophagus, second century CE. Museo Nazionale Romano Palazzo Massimo Alle Terme, Rome, Italy. Photo: DeAgostini/Getty Images.

dextrarum iunctio, or joining of right hands (see Figure 1.5). Because of its prominence on sarcophagi, it has often been taken to represent a gesture performed during the wedding ritual. More recent scholars have questioned this view, since the literary sources do not mention clasping hands at any point in the wedding.[108] Instead, the *dextrarum iunctio* seems to have been a potent symbol of the *concordia* between husband and wife during their married life together.

RITUAL VARIANTS

Not all couples followed all of the Athenian and Roman rites and rituals I have described above. Our fictional brides Timarete and Cornelia took part in a wedding ritual to mark the start of their marriage, but there were other ways to begin a union in the ancient world. One of the most dramatic was what we call "abduction marriage," in which the bride is abducted by her groom without a prearranged agreement between her father and the abductor.[109] Such unions may be ratified after the fact. For many, these may have been assault pure and simple, and it seems that in some cases women were expected to marry their rapists.[110] In other cases, such abductions may have been the result of collusion between the bride and the groom and were a way to arrange for marriages of passion. In fact, our opening example of the eventual marriage between Clitophon and Leucippe in Achilles Tatius's novel could be considered an abduction marriage, since the bride and groom run away together but later gain the blessing of her father.

Another version of the wedding ceremony is found in Sparta, although it is worth noting that most sources for unusual Spartan practices are late and may exaggerate the idiosyncrasies of the Spartans for dramatic effect.[111] Spartan society was based on the military, and the young groom maintained his role as a soldier living alongside his companions rather than living together with his wife. According to Plutarch, the bride's head was shaved on her wedding night.[112] The masculine grooming of the bride may serve to make the groom, accustomed to life in the barracks, more comfortable, or could have served as a rite of passage for the bride. Her groom would sneak out to visit her at night, and the marriage was not officially announced until she bore him a child.[113] Many other elements of the preparations for the wedding, however, including the tradition of bridal offerings, would be the same as in other Greek cities.

I have painted with a broad and synchronic brush, since the traditions associated with the wedding are extraordinarily resilient. But change is inevitable, albeit gradual, and late antiquity saw increasingly fraught interactions between traditional customs and Christian ideals. Religious officials were late taking control of regulating marriages, and in Western Europe marriages could begin and be recognized by communities without the input of priests until the medieval period.[114] Many of the rites and traditions of weddings from antiquity survived long into the Christian period, and there may not have been a "religious" marriage ritual until the fourth century, when the sources first refer specifically to Christian nuptials, mentioning a benediction by a priest and the continuing prominence of veils.[115] Since the wedding was a primarily private affair, organized by individual households and with little formal religious behavior or state intervention in both Greek and Roman traditions, its customs were durable.

CONCLUSION

We can discern at least four different narratives in the wedding ritual: transferal, transformation, seduction, and reproduction. First, the bride's father or guardian transfers her publically to the home of her new husband, along with goods for her upkeep designated as the dowry.[116] Second, the bride undergoes a rite of passage, and the wedding contains rituals of separation, transition, and incorporation that mark her change in status.[117] The Greek ritual could be seen as parallel to a religious initiation for her and uses similar terminology.[118] Hera's epithet as marriage goddess was Hera Teleia, and the marriage was seen as a sort of *telos*, the same word used for initiations. A similar conflation of marriage and initiation may occur in the frescoes from the Villa of the Mysteries in Pompeii, which depict both a Dionysian ritual and a woman dressed as a bride (see Figure 1.6). Removed from her family home, the girl is transformed into a wife.

Third, the wedding included a dramatic seduction of the bride. Scattered references assume that brides look forward to their wedding, but the ceremony itself places great importance on persuading the bride to marry, implying a resistance on her part. Fragments from wedding poems by Sappho present the voice of a bride mourning the loss of her *parthenia*, or maiden status, which has departed never to return. In turn, wedding songs and vases emphasize the bride's and groom's desirability, and feature the influence of the erotic deities Aphrodite or Venus and Eros. Many aspects of the wedding highlight her agency and persuade her to willingly consent to the union.[119] This dichotomy between chaste seclusion and willing acquiescence can be seen in the importance of the veil in both cultures.[120] Marriage, an institution geared toward the reproduction of the male line, is inaugurated by the wedding as a romantic connection between bride and groom. This

FIGURE 1.6 Fresco from the Villa of the Mysteries, detail of young woman in bridal yellow arranging her hair, while a cupid holds the mirror, second half of first century BCE. Pompeii, Italy. Photo: Werner Forman/Universal Images Group/Getty Images.

courting of the bride, however, is done by the community on behalf of the groom, who appears as a participant along with the bride. Finally, the wedding prepares for procreation with elements that encourage fertility and reproduction, seen in the use of fruits and domestic equipment in both Greek and Roman rites. The communal and familial necessity for heirs is a primary motivation for the institution of marriage, and elements of this goal can be found in the ritual celebrating it. Such elements are not as prominent in wedding poetry but do appear in scattered images and descriptions of the ceremony, designating their traditional importance. Throughout antiquity, courtship and wedding rituals negotiate the social and personal needs of couples, families, and the wider community.

CHAPTER TWO

Religion

The Gods and Rituals of Greek and Roman Weddings

MATTHEW P. J. DILLON

Ancient Greeks and Romans observed specific wedding rituals that invoked numerous deities whose assistance was called upon to ensure both that the marriage resulting from the wedding would be successful and that the marriage would be publicly acknowledged. While there were differences among weddings in the two societies, in both cases these rituals focused largely on the bride rather than the groom, reflecting the gendered nature of these societies. Weddings also highlighted the bride who entered into and was to dwell in the husband's house, leaving her own family and household. Various rituals ensured the approbation of the gods and prepared the bride for her transition to wife, while the groom performed others which marked her acceptance into his home. Friends and relatives acted as witnesses to the wedding and played a role in the various ceremonies, which called upon specific deities associated with weddings and marriages. For Rome, the evidence centers on elite families, while much of what is known of Greek weddings comes from scenes on vases from Athens. These latter depictions might well reflect the weddings of prosperous rather than poor Athenians, and the rites performed at Athens do not necessarily reflect practices across the Greek world. In neither society was there such a thing as a "standard" wedding; moreover there would have been variations in nuptial practices depending on economic and social status, geographical location, and local customs.

THE GODS AND RITUALS OF THE GREEK WEDDING

In the *Odyssey*, the ship-wrecked Odysseus says to the young Nausikaa, who has gone to the seashore to wash her clothes in the expectation of a forthcoming marriage to some suitable young man, that he hopes the gods grant her a lifetime union with "a husband and a home and unity of mind and feeling." In turn, Nausikaa is shown by Homer praying to the gods for a husband.[1] There was a very real sense in which it was believed, at least in the case of heroes and semi-divine mortals, that the gods were responsible for arranging a marriage. For example, Homer relates the tale of the orphaned daughters of Pandareus (killed by Zeus for stealing the golden hound guarding his sanctuary), for each of whom Aphrodite intended to ask Zeus to bring about a "blissful marriage."[2] The marriage between Zeus and Hera was described as sacred—a *heiros gamos*.[3] Material evidence attests to a popular belief that gods were involved in mortal marriages: dedications of hair and toys, the *proteleia*, and wedding sacrifices, all signal a belief in the interest and involvement of the divine in the weddings of mortals, not just in the world of epic but in the present time.

Diodoros, in describing the attributes of various gods, has Zeus giving to Aphrodite the care of maidens in the years in which they would marry, and superintendence of "wedding matters," and Plutarch lists Aphrodite among the gods most closely involved with weddings: Zeus Teleios (Fulfillment), Hera Teleia, Aphrodite, Peitho (Persuasion), and Artemis, and seems to be applying this across the panhellenic world.[4] Zeus and Hera here obviously stood metonymically for divine marriage, but their *epikleseis* (epithets) given here (Teleios and Teleia) also point to their role in the fulfillment of the married state. Peitho was worshipped as the goddess of persuasion in love, and she and Aphrodite were thought of as persuading the bride and groom of their mutual love, while Artemis oversaw the transition of the bride from maiden to adult spouse. Hera as Hera Gamelia, "Hera of the Wedding," received offerings at the wedding itself.[5] In addition, the chorus of Argive soldiers in Aeschylus's *Supplians* mentions, in connection with the marriage of the daughters of Danaos with the sons of Aigyptos, several female deities who must be honored: Aphrodite, Hera, Pothos (Longing), Peitho, and Harmonia. A fragment of the next play in the trilogy to which the *Supplians* belongs, the *Danaides*, has Aphrodite singing of the marriage of Ouranos and Chthonie (Heaven and Earth), praising the rain resulting from the union, as it provides mortals with fodder for their flocks, and grain and fruit (the works of Demeter).[6] The importance of goddesses in the wedding ritual is also reflected in their role in helping a marriage to prosper: Plutarch advises that when a husband and wife sleep apart after they have quarreled, they should invoke Aphrodite; he then paraphrases a passage from the *Iliad* in which Hera comments that she will resolve the dispute between Okeanos and Tethys, and send them back to their shared marriage bed reunited in love.[7] After the wedding, with all the divine involvement that it entailed, Plutarch advises that the bride and groom should have the same friends—and worship the same gods; that is, the wife should worship the same gods (and have the same friends) as her husband.[8]

PRE-WEDDING DEDICATIONS

Many ancient Greek states had a month in the season of winter named Gamelion, "Marriage Month," in which many weddings were presumably celebrated.[9] Bridal preparations in ancient Greece commenced with ceremonies involving the cutting and dedication of girlhood hair, and ritual bathing. Most of the religious rituals performed prior to the actual marriage celebration were undertaken by the bride, rather than the groom, to prepare her for the wedding ceremony and her new role as wife. Cutting the bride's hair and its dedication to a deity might appear to have been a initiation ritual for girls, but in all cases the deity to whom the hair was dedicated was concerned in some way with fertility or marriage: this was a rite of transition. The first evidence for a dedication relating to marriage is from the poet Archilochos from the island of Paros in the sixth century BCE: "Alkibia dedicated to Hera the sacred veil of her tresses, when she met with a lawful marriage." He deliberately uses the word "veil" to signify Alkibia's long hair, as this was a specific accoutrement of the bride. Dedications of the hair of brides prior to their marriage are known from throughout Greece, when the pubescent girl shed her girlish locks and pig-tails (as seen on the *korai* of the Athenian Erechtheion) and shortened her hair, which could then be bound in a bun and hidden under the close fitting cloth cap which women are routinely shown wearing on Athenian vases. Hence in Antipater's epigram in the *Anthologia Palatina* (or *Greek Anthology*) the girl Hippe, otherwise unknown, "put up" her hair at the time of her wedding.[10]

The custom of hair dedication is known from Herodotus for the girls on the island of Delos, while Pausanias six hundred years later refers to the same practice there in his own day. Prior to their wedding, girls would go to the tomb of the (mythical) Hyperborean maidens, where they would cut off their hair and dedicate it. Because the Hyperborean maidens had died virgins, and hence were childless, their assistance was sought to ensure that the young women about to be married would not enter the same childless condition but give birth to many children.[11] As the girls left behind their virginal state and made the transition to married life, they sought the aid of virginal deities whose status they would no longer share but upon whose favor and goodwill they relied in this transition. Some of these deities, as in the case of the Hyperborean maidens, were clearly seen as potent chthonic entities who could assist these prospective brides. Boys on Delos performed the same ritual, but Herodotus does not connect their hair cutting and dedication with marriage, since most of the boys would have married considerably later than the girls, and theirs was a rite of transition to manhood.

Virgin deities were, therefore, particularly the object of hair dedications. For example, before their weddings, maidens in Megara would visit the local tomb of the virgin Iphinoe, who had the status of a semi-divine heroine, and dedicate their hair to her as well as offer her libations: both types of offerings were designed to secure her favor. A male deity could also be involved: Hippolytos had worshipped Artemis exclusively and was punished by Aphrodite with death for this reason: as he dies, Artemis promises him that in recompense he will receive the locks of young girls prior to marriage. At his temple on the island of Troizen, all brides prior to their wedding cut off, and dedicated, a lock of their hair to Hippolytos—once again on the same apotropaic principle that he, as a divine hero, would ward off his own fate from the maidens supplicating him and assist them in their transition to the married state, their loss of virginity, and in their new role as wife.

Prior to her marriage, Nausikaa as a young girl in the *Odyssey* washes her clothes and afterwards plays a ball game with her maiden servants.[12] This is a deliberate juxtaposition, for Nausikaa will soon have to leave aside her ball games and would be expected to wash garments as part of her duties as a married woman. Girls put away their childhood toys when on the point of marriage, not simply to mark a transition but to invoke the protection of the goddess Artemis or the nymphs as they left their pre-adolescent, virginal life to encounter sexuality and childbirth. An anonymous epigram details some of the items a maiden might have dedicated: Timarete dedicated to Artemis Likmatis ("of the Lake," at Sparta) her tambourine, pretty ball, hair net, and her dolls and their dresses: as the epigram states, these were the gifts of a virgin to the virgin goddess. In passing from the virginal to the married state, Timarete propitiates the virgin goddess as she passes from virginity and her childhood toys to adulthood. Similarly Hippe, mentioned above, has put away her knucklebones in preparation for her wedding, and Artemis is invoked to grant her a husband and children.[13] Artemis was a kourotrophic deity, a "child-nurturer," caring for the health of infants and their sustenance: as dedications to her were crucial after the weddings, so were dedications prior to marriage which were obviously considered essential for the success of the union.[14] Similarly, a groom would make a sacrifice to Aphrodite Kourotrophos before bringing the bride to his home in the hope of ensuring his bride's fertility.[15]

Brides would also customarily dedicate their girdle (*zonê*) to Artemis prior to the wedding, as part of the transition to married woman: girdles, like the hair net, were part of a girl's dress. An Athenian red-figure lekythos depicts a young woman loosening her girdle, presumably to take it off, in front of the goddess Artemis who is holding her bow and arrows in her left hand and a flaming (wedding) torch in her right; the logical interpretation of this scene is that here the bride is dedicating her maiden's girdle, which bound her dress, and that Artemis (with the wedding torch) is ensuring the success of her marriage. Similarly, at Troizen, girls dedicated their girdles to Athena before marriage.[16]

PROTELEIA: PRE-WEDDING SACRIFICES

Before marriage the bride participated, presumably accompanied by her mother, in the rite of *proteleia*, that is, making a premarriage sacrifice or dedication.[17] In a love story related by Plutarch, the bride-to-be made her way to a spring called Kissoessa, in Boiotia, to make this *proteleia*, or "preliminary sacrifice," to the nymphs of the spring, who were traditionally associated with marriage and, in particular, childbirth. Weddings were said to be impossible without the assistance of the nymphs,[18] and Hera in addressing the nymphs of the Argive river Inachos refers to them as associated with weddings (with their joyful music) and maidens new to the marriage bed.[19]

In Athens, prior to the wedding, the bride and her parents went up to the acropolis and sacrificed to Athena Parthenos at her temple there; presumably only the wealthier citizens could afford to perform this rite. A monetary offering might be made to Aphrodite: a fourth-century inscription on a *thesauros* (treasury box) at Athens stipulates a monetary *proteleia* to Aphrodite Ourania, heavenly Aphrodite: "Thesauros, first fruits to Aphrodite Ourania as *proteleia* for marriage: one drachma." The Erinyes (Furies) also received offerings for weddings at Athens, as Zeus did on Crete (possibly due to his prominence as the island's deity). On the island of Kos, Nike received sacrifices at the time of a wedding, and a law stipulated that all free women were to make a sacrifice to Aphrodite Pandemos, according to their financial ability, within one year of their marriage.

Similarly, at Cyrene, a decree recorded, amongst various provisions for purity, that brides were to make a compulsory sacrifice to Artemis. If a bride did not do so, she was debarred from participating in Artemis's festival, the Artemisia, and had to pay for the sacrifice of an animal to Artemis as a fine. In addition, she was to perform the sacrifice she should have made earlier, with the law designating the place in Artemis's temple where the wedding sacrifice was to be made as the *nymphaion*, the "bridal-room" (a unique designation and prescription), presumably where dedications relating to marriage took place, implying considerable usage.[20]

In Euripides' *Iphigenia in Aulis*, Agamemnon prepares to sacrifice his daughter Iphigenia, who has been brought to Aulis by her mother Klytemnestra in the expectation of marrying her to Achilles. Euripides makes a special point of referring to Agamemnon's daughter as a *proteleia*, a sacrifice before marriage, made to Artemis so that the Greek fleet can sail to Troy: in this case the would-be bride is herself the sacrifice.[21] Sacrifices and dedications could also be made to local deities: the goddess Eukleia had an altar and statue in every marketplace throughout Boiotia and Lokris, and both men and women who were about to be married performed preliminary sacrifices to her there.[22]

DIVINATION

Lucian in the second century CE wrote that in "ancient times" (presumably the classical period) men would engage in divination before all major undertakings—whether founding cities or getting married. An unmarried girl could look for omens in her daily life which might suggest a potential husband, as in Aristophanes' *Lysistrata*, where a girl, unmarried despite her age because of the Peloponnesian War, "sits at home looking for omens," hoping, presumably, that she will see signs predicting a future marriage. In a love story set in Boiotia, Plutarch describes a father considering whether to consult the oracular center of the hero-god Trophonios in order to have the god's opinion as to which of two suitors he should choose as a husband for his daughter. Theokritos the poet, in the third century BCE, suggested that when Menelaos came to Sparta competing for the hand of Helen, someone must have sneezed, for he was successful in his suit, since a sneeze was a good omen from the gods.[23] Marriage was an important undertaking, and much was expected from it: children, happiness, and an increase in wealth for the household: having the approval and sanction of the gods was therefore crucial.

LOUTROPHORI AND RITUAL BATHING

Part of the bride's preparation involved ritual bathing, for which water was drawn in a special vase with handles and an elongated neck, a *loutrophoros* (pl. *loutrophoroi*). From about 480 BCE, *loutrophoroi* were often decorated with wedding scenes. Water for filling the loutrophoros was drawn from a sacred source: Thucydides, for example, indicates that the *enneakrounos* spring at Athens (once called Kallirrhoe) was still used, as in the ancient past, for the wedding ritual. At Thebes water was drawn for the bride's bath from the river Ismenos.[24] Whether all streams and rivers were regarded as sacred in the context of drawing water for bridal baths is unknown, but it seems likely that each community had sources of water which were of special significance to brides.

An Athenian red-figure loutrophoros of 430–420 BCE depicts a bride and her female companions leaving a fountain house and returning home, with one of them carrying the loutrophoros, filled from the fountain, while a wreathed boy plays the double flute.[25] A winged Eros (pl. Erotes) often accompanies the bride in wedding scenes on loutrophoroi: Eros is the companion of the goddess of amours, Aphrodite, and is symbolic of the presence of love; often several winged Erotes gather around Aphrodite as part of wedding scenes. The best example, from a loutrophoros of 430–420 BCE, depicts a procession of four women, behind a boy playing the double flute. He is followed by a woman carrying a loutrophoros, then the bride, and finally two other women; they are met at a house by a woman holding two torches. A wingéd Eros hovers at the side of the loutrophoros, as if to receive it.[26]

Scenes of weddings can also be found on boxes meant to hold items for a woman's toilette (*pyxides*; sing. *pyxis*). On an Athenian red-figure *pyxis* from 420 BCE comprising a terracotta cylindrical box with lid, there are three scenes, each with a winged Eros. On one panel, a standing Eros pours water over a crouching naked woman who wrings out her hair; in the next panel, an Eros holds a box from which the bride's attendants take ribbons, one of which the bride binds around her forehead; and in the third panel, the bride, her toilette complete, has a winged Eros sitting on her lap, both resting from their preparations.[27] Depictions of the naked bride appear from the close of the fifth century.[28] The Erotes' involvement in the bride's preparations following her ritual bath can also be seen on a vase featuring an Eros fussing over her headgear even as the groom leads her into his home.[29] In Aristophanes' *Birds*, the chorus sings of how a golden winged Eros held the reins and guided the chariot for Zeus and Hera at their wedding:[30] the divinized and personified love inspired by the Erotes was crucial to the success of the marriage of both gods and mortals. Finally, an Athenian red-figure loutrophoros dating to 475–425 BCE depicts a procession led by a wreathed young man to obtain water for the ritual, who is shown returning from a fountain house to the bride's home, with an ithyphallic herm and a flaming altar outside the door, which is normally interpreted as a sign of this god's apotropaic powers and good will for the upcoming wedding.[31] Due to the ritual significance of the loutrophoros and the consequent bridal bath, loutrophoroi were dedicated by brides at Athens after their wedding to the goddess Nymphe, "Bride," at her shrine on the southern slope of the acropolis as well as at caves where Pan and the nymphs were honored throughout Attica, at Parnes, Vari (where miniature loutrophoroi were found), Daphne, and Eleusis. Loutrophoroi were also dedicated at the shrine of Artemis Brauronia on the Athenian acropolis and at the shrine of the healing hero Amynos.[32]

THE WEDDING FEAST

On the following day, the sacrifice and wedding feast took place at the house of the bride's father, and these feasts were synonymous with marriage—without one there was no wedding. In the *Odyssey*, the goddess Athena, disguised as the mortal Mentes, advises Telemachus that his mother Penelope, if she should decide to remarry, should return to the home of her father, who will prepare for her a wedding feast and provide the gifts which will accompany her to her new home.[33] After a sacrifice, the wedding feast could begin and customarily included dancing and drinking as well as libations and prayers of blessing for the bridegroom and bride. Plato advises that in his ideal state the bride and groom should remain sober at their wedding, which indicates that this was not always the case.[34] This too is how Homer describes Menelaos celebrating the wedding feast (but not the weddings themselves) of his son Pleisthenes and of his daughter Hermione. His daughter was being married to the son of Achilles, to the accompaniment of feasting, music, a god-like singer, and two acrobats, and he was sending her to her new home accompanied by horses and chariots. Menelaos had promised his daughter to Neoptolemos at Troy; now, Homer writes, "the gods brought their marriage about," with this marriage clearly being thought to have been blessed by such divine favor.[35] Similarly, at Thespiai in Boiotia, a sacrifice at a temple (to an unnamed god) occurred as part of a marriage ceremony described briefly by Plutarch.[36]

Another ritual, that of the *anakalypteria*, which probably took place after the meal, involved the removal of the bride's veil prior to her leaving her home, and the bride being transported by cart or wagon to the groom's house. Aetiologically, it related to the wedding of Zeus and Chthonie, and is first mentioned by the sixth-century BCE mythographer Pherekydes of Syros, who has this ceremony taking place on the third day of the wedding ceremony rather than after the marriage feast. Zeus made a robe for Chthonie and gave it to her: this was the occasion of the first anakalypteria, when she unveiled herself to her husband, and the word hence came to denote the gifts a groom bestowed on his bride when she unveiled herself to him.[37] This divine pedigree for the rite underlined its symbolic overtones. In Hesiod, Pandora is also adorned by Athena with a patterned veil, as if she is a bride, and similarly the well-known Athenian sixth-century BCE kore statue of Phrasikleia portrays her adorned like a bride in a wedding dress.[38] The father then gave away his daughter to the groom, and this handing over (*ekdosis*) of the bride was the culmination of the marriage itself.[39] This formal transferral of the new wife to her husband completed the legal formalities begun with the betrothal and signing of the marriage contract. Rituals themselves, though customary, were not necessary for a legal validation of the marriage.

THE PROCESSION TO THE GROOM'S HOUSE

The seventh-century BCE pseudo-Hesiodic poem, *The Shield of Herakles*, in describing the scenes inlaid on the shield, provides a colorful description of perhaps the most crucial aspect of a Greek wedding, the wedding procession, when the bride left her home for that of her husband:

> Beside them was a well-towered city of men, and seven golden gates, fitted to the lintels, encompassed it. The men were at pleasure, in revelries and choruses; some were leading a bride to her husband on a well-wheeled wagon, and a great wedding-song (*hymenaios*) rose up. From afar rolled the blaze of burning torches in the hands of slaves, who walked in front, blooming in revelry, and performing choruses followed them. Men sent forth their voices from their soft mouths, accompanied by shrill panpipes, and around them spread the echo; while the women led the lovely chorus to the accompaniment of lyres. On the other side from there, young men were carousing, accompanied by a pipe, some performing in dance and song, while some walked in front, laughing each one with the pipe-player. Festivities and choruses and revelries filled the whole city.[40]

The wedding hymn (*hymenaios*) scene depicted on Herakles' shield was also part of Homer's description of the shield of Achilles in the *Iliad*, on which amongst other scenes marriages were depicted, with brides led from their homes through the city, and young men dancing to flutes and lyres. So traditional was the revelry comprising an integral part of such festivities that Odysseus, having slain the suitors who wished to marry his wife Penelope, decided to pretend that a wedding was being celebrated, in order that a rumor that the suitors had been killed would not be bruited abroad. Hence a "god-like singer" was to play the lyre, while others danced, so that anyone passing by or hearing the noise would believe that Penelope had chosen one of the suitors as her husband and that her wedding was being celebrated. So music and dancing were present at the wedding feast and during the procession, when the bride, proceeded by torches, was escorted during the evening to the house of the groom. An Athenian black-figure *lekythos* by the Amasis Painter (active *c*. 550–500 BCE) includes a wedding scene on both its sides, while around the spout a circular scene depicts three groups of three women dancing to the music of a male double flute player and a male lyre player.[41]

Sappho describes the wedding procession of Hektor and Andromache: the whole city of Troy came out to meet them, the maidens gave voice to a sacred song, the scents of myrrh, cassia, and frankincense filled the air. Pipes, castanets and the lyre were played, and the men sang the hymn (the *paean*) invoking Apollo, the god of the lyre.[42] According to the (seventh- to sixth-century BCE) lyric poet Stesichoros, as part of the wedding procession of Menelaos and Helen, spectators threw apples, myrtle leaves, wreathes of roses, and garlands of braided violet flowers.[43] Throwing flowers at the couple in the wedding procession was apparently common.[44]

Wedding processions from the bride's to the groom's house were a common motif on Athenian vases,[45] with the bride depicted seated on a cart drawn by mules (or horses or oxen) or shown on foot. Leading the procession was the mother of the bride, accompanied by friends, attendants, and musicians, and the bride carried a number of items with her, including a pan for roasting grain and a sieve, foreshadowing her household duties. At the groom's house, the bride was met by the groom's mother, standing at the doorway carrying a sprig of vegetation in her hand, while the bride's mother likewise carried sprigs of vegetation, with one in each hand, presumably as fertility tokens.[46] Plutarch notes that a pestle was fastened to the door of the bridegroom's house, and the bride was given a portion of a special cake, baked with honey and sesame seeds, as well as a quince or date as a fertility symbol, by her new husband.[47]

Vegetation played an important role in the wedding ceremony, symbolizing the hope for marital fertility. A *korythale* was placed at the groom's door: this was a sprig usually from an olive tree but also could be of laurel. Korythale (deriving from *koros* and *thallein*) may be translated as "youth-blossom," and invoked fertility and future offspring.[48] Male children in particular were needed for the continuation of the family and the inheritance of the *oikos*.

Children make an appearance at the wedding in the form of Eros *amphithales* "with both parents living" (or "flourishing on both sides"). In ancient Greece, a child who was amphithales had several important religious roles, and it is therefore not surprising to find such a child as having a role in weddings: a child who had lost one or both of its parents would have been thought unpropitious at a union entered into for the sake of children. Zenobios the paroemiographer in his entry to explain the expression, "I escaped the bad, I have found the better," refers to the role of this pais at weddings: a child amphithales, crowned with thistle intermingled with acorns, would carry loaves of bread in a winnowing basket and distribute them to the guests, and repeat that saying. A young boy who is shown sitting behind a bride and groom on a cart in a wedding procession on an Athenian black-figure lekythos of about 540 BCE might well be a pais amphithales, but he is not carrying his ritual objects.[49] Callimachus writes that a bride on the night before her wedding slept with a pais amphithales and that it was connected to an incident involving Hera—but that he cannot write of that, for it would be impious to do so.[50]

THE WEDDING HYMN

As seen in the Hesiodic *Shield of Herakles'* description of a wedding, the wedding hymn was sung to accompany the bride in the torch-lit procession to her new husband; Homer too, describes such a hymn. But, as seen above, there were other occasions as well which featured the hymn; the wedding feast was naturally one of these, as was the arrival of the bride and groom at the bridal chamber. Kassandra also sang a solo hymn as a lament when she heard of her impending "marriage," her concubinage with Agamemnon.[51]

Yet the wedding hymn (*hymenaios*) was not simply a song. Hymenaios was a deity, a personification of the wedding hymn itself, as in Pindar, who refers to the funeral dirges sung when the mortal Hymenaios died and gained heroic semi-divine status. When Kassandra is preparing for the "marriage" between Agamemnon and herself, she calls upon Hymen and Lord Hymenaios, and ironically bids her mother to join in a wedding dance. Theokritos writes of the wedding of Menelaos and Helen, "Hymen o Hymenaios, may you rejoice in this marriage."[52] At the end of Aristophanes' *Birds*, a wedding hymn for Peisetairos and his "Princess Bride" is sung by the chorus, who invoke the marriage of Zeus and Hera, intoning "Hymen Hymenaios."[53] A *hymenaios* was also sung by the fifty daughters of Nereus (Thetis's sisters) at the wedding of Peleus and Thetis, parents of Achilles.[54] Hymen was invoked for his divine blessing on the marriage and his assistance sought at the every stage of the ceremonies.

Hymns sung in front of the bridal chamber were referred to by the Alexandrian scholars as a subset of *hymenaioi* and they termed them *epithalamia* (to the bridal chamber), a distinct literary genre: Sappho composed a book of *Epithalamia*, as did Anakreon, Pindar, and Stesichoros, none of which are extent.[55] While these books of epithalamia are lost, fragments of Sappho's poems suggest a widespread popularity for the genre. Catullus's Latin *epithalamium* (poem 62) is almost certainly derived from Greek models, possibly one of Sappho's, and in it "Hymen, Hymenaeus" is invoked several times by the choirs of youths and maidens. This hymn is structured as a singing contest between the two choirs, the former extolling and the latter deploring marriage.[56] Choirs of virgins are presented as singing the *hymenaios* outside Menelaos and Helen's bedroom by Theokritos (and this is surely an *epithalamion*), with similar occasions recorded by Pindar, Aeschylus, and Callimachus.[57] Lucian describes a wedding scene with garlands, female flute players, hustle and bustle, and the singing of the wedding hymn, all as evidence that a wedding was taking place.[58] A further hymn was sung on the morning after a wedding, an "awakening hymn" (*diegertikon*) outside the bridal bedroom, by a choir of youths and virgins (*kouroi* and *korai*).[59] Torches, as noted above, were also a customary feature of weddings: Kassandra brandishes torches "as custom requires" when she sings the *hymenaios* for herself,[60] while Iokaste will not carry the "customary" wedding torches for her son Polyneikes, as he has arrived home already married and hence his wedding will not take place in his home town.[61]

THE WEDDING SACRIFICE AT THE GROOM'S HOUSE

In two wedding scenes on Greek vases, the presence of an altar is not incidental but relates to sacrifices made to the gods at the groom's house, stressing that as the wedding rituals come to a close, seeking the favor of the gods was a paramount concern. So the flaming altar past which participants in the wedding procession on an Athenian white-ground pyxis process is a significant detail. A lit altar also stands outside the door of a house into which an eager groom is leading his wife in a scene from a wedding on a Boiotian red-figure pyxis, as a sign of sacrificial activity, denoting an offering made to ensure the goodwill of the gods.[62]

At a sacrifice, the gall bladder of the victim was ordinarily placed on the altar's flames, to be burned along with the rest of the offerings to the gods, and its juice was often squeezed onto the flames first.[63] Plutarch, however, is quite specific that in any sacrifice to Hera in her capacity as "Protector of Marriage" the gall bladder—as it contained bile—was not burnt but thrown down next to the altar: bile represented anger and bitterness, and therefore had no role to play in marriage. He presumably is implying that this was a Greek practice generally, for the burning of the gall bladder on the altar was otherwise a typical feature of an ancient Greek sacrifice. Elsewhere, he has Hera as the symbol of the marriage of men and women, and as the leader of the bridal procession (calling Hera *nymphagogos*, "Bride leader").[64]

THE KATACHYSMATA

The *katachysmata*, a rite in which bride and groom were showered with coins, nuts, figs, dates, and dried fruits, occurred within the groom's house after their arrival.[65] Perhaps the scene is best represented on an Athenian red-figure loutrophoros from 430 BCE, which shows a basket of items being held above the groom's head, as his wife stands before him and is being unveiled.[66] A katachysmata ritual can also perhaps be identified in a wedding scene on a Boiotian red-figure pyxis vase of 475–450 BCE, which shows a woman carrying a long tray filled with various round-shaped objects, fruits, and similar items.[67]

Into the bedroom

One Athenian red-figure loutrophoros depicts a young man leading his wife toward a door, while two winged Erotes hover at the bride's head, adjusting her wedding tiara (Figure 2.1). A woman just inside the door looks down at another Eros hovering in a seated position at the door and raises her hands in an epiphanic gesture: that is, she sees the divinity and recognizes him. Just inside the door a bed is depicted—the marriage bed to which the groom is leading the bride.[68] This Eros can, perhaps, be assumed to have just hopped off the bed to welcome the newly married couple. While the presence of Erotes in such scenes as this one—and there are others—could be viewed as purely conventional, the artists who produced these scenes, and the viewers (presumably the husband and wife-to-be) thought it was important that the presence of the divinity Eros was a crucial aspect of the wedding rite. The bride and groom were led into the bridal bedroom, to the accompaniment of lewd jokes and the singing of *epithalamia*.[69]

The bedroom was guarded throughout the night and on the following day the ceremonies concluded with the *epaulia*, in which gifts were given to the bride, and sacrifices were made and a feast held at the groom's house, when the newly married couple received presents from family members and friends. Athenian vases depict the epaulia, with women bringing gifts to the seated bride; winged Erotes are present in some of these.[70] On a red-figure Athenian pyxis of 350 BCE, a line of women, as if in a procession, come toward a seated woman, with Eros flying along in the line with them, bringing his gift: a loutrophoros with a ribbon.[71]

Another sacrifice was also held some time after the wedding, but not in the newly-wedded couple's home: the husband now celebrated this with the members of his *phratria* (which loosely translates to "brotherhood"; *phratriai* were one of the ancestral groupings to which Athenian citizen men belonged). This was called the *gamelia*, and while the wife was not present, the sacrifice indicated to the new husband's phratria that he was now legally married.[72] With these various rituals complete, the bride and groom were now wife and husband.

FIGURE 2.1 Athenian red-figure *loutrophoros* showing details of wedding rituals. Boston Museum of Fine Arts, 03.802.

PRIESTLY PERSONNEL

The extent to which an officiating priest or priestess was necessary at weddings is unclear, and it appears that a wedding did not necessarily involve religious personnel. Plutarch writing his *Advice to the Bride and Groom* in second-century CE Boiotia provides advice to the newly wedded Pollianos and Eurydike, which he argues will be useful, following as it does upon "the ancestral rite, that Demeter's priestess performed for you, when you pair were going together (to your wedding bed)." This appears to be some kind of ritual blessing upon the newly married couple as they went to bed, in the same sense that the chorus of young maidens who accompany Menelaos and Helen to their marriage bed, in Theokritos's *Idyll* 18, invoke in the *hymenaios* the goddess Leto ("good mother Leto"; she had born the twins Apollo and Artemis) to grant them fair children, Aphrodite to give them love for each other, and Zeus to bestow on them indestructible happiness.[73]

A Greek wedding was the culmination of various ceremonies, most of which centered on the bride rather than the groom in terms of personal preparations for the wedding. The legitimizing element of the wedding was the handing over of the bride to the groom by her *kyrios*, while the procession to the groom's house provided a public witness that a wedding was taking place. The performance of the various rituals, as evidence of the publicly demonstrated agreement of the two families, confirmed that a wedding had taken place with the consent of all parties.[74] Preliminary sacrifices, and the deities to whom they were made, clearly varied between cities, but it was customary to make offerings to the gods on the occasion of a wedding, both at the bride's home and at the house of the groom on the couple's arrival.

THE GODS AND RITUALS OF THE ROMAN WEDDING

Roman weddings, like Greek ones, had a number of accompanying rituals and ceremonies invoking the gods, whose blessings were requested for the wedding itself and the bridal couple.[75] *Auspices* (omens) were taken at the bride's house early on the wedding day, followed by a sacrifice at an altar, at which the goddess Juno Pronuba was thought to be present. As part of the ritual the hands of the couple were joined by a *pronuba*,[76] while nuts were showered on those present by the groom, and a procession to the house of the groom took place in the evening. Three boys with lighted torches led the way, accompanied by the wedding cries of "Talassio!" and the singing of bawdy verses, the *Fescennina iocatio*. A woman, known as the pronuba, who had arranged the marriage bed, led the bride into the nuptial chamber.

Lucan (writing in the second half of the first century CE) indicates some of the most important wedding rites in his description of the remarriage of Cato the Younger and the now widowed Marcia (at the beginning of 49 BCE; they had previously been married to each other, but Marcia and Cato had divorced so that Marcia could marry Hortensius). Lucan places the marriage during the civil war with Caesar, which he gives as the reason for the wedding being a plain affair, without the usual rituals and ceremonies. It is probable, however, that the reason for the lack of display was that Cato was marrying her for the second time, but nevertheless Lucan's description serves to highlight the usual ceremonies attending a wedding:

> They resolved to wed simply and perform no useless display; the gods alone should be present to witness the ceremony. No festal garlands, no wreath, hung from the lintel; no white fillet ran this way and that to each post of the door. The customary

torches; the high couch supported on ivory steps and displaying a coverlet of gold embroidery; the matron, wearing on her head a towered crown, and careful not to touch the threshold when her foot crosses it—all these are absent. No saffron veil, intended lightly to screen the bride's shy blushes, hid the downcast face; no belt bound the flowing raiment with jewels, no fair circlet confined the neck, nor did a scarf, clinging to the tip of the shoulder, surround the bare arms with narrow band. Marcia made no change but kept the solemnity of her widow's weeds, and embraced her husband just as she did her sons. The purple band was covered and concealed by wool of funereal color. The customary light jesting was silent, nor was the sullen husband greeted by the ceremonial abuse in Sabine fashion. No members of the family and no kinsmen assembled: their hands were joined in silence, and they were satisfied with the presence of Brutus as augur.[77]

JUNO PRONUBA AND OTHER WEDDING GODS

Each of the last three centuries of classical scholarship has proposed a name for the female figure who joins a husband and wife on Roman sarcophagi: a Vestal Virgin was suggested in the eighteenth, Juno Pronuba in the nineteenth, and most recently the *communis opinio* has settled, less convincingly, on the goddess Concordia.[78] Yet few would argue that Juno, in her manifestation as "the joiner" (Iuno = *iungo*) was held to be responsible for the "joining" of couples in marriage.[79] Since Juno as Juno Pronuba ("of the nuptials," or "she who prepares the bride") has a strong attestation in Roman poetry as a goddess of Roman weddings,[80] it is probable that the female figure is in fact Juno Pronuba and as such is shown on several Roman sarcophagi standing between the groom and bride, with her hands on their shoulders. It seems certain that on some sarcophagi the couple join hands to signify that a wedding is taking place (the so-called *dextrarum iunctio*, or "joining of the right hands").[81] In one example of such a scene from a sarcophagus of the second century CE, Juno stands between the couple; a sacrificial beast is present, to be sacrificed in the ceremony, while a small altar is also shown.[82] While Juno is given the epithet "Pronuba" only in Latin poetry, and it is only found in relation to the weddings of gods and heroes,[83] it is possible that mortals would have wished to have their marriages blessed by Juno Pronuba. For example, few are unaware that Vergil mentions Juno Pronuba in connection with the fatal love of Dido, queen of Carthage, with Juno Pronuba and the god Tellus (as *auspex*) giving a sign as Dido and Aeneas enter a cave together, to the accompaniment of lightning, symbolizing wedding torches,[84] while Ausonius's *Epithalamium* has Cythera (Venus) and Juno Pronuba arousing sensuality in the wedded pair in the nuptial bed.[85]

At the wedding itself, a married woman (often the mother of the bride), who was still married to her first husband, took on the role of the pronuba. Just as Juno Pronuba presides in iconography over the *dextrarum iunctio*, in the actual wedding the pronubic role may have been the responsibility of this married woman, who joined the hands of the bride and groom.[86] Her other chief role was to prepare the bridal bed in the new husband's home on the wedding night, lead the bride to the bed, pray to the gods on behalf of the new couple, and undress her. Cicero indeed intends to shock his audience when he relates how, when Melinus married Cluentia, her mother prepared the bridal bed for her, but when Melinus divorced Cluentia two years later, her mother took over that very bridal bed and married Melinus in her

FIGURE 2.2 Roman marble sarcophagus, c. 180 CE, showing a goddess between the couple being married, with a small flaming altar in front. The "Belvedere sarcophagus." Vatican Museum, Belvedere Court 38. Alamy Stock Photo.

turn.[87] Another manifestation of Juno, this time with the epiklesis (epithet) Lucina, was believed to assist in childbirth, and for this reason a coin was to be deposited into her temple treasury for every child born.[88] In this guise Juno should also be considered connected to the wedding, since legitimate children were one important goal of Roman marriage.

Romans had the habit of personifying as deities, major and minor, various phenomena—such as the manuring of crops or the rust on grain. Therefore it should not be a surprise that many aspects of the Roman wedding were associated with a presiding deity. Venus brought couples together in marriage,[89] but Juno most especially, as Vergil states in his narrative about Dido and Aeneas in the cave, was concerned with marriage.[90] As noted above, Juno Pronuba was thought to play a crucial part of the wedding ritual, while when in the wedding bedroom the husband untied the complicated knot of the bride's girdle, the action was presided over by Juno Cinxia (Juno of the knot).[91] There were many gods concerned with weddings, and they could be expressed collectively as the *Di coniugales*, the deities of marriage.[92] Tertullian, Arnobius, and Augustine write derisively of these numerous deities: Afferenda who presided over the dowry as well as the deities Mutunus and Tutunus (or these two could be the same deity), Pertunda, Subigus, Prema, Perfica, Noduterensis, Virginiensis, Vesus, and Priapus.[93] Christian authors add the questionable assertion that the Roman bride, once inside the groom's house, sat on a phallic image of Priapus, in the guise of the Roman phallic deity Mutunus Tutunus (also spelled Mutinus Titinus),[94] who was worshipped by Roman matrons in his sanctuary at Rome.[95]

BRIDAL PREPARATIONS

The bride, on the evening before her wedding, laid aside her girl's clothing in her home and dedicated her toys to Venus.[96] Arnobius refers to an ancient Roman practice, no longer observed, of dedicating the virgin bride's clothes after her wedding in the temple of Fortuna Virginalis.[97] On the evening prior to the wedding she donned (in the place of the clothes now set aside) a *tunica recta*, a tunic she had probably woven herself.[98] This she wore to her wedding, fastening it with a girdle which had been woven from the wool of a ewe (presumably because of the ewe's fecundity) fastened with an elaborate knot, aptly titled the *nodus Herculaneus*, tied by her mother in the capacity of Juno Cinxia. The husband "released" her chastity by untying this Herculean knot on the wedding night. As Festus notes, in this way the couple could hope for children, just as Hercules himself had sired seventy offspring.[99] Her hair was arranged in the same style as that of the Vestal Virgins, the six plaits known as the *seni crines*.[100] A Roman bride's hair was parted with a spear (*hasta caelibaris*)—for three possible reasons, according to Plutarch, either because the first Roman weddings, those with the captured Sabine virgins, were the result of war, or because the marriage could only be dissolved at the point of a spear, or because Juno was the patroness of marriage and she was associated with the spear.[101] It will have been a dramatic part of the wedding preparations, whatever the origin of the ritual. She wore a crown or wreath, and a bridal veil (the yellow *flammeum*) completed her toilette.[102]

DIVINATION AND THE OMINOUS WEDDING

Divination played a role in the choice of date for weddings in Rome, as there were many inauspicious days in the Roman calendar, days that the Romans called *nefasti*, such as the date of the disastrous defeat at Cannae in 216 BCE, when private and public business was avoided.[103] Macrobius relates that weddings were banned on the Nones of each month, because the day that followed was ill-omened (as was the day after the Kalends and Ides). Marriages were celebrated over two days, with the sexual consummation on the first day, while on the second the bride began to exercise her authority (*dominium*) and offer sacrifice to the gods in her new home. Ovid cautions those marrying to delay their marriage torches until after the Parentalia, the Roman festival when deceased parents and relatives were remembered since, as a festival of the dead, it was not an appropriate time for weddings. Likewise May was not a suitable month in which to marry, and it was advisable to wait until June. Plutarch gives as one possible reason that April was sacred to Venus, and June to Juno—a May wedding would fall between months sacred to the two goddesses concerned with marriage. Ovid warns against a May wedding—a bride who weds then will not live long—but on the grounds that offerings were made to the dead in this month, another possible reason also given by Plutarch.[104]

In addition to the choosing of a well-omened date for a wedding, other divinatory practices occurred at the wedding. Tacitus, in describing the bigamous "marriage" of Messalina (while wife of the emperor Claudius) to Gaius Silius indicates that the bride listened to the pronouncement of the *auspices* as part of the legitimization of a marriage:[105]

> It will seem, I am aware, fabulous that, in a city cognizant of all things and reticent of none, any human beings could have felt so much security; far more so, that on a specified day, with witnesses to seal the contract, a consul designate and the emperor's wife should have met for the avowed purposes of legitimate marriage; that the woman

should have listened to the words of the *auspices*, have assumed the veil, have sacrificed in the face of Heaven; that both should have dined with the guests, have kissed and embraced, and finally have spent the night in the license of wedlock.

In a section of Cicero's *de divinatione* related by his brother Quintus, he recounts how a certain Caecilia Metella assisted in the arrangement of the marriage of her sister's daughter (unnamed); she went with her niece to a *sacellum* (small shrine) at night as was customary, to seek an omen, and in the event did receive a prediction. As her niece grew tired of standing while her aunt occupied the only chair, she asked Caecilia if she could sit on her seat; the aunt kindly obliged with the words, "You can have my place." Soon after, Caecilia died, and her niece married her now widowed husband. Quintus argued both that this was an omen and, while such signs might be ridiculed, that to disbelieve them was to disbelieve in the gods who sent them.[106]

Pliny comments on divination at Roman weddings, as Lucian does on Greek ones, that "neither marriage, nor having children, nor anything else in fact do they decide except by the verdict of sacrifices." This clearly indicates that many weddings would only have been allowed to proceed after divination from the entrails of a sacrificed beast had been performed. Incidental omens also, of course, played a part, and Pliny elsewhere notes that the sight of the *aegisthus* hawk, if lame in one foot, was a very good omen for marriage contracts (although he does not explain why).[107] The call of an owl, in contrast, was a bad omen. Ovid describes Myrrha's coming to the bedroom of her father as like a wedding rite: thrice did the funereal screech owl warn her not to proceed; thrice in ill-omen she stumbled on the threshold of his bedroom; and she made her way without light (i.e., without wedding torches). Similarly at the wedding of Procne and Tereus, the screech owl was present (but did not call), and with this omen (*hac ave*) they were wedded. Yet Juno Pronuba, Hymen, and the Graces were not present, and it was the Furies who lit the wedding torches—and from a funeral pyre—and the Furies who spread the coverlet on the bed. These ill-omens and omissions reflect an inversion of what would normally have taken place at a wedding.[108]

Torches and Furies combined signified that other weddings were disastrous. In Ovid's *Heroides*, Phyllis complained of her wedding to Demophoon that it was attended by ill-omens predicting that the marriage would be unsuccessful: one of the Furies, Tisiphone, was pronuba in the bedchamber (that is, instead of Juno Pronuba), a bird of ill-omen sang sadly, while Alecto, another Fury, with serpents about her neck, was present, and the wedding torches were sepulchral. Ill-omened wedding torches feature elsewhere: while Hypsipyle has both Juno Pronuba and Hymen attending her wedding, "sad Erinys" (sing. of the Erinyes, the Furies) carried before her an ill-omened bloodstained torch, suitable for lighting Hypsipyle's funeral pyre.[109] Well-omened wedding torches, suggests Pliny, are made from the black-thorn (*spina*) tree (modern *prunus spinosa*), because, according to Masurius, the shepherds who abducted the Sabine women carried such torches: it is therefore the most auspicious (*auspicatissima*) wood to use. The associations of the fecundity of the Sabine women's marriages to Romans were invoked with this wood.[110] Celestial divination also had a nuptial role, and the cave "wedding" of Dido and Aeneas in the *Aeneid* was ill-omened as it was attended by hail, storm clouds, and thunder.[111] In contrast, Statius describes a wedding so well-omened that hardly had dawn broken when propitious signs appeared. Octavian's marriage to Livia was said to have been well omened for the Roman state.[112] A sneeze, to the left or right, was a good omen for strong and continuing love between a couple but was not specifically connected with Roman weddings as an omen.[113]

At the wedding itself, there were diviners known as *auspices* (sing. *auspex*) responsible for taking the omens.[114] At her bigamous wedding to Gaius Silius, Messalina listened, as presumably did all those present, to the words pronounced by the attendant auspices, and even though Cato and Marcia had a frugal wedding it is specifically noted that Brutus attended and was present as an auspex. This omission highlights the deficiency of their wedding ritual: in normal circumstances, there would have been several auspices present, while none at all were present at the infamous marriage of Sassia to her ex-son-in-law Melinus.[115] Tacitus describes the wedding of Nero, in the role of bride, to one of his favorite freedmen:[116]

> Nero became, with the solemn rites of marriage, Pythagoras' wife. The veil was drawn over the imperial head, *auspices* were present; the dowry, the couch of wedded love, the nuptial torches, were all there.

As in Greece, the Roman bride was led to her husband's house: this was the *deductio in domum mariti*, which gave legitimacy to the marriage and was recognized as its beginning.[117] Even when the groom was not present at his house, the leading of a woman to it constituted a marriage.[118] As in Greece, in this procession to the house, there was a role for children whose parents were still living, as three boys who were *patrimi et matrimi* (possessing fathers and mothers), and still wearing *the toga praetexta* (i.e., not yet adults), led the bride to her new home. One went in front with a hawthorn torch (considered to be a lucky wood), while the other two supported the bride, for the procession to the bridegroom's house occurred at night. They, in roles similar to the *paides amphithaleis* in Greece,[119] were thought to imbue the bride with a potent life force for the promotion of children and their well-being, and represented of course the expectation that the bride and groom would live to rear their own children.[120] Plutarch indicates that "five torches, no more, no less," were lit for the wedding rites and that one of the possible reasons for this was that the new husband and wife had need of the goodwill of five deities: Zeus Teleios, Hera Teleia, Aphrodite, Peitho, and finally Artemis. Here he is naming Greek gods, and for Zeus Teleios and Hera Teleia as well as for Peitho there were no Roman equivalents.

TALASSIO AND FESCENNINA IOCATIO

Plutarch in his *Roman Questions* asks five different questions concerning Roman wedding practices. One concerns the bride and groom entering the house to the sound of the cry of "Talassio," regarding which he asks, "Why is the far-famed 'Talassio' sung at the marriage ceremony?" He gives two possible reasons: the first is an etymological explanation, with *talasia* meaning spinning and *talasus* the wool-basket. When the bride was brought into the husband's house a fleece was placed beneath her; she brought her distaff and spindle, the main instruments for spinning, and in addition she wreathed the door of her new husband with wool. It was clearly important that the bride be accompanied by the symbols of wool-working and women's craft, associated as they were with female virtues, as she was taken to her new home in this transition to matronhood.[121] In his second possible reason, he cites the authority of "the historians" in what is obviously an invented aetiology: when the Romans were carrying off the Sabine women in the incident known as the rape of the Sabine women, the plebeian clients of one Talassius stole away a particularly beautiful maiden. To prevent any other Roman from attempting to carry her off, the clients kept calling out that she was "for Talassius" ("Talassio!"). As this marriage turned out to be a successful one, the Romans therefore started shouting Talassio at all their weddings doing so, as Plutarch continues, just as the Greeks would call upon Hymen. Whatever the meaning, Plutarch's analogy with the Greek Hymen cannot be taken too far, as Talassio was not a deity, unlike Hymen. This cry is certainly an invocation: but whether for a happy marriage, or for a prosperous one (the woman's spinning), or both, is unclear.[122] It becomes a motif describing marriage in Rome for Catullus: the bridegroom Manlius must give away his boyish fondness for nuts, as now he must serve Talasius.[123] Catullus also features the Greek invocation of Hymenaeus in his wedding hymn (Poem 61), but this detail derives from Greek literary models; later, following Catullus's lead, Hymenaeus is invoked by many writers of epithalamia.[124]

Another ritual pronouncement at the Roman wedding was the *Fescennina iocatio*, which Catullus in his epithalamium forbids to "be silent for long."[125] These Fescennine jokes or verses (*Fescennini versus*), which were ribald or bawdy songs, were an important and noisy part of the wedding celebration, and presumably were the "Sabine abuse" that Lucan writes was absent from the unpretentious wedding of Cato and Marcia. These presumably took place during the wedding procession, and were festive and convivial, adding to the joyful atmosphere of the occasion. Seneca writes in the wedding hymn for Jason and Medea: "Let the sharp-tongued Fescennine verses pour their festive abuse (*festa convicia*), let the crowd give rein to jokes." These verses were almost certainly apotropaic in character, and Ausonius in his *Epithalamium* writes that "the crowd at a wedding loves Fescennine songs."[126] Varro notes that boys shouted obscenities,[127] and Livy notes that the Fescennine verses were improvised on the spot in the context of his account of 365–364 BCE.[128]

At some stage in the festivities, the bridegroom would scatter nuts, a ritual element that evidently occurred at his house when the procession arrived there. Pliny advanced two reasons as to why walnuts were used: the first, which he thought more probable, was that the flesh of the walnut was doubly protected, with the hard outer shell and an inner woody one; it therefore served as a suitable symbol for a marriage which successfully produced children as it protected its young in this double way. He thinks the second reason less likely: that when the walnuts bounced on a floor they made a "rattling" noise, which was taken as a good omen, although this second suggestion has been more convincing to scholars. Festus writes that nuts were auspicious for the new bride entering her new home.[129] When a bride was being led to her new home, she was told to say, "Where you are Gaius, there I am Gaia" (*Ubi tu Gaius, ego Gaia*). Plutarch offers two reasons: Gaius was a name used by jurists in proving an example (like "John Smith" today). Another possibility he raises is that the bride in saying she is Gaia is referring to Gaia Caecilia, a woman of beauty and virtue from the regal period, a bronze statue of whom stood in the temple of Sancus, and whose sandals and spindle had been dedicated there to represent her love of home and her industrious nature.[130]

At the door of her new home, the bride anointed the door with pig or wolf fat, and attached woollen fillets (*vittae*) to it. A pig was a suitable sacrifice at a wedding, according to Varro, for it was a symbol of fecundity. While some sarcophagus scenes show a sacrificial bovine about to be sacrificed in the presence of Juno Pronuba, most people being wed would have found a pig much more affordable.[131] The woollen fillets may again refer to the bride's skill at wool-working.

When the bride entered her new home, she brought three coins with her. One, held in her hand, she gave to the bridegroom, perhaps "paying" for her entrance into his house. Another, secreted in one of her shoes, was for the *Lares familiares* of her husband's house, while the third coin, carried in a purse, was for the *Lares compitales*, the Lares of the crossroads of her new neighborhood, to whom she would soon give it. Entering into a new household, the bride needed to pay worship and respect to its *Lares*, for they were the protectors of the house to which she now belonged, and she needed to engage with their worship for the house and household to prosper. In a similar way, she needed to venerate the Lares of the crossroads in her new neighborhood to mark her entrance into the community as a new resident.[132]

In Catullus's epithalamium, which is modeled on a Greek wedding hymn, there is, however, at least one Roman, non-Greek element. He tasks the bride to lift her feet as she walks over the threshold of her new home, so as to do so with "good omen." Servius explains that to kick the threshold was bad luck, for it was the province of Vesta, a chaste goddess, whereas the bride was about to lose her virginity and wished to do so. Plutarch in his *Roman Questions* asks why those escorting the bride carry her across the threshold and gives three possible explanations: because the Sabine women were abducted and forced into Roman homes; or to make it appear that the women were unwilling to enter and surrender their virginity; or that she entered the home under constraint and could not abandon it willingly. Lucan, as noted above, comments that the bride was normally carried over the threshold, and in Plautus's *Casina*, the groom asks the bride to lift her feet over it.[133] Catullus has the modest bride hesitating on the threshold of her husband's house.[134]

Plutarch asked, in the very first of his *Roman Questions*, why was the bride required to touch fire and water within her husband's house when first she entered it? This was the final and conclusive ritual of the marriage, the *aqua et igni* ceremony, as the jurist Scaevola argued that any gift given to the bride prior to this event remained hers in case of a divorce, but a gift made after this rite was considered part of the dowry and was to be taken into consideration as such. Ovid gives a similar explanation: it is the fire and water ceremony which transforms a bride into a wife. Plutarch answers his own question, as usual, with several possibilities: fire and water are gendered, with fire male and water female; fire causes inert water to be active, but without water, fire has no material with which to work; fire purifies and water cleans, and it is necessary for a married woman to always be clean and holy; fire by itself is arid, and water by itself is inactive—accordingly, male and female must unite to produce a perfect life in marriage; and the couple must stay together even if they are reduced to having nothing but fire and water. Varro also explains the ritual on the grounds of gender: sperm is male and the embryonic egg female, and he specifies that fire and water are "used" on the woman at her new home's threshold to promote fertility. Despite these various explanations, it is more probable that fire and water as the main symbols of domesticity signified the married state, and this was the bride's first act of participation in the domestic cult.[135] Arnobius, in his questions concerning Roman wedding customs no longer practiced, asks whether the ritual of invoking the genius of the husband continues to his day: this invocation may well have been the responsibility of the bride.[136]

CONFARREATIO: MARRIAGE AS A SPECIFICALLY RELIGIOUS CEREMONY

These various rituals, which recalled ancient traditions and involved the participation of the gods, were common to all wedding celebrations. There was also a rite of Roman marriage which like the two other legal forms, *coemptio* and *usus*, involved the bride being placed in the *manus* (power) of her husband (although *usus* had special provisions by which the wife could avoid being in manus) but had an overtly religious character: this was the rite of *confarreatio*,[137] a peculiarly religious ceremony, which the Roman jurist Gaius in about 170 CE described in his *Institutes*:

> Women are placed in the hand (*manus*) of their husbands by *confarreatio*, through a kind of sacrifice made to Jupiter Farreus, in which a cake is employed, whence the ceremony obtains its name; and in addition to this, for the purpose of performing the ceremony, many other things are done and take place, accompanied with certain solemn words, in the presence of ten witnesses. This law is still in force in our time, for the principal *Flamines*, that is to say, those of Jupiter, Mars, and Quirinus, as well as the chief of the sacred rites (*Rex Sacrorum*), are exclusively selected from persons born of marriages celebrated by *confarreatio*. Nor can these persons themselves serve as priests without marriage by *confarreatio*.[138]

Confarreatio must date back at least to the time when the offspring of such marriages, as patricians, were the only ones eligible to fulfill several important priestly offices (see below). While the rite was presumably ancient, it is doubtful that it was the "oldest" form of marriage, or even that significant numbers of people were ever married by it. The term relates to a special bread (*panis*), which was *farreus* "made of far (spelt)," with the "con" meaning "with"—and from this the ceremony took its name. Spelt was used, Dionysios of Halikarnassos relates, because it was an ancient food and for a long time constituted the usual food (bread) of the Romans. Because of this, *far* was used at all sacrifices, while Ulpian adds that it was employed as a part of a "solemn sacrifice" (*sollemne sacrificium*).[139] Bride and groom shared a cake made of this flour (a *farreum libum*), and a sacrifice of *panis farreus* was made by the *Flamen Dialis* to Jupiter *Farreus*—a special aspect of this god, who was crucial for the legitimacy of the wedding. Bride and groom were married at the altar of Jupiter at the Capitoline temple in the presence of ten witnesses, with the invocation of "solemn words," and the Flamen Dialis as well as the Pontifex Maximus had to be present at the marriage ceremony, demonstrating that this was a religious ceremony that needed public recognition by these religious personnel and was of importance to the state.[140]

In the confarreatio ceremony performed for the Flamen Dialis and *Flaminica*, the bride and groom, with their heads covered, sat on a single sheep-skin stretched across their two chairs, the sheep having been sacrificed to Jupiter Farreus as part of the ceremony.[141] While Festus claimed that this was the case for all weddings by confarreatio,[142] this is probably a misunderstanding, for Plutarch records that for Roman weddings, when the bride was first seated in the bridegroom's home, a fleece was spread beneath her.[143] The bride in the confarreatio ceremony was veiled,[144] as in other wedding ceremonies.

To hold the priestly office of *rex sacrorum* or those of the three principal flaminical positions (the *Flamines Dialis, Martialis,* and *Quirinalis*), it was necessary for the parents of the priest to have been married by this rite of confarreatio. In turn, the priests had themselves to be married by this same rite.[145] These religious positions were held only by patricians. Above all, this was a religious rite, with features—particularly the panis farreus, sacrifice, and special formulaic prayers—which were missing from the other forms of marriage (coemptio and usus).

A marriage formed by confarreatio (as was mandatory for the Flamen Dialis) could not be dissolved: Plutarch records that the emperor Domitian (who reigned 81–96 CE) was successfully petitioned to dissolve one such marriage. This occurrence was, however, isolated and unique, and this form of divorce was still illegal, Plutarch writes, in his own day. On that occasion, Plutarch records, "The priests were present at that ceremony of divorce and performed many horrible, strange, and gloomy rites."[146] He unfortunately gives no details, which, given that a divorce in a confarreatio marriage had never occurred before in the case of a Flamen Dialis, must have been an "improvised" religious ceremony, breaking the marriage bonds made before Jupiter. Otherwise, a confarreatio marriage could be dissolved, by *diffarreatio*—and only Festus provides the technical term and indicates that it involved a sacrifice. These rites must have been required to "undo" the religious commitment that had taken place at the confarreatio ceremony itself, including the special formulae Gaius and Ulpian refer to, and atoning with a sacrifice to Jupiter Farreus for the negation of the original ceremony. Pliny commented: "there was no religious bond more sacred than *confarreatio*."[147]

In the reign of Tiberius (14–37 CE), the choice of a successor for the recently deceased Flamen Dialis, Servius Maluginensis, caused the issue of marriage by confarreatio to be raised in the Senate by the emperor. The successor of the Flamen Dialis had to be chosen from amongst men whose parents had been married by this rite. But Tiberius pointed out in the Senate that, whereas previously three patricians had been nominated for the position, now there were not three candidates available, as the rite of confarreatio was employed by only a few, due to the "difficulties" involved (which are not specified) and that the husband in a confarreatio marriage was transferred out of his father's jurisdiction, if alive, while the wife (*Flaminica*) came into the manus of her husband. After discussion, it was decided not to alter the office of the Flamen in any way but to change the legal aspect of the relationship between Flamen and Flaminica: the Flaminica was to be in her husband's authority with regard to sacred rites but otherwise was to possess the normal legal position of a wife.[148] No changes were made to the confarreatio ceremony itself.

Confarreatio emerges as the only form of Roman marriage that was seen as a formal religious procedure involving not just religious rites but the priesthood. Coemptio and usus marriages were processes by which the wife entered into the manus of her husband (as with confarreatio), but these were not formal religious ceremonies which needed priestly validation. All Roman weddings, however, were accompanied with religious observances, which played a very real role in the social recognition that a wedding had taken place and involved calling upon the assistance of many and diverse deities.

CONCLUSION

In both Greece and Rome, weddings were essentially legal transactions, which involved the transference of a young girl from one family into another. This public relocation of the bride from one household to another was in both cases the main demonstration that a marriage had taken place, and, except in the case of confarreatio in Rome, the marriage itself was not sacramental but transactional, a compact between the families without any official religious validation. Although not all weddings would have been equally elaborate depending on the couple's socioeconomic status, there were, however, a number of customary rituals, including pre-wedding dedications and the offering of sacrifices, which could be undertaken to ensure the support of the gods for the welfare of the new family and household, and to mark the major rite of passage for the bride: her transition from child to wife and mother and entry into a new social group. In all marriages in Greece and Rome families called upon the goodwill of the gods, in the hope that the union of the new husband and wife would be successful and produce offspring to continue the family line and further its economic interests. Marriage was one of the mortal activities in which the gods were believed to take an interest, with specific gods in both societies having oversight of wedding and pre-wedding rituals. Hence it was considered important to invoke the goodwill of these various deities as part of the ceremonies associated with weddings to ensure a successful outcome for the new couple and their families.

CHAPTER THREE

State and Law

MATTHEW J. PERRY

In the second century BCE, Antipater of Tarsus, the head of the Stoic school of philosophy in Athens, wrote an essay on marriage that emphasized the civic importance of the institution. He began:

> The noble and courageous youth, being, moreover, civilized and political, perceiving that household and life cannot otherwise be complete except with a wife and children— for it is incomplete as in the case of a city-state, not only one composed entirely of women but also one composed of single men: in the same manner that a flock is not good when it has no increase, nor a herd when it does not thrive, much more so neither a city-state nor a household—and so, having observed these things, and that he is political by nature, the noble person [holds] that he must assist in increasing the fatherland. For, surely, the city-states would not otherwise be able to prosper unless the best children, with regard to character, of the true citizens—even as the predecessors of the latter "wither and fall off," just like leaves of a good tree—unless these children would marry in due season, bequeathing, just like some true shoots, successors to the fatherland who would make it thrive eternally and protect its vigor to the extent it depended on them, never exposed to its enemies. *Endeavoring, both while living and having passed away, to bolster the fatherland and assist it, they consider being united in marriage among the primary and most necessary actions that are fitting*, being eager to fulfill every task laid on them by nature, most especially that which furthers the safekeeping and proper growth of the fatherland, and, even more, the honor of the gods—for if the race would die out, who will sacrifice to the gods?[1]

Two hundred years later, another Stoic philosopher, Gaius Musonius Rufus, wrote a similar treatise, in which he maintained that it was:

> Each man's duty to take thought for his own city, and to make of his home a rampart for its protection. But the first step toward making his home such a rampart is marriage. *Thus whoever destroys human marriage destroys the home, the city, and the whole human race.* For it would not last if there were no procreation of children and there would be no just and lawful procreation of children without marriage. That the home or the city does not depend upon women alone or upon men alone, but upon their union with each other is evident.[2]

Both authors penned their essays in response to what they believed was a worrisome trend in behavior that placed the state itself at risk: more and more young men were eschewing marriage in favor of a pleasurable or contemplative life of bachelorhood. This chapter seeks to illustrate and explain the meaningful link between marriage and the state—a territory governed by centralized administrative and legislative institutions—that existed in the ancient world.³ Over time, ancient thinkers arrived at something of a consensus, arguing that marriage was a necessary precondition for creating new households as well as the citizens that composed them. Households of citizens, in turn, were the constituent parts from which the state was assembled. It was a sign of both the importance of citizenship and the power of the state when political authorities began to craft new laws on marriage; once merely invested in marriages when they resulted in contractual disputes, ancient states increasingly addressed issues concerning the eligibility of partners, the legitimacy of unions, and the violation of marital bonds.

Law provides inimitable insight into a society's cultural and moral values, and thus lends itself to the study of marriage's private and public meanings. Yet modern scholars who investigate marriage in ancient law must draw examples and anecdotes from a variety of surviving sources: personal documents, public inscriptions, forensic speeches, literary texts, and edited compilations of laws and juristic interpretations. The patchwork nature of the evidence makes it difficult, if not impossible, for scholars to develop authoritative accounts that are unequivocally comprehensive and accurate. The study of the legal regulation of marriage is further complicated by the fact that there is little data regarding how people received these laws or if they abided by them. Scholars must always consider the possibility that individuals might have been unaware of the law or chose to disregard it, especially since the means of enforcement were quite limited in the ancient world.

MARRIAGE AND THE STATE

Marriage became a vital state institution through its connection to the household, the fundamental social and economic unit in the ancient world.⁴ A household, consisting of a family and its property, was a perpetual entity (at least in theory) that outlasted the lives of its individual members. Marriage either led to the creation of a new household or functioned as a mechanism to incorporate outsiders into an existing one (and thereby allow the original household to continue). Intermarriage between families served to link households together, establishing bonds of common economic and civic interest.⁵ Furthermore, since the household was the locus of property ownership in the ancient world, marriage also created the framework for the generational devolution of property. Through marriage, a man and woman produced "legitimate" children, a status that marked offspring as authentic members of not only the household but also the civic community in which the household was located.

Marriage's unique ability to legitimize and link together both individuals and families made the institution essential to the operation of ancient states, especially hereditary monarchies, where rulers often adopted the "state as household" model of governance. Royal marriages were critical first and foremost because they were the primary mechanism by which political successors were produced. Monarchs frequently sought unions for themselves or their family members with local aristocrats in order to solidify their power, or with foreign nobles in order to cement diplomatic agreements.⁶ One of the most famous diplomatic marriages occurred in the thirteenth century BCE, when the Egyptian pharaoh Ramses II wedded the daughter of the Hittite king Hattusilis in order to confirm a new peace treaty ending decades of intense warfare.⁷ Much later, King Herod of Judea, whom the Roman Senate elevated to the throne in 37 BCE, attempted to legitimize his position by marrying one of the last members of the preceding Hasmonean dynasty.⁸ Other politicians and social elites likewise used marriage as a means for establishing alliances on both a personal and national level (see Figure 3.1). Julius Caesar famously married his daughter to Gnaeus Pompeius and himself wedded the daughter of a close friend of Marcus Crassus in order to unite the powerful coalition known as the First Triumvirate that would dominate Roman Republican politics for nearly a decade.

Arguably the most important function of marriage within the state was its role in the transmission of legal status, especially citizenship. While there were gradations of official classifications in the Near Eastern states, often linked with an individual's ethnicity or community of residence, the distinction between citizens—persons who embodied the state and had a stake in its operation—and outsiders sharpened in both Greek and Roman culture.[9] A pivotal moment in the development of this concept was the abolition of debt-slavery in Athens by Solon, who justified his ban in terms of the special bond between

FIGURE 3.1 Scarab commemorating the marriage of Egyptian King Amenhotep III and Queen Tiye, *c.* 1390–1352 BCE. Metropolitan Museum of Art, 10.130.1643. Public Domain, CC0.

individual Athenians and the city-state (*polis*) itself.[10] This connection between individual and state, and the privileges and responsibilities it entailed, separated citizenship from mere residency. The primary mechanism for creating new citizens in the ancient world was the production of "legitimate" children by a married couple.

Many ancient authors, including Antipater of Tarsus and Musonius Rufus quoted above, connected the success and perpetuation of the state to marriage, casting it as the duty of patriotic citizens.[11] The Roman rhetorician Titus Castricius supposedly remarked that a "state could not survive without numerous marriages" and named this the truest and most valid principle of all.[12] Correspondingly, many lawmakers and philosophers characterized violations of marital unions as assaults upon the state.[13] Laws promoting marriage and criminalizing adultery often became the cornerstones of governmental policy, especially in times of crisis and rebuilding. The pecuniary consequences of marriage provided the initial grounds for legislation, but it was the rise of citizenship that promoted greater state involvement and regulation.

MARRIAGE AND LAW

Ancient states had a very limited role in the actual formation of a marriage, which was a private arrangement between two individuals or families. Involved parties began seeking state assistance to resolve problems regarding the terms and execution of the agreement. Ancient lawmakers and jurists addressed a variety of potential points of conflict including the fulfillment of betrothals, the payment of dowries, and the merger of family property, which located marriage (or aspects of marriage) within the law of contracts. This provided the first context for the rise of what might be called a "legitimate" or "lawful" marriage: unions in which the involved parties had access to the legal remedies offered by the state. This right of use derived from the conditions under which the union was formed, and the status of the involved parties. States began to refine the latter category over time, establishing requirements for individuals wishing to wed based on criteria such as age, social standing, legal capability, and eventually citizenship. Finally, ancient lawmakers sought to ensure the success and stability of the state by creating incentives for citizens to marry and penalties for individuals who violated the marriage of another. As the economic and political stakes of marriage began to increase, ancient states assumed a larger role in regulating the institution through law.

THE NEAR EAST

The first states emerged around the year 3500 BCE in Egypt and Southwest Asia.[14] Ranging in size from cities to multiethnic empires, the monarchical Near Eastern states flourished until the campaigns of Alexander the Great and the advent of the Hellenistic world in the third century BCE. Near Eastern kings utilized the new technology of writing in order to publish collections of laws, which codified existing practices and royal judgments relevant to the community, including those regarding matrimony (see Figure 3.2).[15] There were few official prohibitions placed upon marriage—both in terms of which individuals were able to form a legitimate union and whom they could wed—and intermarriage between couples from different states/cultures does not appear to have been problematic from a legal perspective.[16] Even slaves could enter into valid marriages, either with fellow slaves or with free individuals, due to the fact that Near Eastern lawgivers traditionally explained legal status in terms of personal relationships (i.e., that a woman could be a

FIGURE 3.2 Law Code of Babylonian King Hammurabi, *c.* 1792–1750 BCE. Louvre. Public Domain, CC0 3.0.

slave to one man and a wife to another). This meant, however, that an individual could not be both slave and spouse to the same person.[17]

The establishment of a lawful marriage in the ancient Near East resulted from an agreement between two individuals (or families) and required neither formal sanction nor the involvement of state or religious authorities. The defining attribute appears to have been cohabitation, which occurred when a man received a woman into his house to be his wife. Sources indicate several means of demonstrating cohabitation with conjugal intent: an oral statement accepting a woman as a wife, a bride physically entering her husband's house, consummation, or a couple living together for a set period of time.[18] Both social convention and law allowed men to have multiple wives, although the practice of polygamy varied across cultures and economic statuses.[19] Women were only ever allowed one husband at a time.

Families frequently established an oral or written betrothal agreement prior to the formation of a marriage in order to document the intent to wed and the financial stipulations of the union (see Figure 3.3). Near Eastern states first became involved in the matrimonial process by agreeing to aid in the enforcement of these provisions. A betrothal contract did not in itself produce a marriage but instead recorded the legal and financial transactions associated with the bride's change in status.[20] A woman was always subject to the authority of a male head of household; a betrothal contract recognized the impending transfer of the woman from her father's power to that of her husband. Such an agreement might make provisions for a dowry, money or items to be transferred from the bride's household to her husband. It was also common for a groom to pay a sum to the family of the bride (frequently called a "bride-price" in English), which came to be regarded as an advance payment for damages in case of breach of betrothal or divorce without cause.[21] The significance of this payment is highlighted by two of the Hittite laws, which distinguished between betrothed women who were "promised" and those who were "bound," with the latter status arising when the groom had paid a "bride-price."[22] If a bride's family broke the betrothal, they would owe greater restitution for a "bound" daughter as opposed to one who had been "promised." Betrothal contracts might also lay out an economic arrangement for the dispersal of goods, especially in cases of divorce.[23] Eventually, some states began to require a written contract between parties as a necessary condition for a legal marriage.[24] For example, in the eighteenth century BCE, the Babylonian king Hammurabi ruled: "If a man marries a wife but does not draw up a formal contract for her, that woman is not a wife."[25]

Two surviving contracts illustrate many of these principles. The first, which was roughly contemporary with Hammurabi's declaration, reads:

FIGURE 3.3 Marriage contract from late period Egypt, *c.* 380–343 BCE. Metropolitan Museum of Art, 35.4.1a, b. Public Domain, CC0.

> Warad-Samas, son of I[li-ennam], has taken Taram-Sagila, daughter of Samas-nasir and Risatum, in marriage from Samas-nasir [her father] and Risatum [her mother]. Should Warad-Samas, son of I[li-ennam], say to Taram-Sagila, his wife, "You are not my wife," he will pay (her) 1/2 mina of silver.[26]

With this document, Warad-Samas made a formal declaration that Taram-Sagila was now his wife and promised to pay her a set amount of silver in case of divorce. Another contract from sixth-century Babylonia reads:

> Gūzanu voluntarily spoke to Bēl-uballit and to fGudadadītu, his mother, as follows: "Please give me fKaššā, your daughter (and sister), the lass, in marriage. Let her be my wife." Bēl-uballit and fGudadadītu, his mother, agreed to his (proposal), and they gave fKaššā, their daughter (and sister), the lass, to him in marriage. Should fKaššā be found with another man, she will die by the iron dagger. Should Gūzanu release fKaššā and take a second wife in preference to her, he will pay her six minas of silver, and she may return to her paternal home. Bēl-uballit and fGudadadītu voluntarily promised to give as dowry with fKaššā, their daughter (and sister), to Gūzanu: one-third shekel of (gold?) jewelry, one pair of gold earrings worth one shekel, one Akkadian bed, five chairs, one table, a goblet, and a bronze platter. May Marduk and Zarpānītu decree the destruction of the one who contravenes this agreement; may Nabû, the scribe of Esagil, cut short his long days.[27]

In addition to a statement of marriage, the author also listed both the promised dowry and the payment he would make in the case of divorce.

Marriage fundamentally changed the status of the bride, who was transferred from the legal authority of her father to that of her husband. A husband possessed significant control over his wife's person in ancient Near Eastern law, including the right to pledge her as a surety for a debt or to sell her into slavery.[28] Moreover, a married woman's dependent status seemingly constrained her ability to own property and make contracts.[29] Husbands also could prosecute or directly punish wives who violated sexual mores. One law from twelfth-century Assyria, states:

> If a man should seize another man upon his wife and they prove the charges against him and find him guilty, they shall kill both of them; there is no liability for him (the husband). If he should seize him and bring him either before the king or the judges, and they prove the charges against him and find him guilty—if the woman's husband kills his wife, then he shall also kill the man; if he cuts off his wife's nose, he shall turn the man into a eunuch and they shall lacerate his entire face; but if [he wishes to release] his wife, he shall [release] the man.[30]

Several Neo-Babylonian marriage contracts, such as the one quoted above, included a clause explicitly stating the punishment for an adulterous wife.[31] In contrast, married men were not prohibited from having sexual partners other than their wives, so long as their partners were slaves or other lower-status individuals.

ATHENS AND GREECE

The Minoan and Mycenaean states that formed in the Aegean in the second millennium BCE all collapsed by the year 1150, leaving behind little evidence of their legal systems. After a 250-year period of political and economic depression, new Greek city-states (*poleis*) began to emerge throughout the Mediterranean region. Each of these sovereign *poleis* created their own laws, and, despite a shared Hellenic culture, there appear to have been substantive differences in civic policy.[32] However, the surviving evidence focuses almost entirely on Athens and little is known about the laws of most of the other polities.[33] Whereas the earliest written Athenian law was largely the product of magistrates holding special legislative authority, legislation from the classical era (*c*. fifth to fourth century BCE) was promulgated by the democratic assembly.[34]

The most important development shaping the legal institution of marriage in ancient Greece, and distinguishing it from contemporary Near Eastern models, was the tradition of formal monogamy, whereby Greek cultural norms—and eventually law—allowed individuals to possess only one spouse at a time.[35] The practice of formal monogamy was not grounded in an ideal of romantic commitment, nor did it preclude a married man from having other sexual partners or long-term personal relationships. It instead reflected a particular view regarding the constitution of the household (*oikos*), the foundational social and economic unit in the Greek world.

The roots of monogamy are impossible to discern fully, but the practice appears to have been established by the eighth century BCE. Modern scholars have suggested that resource parity—and the sense of egalitarianism that a lack of economic inequality can promote—was a primary catalyst and identify the post-Mycenaean economic collapse as a likely context for its origins.[36] The treatment of marriage and concubinage in the Homeric poems seemingly substantiates this theory. These works take as their subject Mycenaean era cultures, yet they often reflect the social and economic realities of the post-Mycenaean world. On the one hand, married Greek leaders such as Achilles and Agamemnon are polygynous, cohabiting with concubines while away at war. The poet ascribes the status of *alokhos* (bedmate) to both wives and concubines, signifying that legitimate children could be produced with either.[37] At the same time, the Greek heroes have only one wife, denoted by the title *kouridie alokhos*.[38] Here, the poet clearly contrasts the Greeks with the foreign king Priam, who has three wives.[39]

Marriage became a crucial issue in Athenian law in the sixth century BCE, when the lawgiver Solon reformulated notions of citizenship and personal status. Facing a dire civic and economic crisis, the Athenian people granted Solon extraordinary legislative powers, which he used to reorganize the polis, laying the essential groundwork for the rise of democratic citizenship. One of his reforms was to exclude children born from any woman other than a lawfully wedded wife from citizen status and limit their economic role in the household.[40] Marriage became defined as a union that produced legitimate children, highlighting its critical role in the creation and perpetuation of not only the household but citizenship as well.[41]

Athenian law closely connected marriage with the formation of a new oikos.[42] Each household had a male head (*kyrios*), who legally owned all of the family property. Women and children were also under the authority of a kyrios (usually, but not necessarily, the kyrios of their oikos), who was responsible for their care and maintenance. Boys no longer needed a kyrios after reaching the age of eighteen, but Athenian law required women to remain in lifelong guardianship. This severely restricted women's property rights, which were limited to small-scale market transactions.[43] Marriage, then, not only involved the creation of a new oikos but also the transfer of a woman from the authority of one kyrios to another.

As in the ancient Near East, marriage in Athens resulted from a private agreement between families. The minimum age for matrimony was generally agreed to be fourteen, although there was not consensus about this point. The critical issue for establishing a legal marriage was the consent of the households—specifically the *kyrioi*—involved; a legal marriage could not exist without their approval. The formal consent of a bride and groom (if he was still under the authority of another) was technically immaterial to the agreement.[44]

Athenian law articulated the standard process of marriage as a two-step procedure: betrothal (*engyē*) and then the formal transfer of the bride from one man's authority to another (*ekdosis*).[45] Betrothal served as a pledge to marry, and classical Athenian law recognized it as a type of non-binding contract.[46] The act of engyē does not appear to have been formalized itself, and sources suggest that a simple, oral acknowledgment by the two kyrioi was sufficient. Nonetheless, the establishment of engyē seems to have been necessary to form a valid marriage. According to the orator Demosthenes, the law read:

> Anyone whom either her father or her brother by the same father or her grandfather on the father's side pledges (*engyēsei*) on just terms to be a consort (i.e. wife), the children born of her shall be legitimate.[47]

Both custom and law expected, but did not require, that the betrothal agreement include provisions for a dowry, ostensibly for the bride's maintenance. A husband controlled the dowry, but did not fully own it, since he was obligated to return the funds if the couple divorced. *Ekdosis*, symbolized by the bride's physical movement from her father's house to that of her husband, concluded the act of marriage by placing her under the legal authority of her husband. Engyē and ekdosis could happen at different times, which in fact seems to have been common practice in cases where the betrothed girl had not yet reached puberty.

The judicial procedure of *epidikasia* was an alternative method establishing a marriage for a woman who possessed the status of *epikleros*. Athenian law recognized only male children as direct heirs to a father, and in cases where a deceased man had no sons, a judge's approval was required to settle the dispersal of the estate. If a sonless man had daughters, they each received the status of epikleros and were allocated a portion of their father's property. The closest male relative of the deceased then had the right to marry an epikleros and take possession of the estate assigned to her. If he refused, then the right of marriage passed to the next closest relative, following an order prescribed by law. In these cases, the process of epidikasia itself formed the marriage.[48] If an epikleros already had a husband, a relative could still claim the right of marriage and compel the dissolution of the existing union. Again, both the divorce of the epikleros and her ensuing marriage would occur automatically through epidikasia. A man who married an epikleros possessed the right to use and benefit from the estate assigned to her, but he could not alienate the property as he did not legally own it. The estate was to be preserved for his children, deemed the true successors to their grandfather. A law attributed to Solon purportedly required the husband of an epikleros to engage in intercourse with his wife at least three times per month, in order to ensure the production of an heir.[49] The level of state involvement in the matter of the epikleros demonstrates the importance that Athenians placed on the perpetuation of the oikos and the role that marriage played.[50]

Prior to the year 451 BCE, children born from a marriage between an Athenian man and a foreign woman became Athenian citizens. One notable example was the influential politician Cimon, who was the son of the Athenian aristocrat Miltiades and a Thracian princess.[51] In 451, the statesman Pericles, who not coincidentally had been an opponent of Cimon, promoted legislation that limited citizenship to children born from two Athenian parents.[52] The sheer number of casualties suffered during the Peloponnesian War led to a return to the earlier policy, but Athens reinstituted the terms of the Periclean law shortly after the conflict had concluded. Pericles' measure did not prohibit or invalidate marriages with non-Athenians but instead used the denial of citizenship for children as a deterrent. This changed in the fourth century BCE, when it became illegal for an Athenian man or woman to marry a foreigner.[53] In a famous court case, the orator Apollodorus accused the former courtesan Neaira of falsely representing herself as an Athenian and cohabiting with an Athenian man as husband and wife.[54] There is also evidence to suggest that men who failed to marry and produce legitimate children might suffer financial and/ or political consequences. Solon supposedly introduced a law that penalized men who did not wed by an appropriate time. The orator Deinarkhos seemingly confirmed this rule when he described legitimate children as being a prerequisite for serving as a general or participating in debates regarding public business.[55]

A few sources suggest that Athenian law recognized concubinage (*pallakia*) as a distinct type of official union.[56] It is difficult to definitively define the title "concubine" (*pallake*), as the term was often used imprecisely, and its meaning apparently changed over time. A homicide law attributed to the seventh-century Athenian lawgiver Drakon allowed a man to kill an intruder caught assailing his wife, mother, sister, daughter, or concubine—defined as a woman kept for the procreation of free children.[57] By the fourth century BCE, a "concubine" appears to have been any woman who was in a long-standing relationship (excluding matrimony) with an Athenian man. These women were most likely non-Athenians, whom the law now banned from marrying citizens, or possibly poorer women from Athens whose families lacked the funds to provide a competitive dowry.[58] A passage from a court speech indicates that the parents of a potential concubine would form an agreement with her partner much like a betrothal.[59] Any children born from this union were free but illegitimate (*nothoi*).[60] It seems likely that a man would have sought a concubine after becoming a widower or divorcing his wife, in part to avoid producing more legitimate children who might compete with his existing heirs. Interestingly, a man evidently could have a wife and a concubine concurrently despite the strict Greek views on monogamy.[61] One of the most famous concubines was Aspasia of Miletus, who entered into a relationship with Pericles after he divorced his wife. Years later, when the statesman learned that his two legitimate sons had died, he obtained a special decree from the Athenian assembly that granted legitimacy and citizenship to his son by Aspasia.

Athenian law prohibited a man from having sexual relations with any respectable Athenian woman other than his wife and a woman from having sexual relations with any man other than her husband. An individual who violated these standards could be charged with sexual impropriety (*moicheia*) by any other Athenian citizen.[62] The law did not formally distinguish between sexual assaults and consensual affairs, although jurors at the trial presumably would have taken the context of the offense into account. One orator, seeking to bolster his case, made the argument that a consensual affair was a worse crime than rape, since the adulterer corrupted a woman's mind as well as her body.[63] Husbands and male relatives also had the right to detain an offender personally and inflict their own punishments, up to and including execution.[64] Women themselves were not subject to public charges but faced penalties if their participation was proven. Athenian law compelled a husband to divorce his wife after winning his case against an adulterer; anyone who failed to do so could lose his civic rights.[65] Furthermore, the guilty woman could no longer attend any of the public festivals or religious rites. Athenian law treated moicheia, and the violation of marriage it entailed, not simply as an offense against an individual but a crime against the community as a whole.

FIGURE 3.4 Marriage contract from Hellenistic Egypt, 285–247 BCE. Metropolitan Museum of Art, 27.254a, b. Public Domain, CC0.

THE HELLENISTIC WORLD

Although the campaigns of Alexander the Great in the late fourth century BCE changed the political landscape of Greece and Western Asia, private law in Greek cities remained largely unaffected. Evidence from different cities suggests an increasing uniformity in legal procedure, most likely due to the influence of Athenian practices.[66] Alexander's conquests facilitated the spread of Hellenic customs and law throughout the Near East, which provided a legal foundation for the new states that emerged after his death. These Hellenistic kingdoms also incorporated many existing local rules and traditions into their legal systems (see Figure 3.4), the most notable example being the sanction of marriage between a brother and sister in Ptolemaic Egypt.[67] All inhabitants of these kingdoms were citizens insomuch as they were subjects of the monarch, although "Greeks" and non-Greeks often possessed distinct statuses under the law. Many cities within these states also retained their own forms of citizenship governed by municipal law. Some, such as Alexandria, required that both parents be citizens in order for a child to receive this status, whereas, others required only one citizen parent.[68] Marriages between Greeks and non-Greeks were lawful, albeit discouraged socially.

The transfer of a woman from her father's household to that of her husband (*ekdosis*) remained at the core of Hellenistic legal interpretation of marriages, but there were significant changes from the classical Athenian model, due primarily to the diminishing power of the kyrios. Most importantly, the consent of the bride and groom became a crucial factor. Engyē no longer appears to have been a necessary condition for marriage, and cohabitation with an intent to marry became enough to establish a lawful union.[69] Hellenistic women began to acquire greater property rights, and there is evidence of wives owning land, issuing loans, and selling goods, although in some cases they may have needed to gain the assent of their kyrios before completing the transaction.[70]

ROME

Over a period of five hundred years, the Italian city-state of Rome grew to control a vast multiethnic empire that spanned Europe and the Mediterranean region. According to tradition, the city adopted the Republican model of government in 509 BCE, after a revolution against the existing monarchy. Just over fifty years later, magistrates produced the first written legal code, known as the Twelve Tables, which provided the foundation for Roman marriage law. A watershed moment for both the evolution of the Roman state and the regulation of marriage occurred in 27 BCE, when Augustus effectively seized power as emperor after a series of destructive civil wars. His ensuing statutory efforts, which were intended to help restore "traditional" values and rebuild society, focused primarily on promoting marriage and punishing those who violated the integrity of the institution.

The treatment of marriage in Roman law revolved around the core legal concept of the head of household (*paterfamilias*). A Roman household (*familia*) was under the authority of a paterfamilias, the eldest male in a direct agnatic line. He maintained full legal and economic authority (*patria potestas, manus*) over the members of his familia and the goods that they possessed. All children born within a valid marriage (*matrimonium iustum*) belonged to the familia of their father and were under his *potestas*. Roman law distinguished between marriages contracted "with *manus*" (*cum manu*) and those "without" (*sine manu*). The former involved a transfer of authority, where the wife passed from potestas of her paterfamilias to the manus of her husband, becoming part of his familia.[71] A union sine manu meant that the wife remained under the potestas of her agnatic paterfamilias even after marriage. Marriage cum manu initially appears to have been the more popular option, but it disappeared by the late Republic, as families sought to retain increased control over their property.[72]

A valid marriage under Roman law required three elements: capacity, age, and consent. First and foremost, both individuals needed to possess the "right of marriage" (*conubium* or *ius conubii*).[73] All Roman citizens enjoyed this right, but its significance grew as the city-state began expanding and absorbing neighboring peoples in Italy. While some Italians obtained Roman citizenship, others received a lesser package of "Latin" rights, which included the ius conubii. As the Roman state grew, it continued to grant conubium to either specific individuals or entire communities based on the circumstances at hand (see Figure 3.5). Citizens who formed a conjugal partnership with individuals without conubium were not considered married under Roman law, although legal authorities still recognized the union as valid under the "law of nations" (*ius gentium*). Children born from such couples traditionally inherited the legal status of their mother, but, in an attempt to curtail these unions, the Roman people passed the *lex Minicia* in the first century BCE, which granted children the status of the "inferior" parent.

In addition to the possession of conubium, Roman law placed several other restrictions upon an individual's capacity to marry. Roman culture adopted a model of monogamous marriage similar to that of the Greeks and prohibited lineal descendants (e.g., parent and child) from marrying as well as collaterals who were only one step from a common ancestor (e.g., uncle and niece). This interdiction was later amended by Emperor Claudius, who legalized marriage with a fraternal niece (but not a sororal niece) so that he could marry the daughter of his deceased brother. Cousins originally could not marry, but this ban was later rescinded, allowing second, and eventually first, cousins to wed legally.[74]

The Twelve Tables explicitly prohibited marriage between patricians, the traditional aristocracy of Rome, and the rest of the population (plebeians) in 450 BCE, but popular outrage led to the reversal of this restriction five years later. During the Republican era, marriages between free Romans and former slaves were valid but could result in social opprobrium and censure, especially for members of the political elite. In the first century BCE, Augustus championed a law (*lex Iulia de maritandis ordinibus*) that formally barred members of the senatorial order from marrying freedpersons or individuals working in morally dubious occupations, such as prostitution and entertainment. Yet in doing so, it also sanctioned and destigmatized unions involving former slaves and non-elite Romans. The same law forbade pimps and male prostitutes from marrying any Roman woman other than a freedwoman.[75] Augustus also appears to have banned active soldiers from marrying, but the evidence for this interdiction is vague and problematic.[76] Later

FIGURE 3.5 Military diploma granted to Roman soldier upon his discharge (confirming the veteran's Roman citizenship, including the right of *conubium*), c. 149 CE. Metropolitan Museum of Art, 23.160.32a, b. Public Domain, CC0.

lawmakers, seeking to ward off conflicts of interest, prohibited guardians or their sons from marrying their wards, and high-ranking provincial officers from marrying women from their province.

Slaves, who were defined as property under Roman law, did not possess the capacity to marry but could enter into a de facto relationship called "companionship" (*contubernium*) that gained a measure of legal recognition. Contubernium was not an official union, and it existed only at the pleasure of the slaves' owners. Nonetheless, slaves often considered themselves to be wedded, and free Romans frequently used the language of marriage and family to describe the couples.[77] Lawmakers and jurists began to recognize the existence of contubernium on the grounds that these unions were in slaveholders' best interests.[78] For example, the jurist Ulpian argued that *contubernales* should be treated as family members, because their separation would cause "great inconvenience."[79] He also assumed that a deceased slaveholder would not want contubernales to be split unless he or she had explicitly stated so in a will.[80]

Individuals wishing to form a valid marriage had to be of minimum age, which was generally held to be the onset of puberty. While some jurists believed that this criterion should be determined on a case by case basis, Roman law eventually fixed the minimum age for marriage at twelve for girls and fourteen for boys.

The final criterion for establishing a lawful marriage was the consent of the involved parties. Early Roman law required only the consent of the paterfamilias of the groom and the paterfamilias of the bride; the approval of the bride and the groom themselves was technically irrelevant.[81] By the late Republic, it became necessary to obtain the consent of the bride, groom, and the father of the bride (if he was different from her paterfamilias) in addition to the approval of the *patresfamilias*. Those wishing to marry also gained the ability to initiate legal action in order to compel a paterfamilias to issue consent, on the grounds that his objection was unwarranted.[82] At the most basic level, consent was demonstrated through one's actions, such as participation in nuptial rituals, or simply a lack of dissent.[83] One jurist wrote: "If, because his father compels him, he marries a wife whom he would not have married if he had been acting of his own volition, he has still contracted a marriage, although marriage cannot be contracted by unwilling parties. It is held that he has preferred this course of action."[84] However, the question of precisely what constituted consent was an oft-debated topic among legal experts.

Traditionally, the first step in creating a Roman marriage was the betrothal agreement (*sponsalia*),[85] in which the *patresfamilias* would declare the terms of the impending marriage, including any provisions for a dowry. There are many examples of sponsalia formed for young children, who would then marry when they reached the appropriate age.[86] Early Roman law allowed parties to initiate legal action in cases where the conditions of the sponsalia were not fulfilled. By the late Republic, however, betrothal agreements were no longer considered to be actionable contracts, even in cases where they established stipulations in case of breach. It had become customary to exchange "tokens" of good faith at the time of betrothal, and these could not be recovered if the marriage was not formed.[87] A husband received control over a dowry upon establishment of the marriage, but, by the second century BCE, Roman law recognized that he did not fully own the property since he was obligated to return it in the case of divorce.[88]

A valid marriage was established immediately when two eligible individuals with an intent to marry (*affectio maritalis*) began to cohabitate. Intent might be demonstrated in a wide variety of ways, including existence of a sponsalia, participation in a nuptial ceremony, or payment of a dowry. Roman law recognized several formal processes which resulted in the wife being transferred to the manus of her husband. The first, "sharing of the bread" (*confarreatio*), was reserved for patricians, and was necessary for those who wished to hold important religious offices. The second, known as "purchase" (*coemptio*), was a fictive sale in which the groom "bought" his bride from her paterfamilias. The third was "usage" (*usus*), which occurred automatically after the bride had cohabited with her husband for a year. To prevent the transfer of manus (and thus create marriage sine manu), the woman needed to be absent from her husband's house at least three nights every year. If, at any point, she did not meet the requisite number of absences, she would come under his authority. As the practice of marriage cum manu began to decline in the late Republic, it no longer may have been necessary for a woman to actually leave the house; a fictive departure may have been enough to avoid manus. A statute eventually simplified the issue by eliminating the possibility of the transfer of manus through usus altogether.[89] Coemptio and confarreatio both remained as options, although legal texts suggest that they both fell into disuse by the early Imperial era.

The property rights possessed by Roman women and the rise of marriage sine manu necessitated the articulation of the precise legal and financial relationship between spouses. A woman under the potestas of her father became independent (*sui iuris*) upon his death, with the right to own property in her own name. There was a general expectation that daughters-in-power should inherit a share of their deceased father's estate. This meant that a woman married sine manu likely would have owned her own property, which needed to be differentiated from the property of her husband.[90] As marriage sine manu grew more popular over the course of the Republic, lawmakers increasingly sought to protect the separation of spousal property. Most notably, they forbade the exchange of gifts between husband and wife. Ulpian wrote, "As a matter of custom, we hold that gifts between husband and wife are not valid. This rule is upheld to prevent people from impoverishing themselves through mutual affection by means of gifts which are not reasonable, but beyond their means."[91]

The legislation promoted by Emperor Augustus in the late first century BCE/early first century CE represents a critical development in the regulation of Roman marriage. Seeking to rebuild Italy after decades of civil war, the emperor sponsored a series of laws intended to increase the population and strengthen the household. In addition to the rules governing a citizen's capacity to marry mentioned above, the new laws provided a series of incentives and penalties designed to encourage marriage and the production of legitimate children.[92] Men between the ages of twenty-five and sixty, and women between the ages of twenty and fifty were expected to be married and procreate; those who failed to meet these standards suffered various legal disabilities, such as the ability to claim legacies. The laws nullified any oaths or testamentary clauses that required an individual to forgo marriage or the production of children.[93] There were also substantial inducements to encourage childbirth, the most significant being the "right of three children" available to mothers. Although Roman women possessed the ability to own property, they needed to gain the approval of their financial guardian (*tutor*) for major transactions. The Augustan legislation granted freeborn women who had three children (and freedwomen who had four) release from financial guardianship, allowing them to conduct all business affairs entirely on their own.

The Julian Law on Repressing Adultery (*lex Iulia de adulteriis coercendis*) was another element in the Augustan reform program. Roman social mores allowed married men to have sexual partners other than their wives, so long as their partners, male or female, were not respectable citizens. Conversely, married women were permitted no sexual partner other than their husbands. Prior to Augustus, most incidents involving illicit sexual activity were handled by the families of the involved parties, with a public trial before the popular assembly reserved as an option for particularly egregious cases. The *lex Iulia* effectively criminalized adultery and other forms of sexual impropriety, significantly altering the way that these offenses were handled in Roman law and society. Augustus created a standing jury court to try cases, where any citizen could initiate charges. The law required that a husband divorce his wife before bringing suit against either her or her alleged partner. A husband who refused to divorce an accused adulterer could be prosecuted as a pander—one who sold the virtue of respectable women (which theoretically explained why he did not divorce and prosecute her himself).[94] Penalties for adultery and other forms of sexual misconduct included fines, loss of civic rights, exile, and even execution (although the last does not appear to have been common). In addition, women convicted under the law were required to wear a toga in public, which was the standard uniform of the prostitute.⁹⁵

One interesting byproduct of the new law on adultery was the development of a legal category of "respectable concubinage." Concubinage was originally an informal concept, describing a long-term relationship with a woman, often a former slave, who was not a wife. Roman norms discouraged, and later prohibited, a man from having a wife and a concubine at the same time; concubinage was supposed to be an alternative to marriage.⁹⁶ Roman men most likely sought concubines when they wished to form a union with a woman whose status made her unsuitable for marriage or to avoid the production of legitimate heirs.⁹⁷ The *lex Iulia de adulteriis coercendis* complicated the practice of concubinage by criminalizing any extramarital sexual affair with a Roman woman other than a prostitute, procuress, or actress. Since concubines did not always fall into one of these three categories, jurists needed to establish more formal guidelines for this relationship.⁹⁸ They were divided on whether the Julian Law allowed freeborn women to be concubines, but all agreed that concubinage with a freedwoman was a permissible and respectable union.

LATE ANTIQUITY

The legal treatment of marriage began to evolve in the fourth century CE with the Christianization of the Roman Empire. In the year 312 CE, Emperor Constantine legalized the religion, and seventy years later, Emperor Theodosius established Christianity as the official religion of the Roman Empire. While the framework for establishing a lawful marriage remained largely unchanged, Christian views on sexuality and conjugal unions led to several significant changes in policy.

The issue of conubium had been somewhat simplified by the Antonine Constitution of 212 CE, which granted Roman citizenship to all individuals living within the boundaries of the empire. However, Roman law increasingly had begun to recognize status-based categories within the citizen body, bestowing different rights and responsibilities upon each. Constantine, in an effort to help maintain these distinctions, extended the Augustan marriage ban on the marriage between senators and low-status women to a much wider range of social elites.⁹⁹ Furthermore, in cases where a higher-status woman married someone of a lower standing, she would acquire legal status of her husband.¹⁰⁰ Although Constantine did not ban concubinage between an elite man and a lower-status woman, he did attempt to weaken the institution by prohibiting a man from giving benefits to either his concubine or any children produced by the union.¹⁰¹

The consent of the bride and groom, and their respective patresfamilias, remained the cornerstone of marriage formation, although there was a growing willingness to take the bride's approval for granted.¹⁰² Marriage cum manu, which had been steadily declining, appears to have disappeared completely by the fourth century. Almost universally, husbands and wives would have been legally independent from one another, belonging to different families.¹⁰³ At the same time, new legal connections between the spouses began to appear, reinforcing the unique, hierarchical relationship between husband and wife. For example, while the distinction between the property of the husband and that of the wife was steadfastly maintained, there was a growing trend of requiring a woman to obtain her husband's approval or counseling before conducting a major transaction.¹⁰⁴

Lawmakers in late antiquity made a concerted effort to bring Roman law into conformity with Christian standards. In light of the religion's valorization of celibacy,

Constantine rescinded the penalties for non-marriage and childlessness that the Augustan legislation established.[105] He also banned the partition and sale of slave families living on imperial lands, giving additional legal recognition to contubernium as an institution.[106] Subsequent laws also forbade Christians from marrying Jews and barred Christian clerics from marriage altogether.

Late antique legal sources continued to emphasize the danger that adultery presented to the civic community, with execution becoming a more standard penalty. The best evidence which highlights this view is the list of crimes—labeled "the most serious of offenses"—for which there was no judicial appeal: adultery, homicide, poisoning, and practicing magic.[107] Emperor Constantine also imposed harsh penalties for so-called "abduction marriage," a practice that had occurred in the Greco-Roman world for centuries.[108] In these cases, a man might "abduct" a woman to be his wife (possibly, but not necessarily, with her as a willing partner), in the hopes that her parents might recognize their marriage in the future. Constantine, however, established mandatory penalties for the abductor, the abducted woman, and anyone who provided aid or accepted the union.[109] Perhaps the most noteworthy aspect of this law is the severity of the prescribed penalties. For example, a nurse who aided or encouraged such an enterprise was to have molten lead poured down her throat; other slaves who provided assistance were to be burned alive. The original punishment for the abductor and a willing bride is not recorded in the surviving sources. A later emperor, seeking to lessen the severity of the original law, reduced the penalty to "only capital punishment," which suggests that Constantine had intended particularly painful or degrading forms of execution, such as crucifixion or burning.[110] Even a woman who was abducted unwillingly was to be punished, albeit less severely, because it was believed that she did not do enough to avoid danger.

CONCLUSION

Over the four thousand years from the rise of Near Eastern kingdoms to the fall of the Roman Empire, the evolving treatment of marriage in ancient law highlights the perceived stakes of the institution. Marriage was viewed not simply as an agreement between two families but also a key part of the civic and moral foundation upon which the state was built. Given the political and economic stakes of this institution, it is perhaps surprising to see that the formation of marriage did not involve state participation and only received limited attention in law, which focused more on eligibility to wed, the legitimacy of children, and the devolution of family property. Yet marriage was never a wholly private act. In the words of one scholar writing on ancient Athens, "marriage itself was recognized and validated not by specific legal ceremony or piece of papyrus, but by the communally witnessed rituals and household events which established its legitimacy ..."[111] An ancient marriage gained its legitimacy in part through recognition by the civic community; in the future, the state would co-opt this function, taking on a more formal role in formation of connubial unions.

CHAPTER FOUR

The Ties That Bind

KATARIINA MUSTAKALLIO

In the ancient Greek and Roman world, not everyone was entitled to enjoy the legal benefits of marriage. Slaves were not allowed to have a marriage—or family—recognized by law, and several restrictions concerning different social ranks forbade many marriages even between citizens. Traditionally, Greek and Roman marriage was monogamous, setting it apart from polygamy practiced by barbarian peoples, which was considered exotic and abnormal. Monogamous marriage was a distinguishing feature of Greek and Roman civilization as well as an important part of the Greek and Roman identity.[1] Ancient writers asserted that the state of marriage was the ideal living arrangement for citizens, and remarriages after a widowhood or a divorce were encouraged, sometimes almost obligatory. In the patriarchal societies of Greece and Rome, choosing the right partner for marriage—especially the first marriage—was a decision made by the couple's families and not by the two people involved. Young men were granted far more participation in decisions concerning their own lives than young women, but both sexes usually entered first marriages arranged by their family members. As was the case in most important family decisions, the wishes of the male head of household were accorded priority. The purposes of marriage were clear: to produce children and lawful heirs, and above all to continue the male line of the family. The bride was usually very young when she married for the first time and when she moved to the house of her husband. Central, and all-important, to this process for all social classes was the creation of a formal contract between the participating spouses and their families.[2]

In this chapter, I will outline the stages from betrothal to marriage and the different ways in which families and spouses were bound to each other in the Greek and Roman worlds. Then I will concentrate on the particular role which marriage ties played in Roman religion and identity. The following sections will examine some special cases, for example, *tabulae nuptiales* found in Egypt as well as certain inscriptions describing marriages. At the end of this chapter, I will examine changes in marriage ties through some case studies from late antiquity.

STRATEGIZING FOR A FAMILY'S FUTURE: BETROTHAL

To approach the question of both the role and the social function of betrothal and marriage in the Greek and Roman worlds, we should first consider families and their attitudes toward the future. The survival and maintenance of the family was the primary focus of its members, especially the head of the family, but there were also strong, seemingly immaterial purposes or motivating factors—such as the continuation of the family name and legacy, as Ville Vuolanto has pointed out in his studies. The strategies for economic and social advancement of the family were tightly bound to the production of a new generation and decisions related to the inheritance of the property of the family.³ New marriages played a central role in the continuity of the family, invested with crucial importance in upgrading its status and increasing its wealth. In this context, marriage preparations were accorded major significance, with the fathers or the nearest male relatives of the bride assuming considerable visibility in this process.

Preparations for upper-class marriages began several years before the actual wedding took place through the search for an appropriate family with offspring of suitable age to wed the prospective bride and groom. The preferred candidates of both sexes seem to have been those occupying a somewhat higher social and economic status than those of the family seeking to add him or her to their household. The steps leading up to marriage usually included a ceremonial betrothal, which was arranged between the father, or the nearest male relative of a bride, and the bridegroom. Mary Harlow and Ray Laurence have closely examined the importance of the betrothal as a central and formative experience in mid–late childhood, especially for young women. Without this stage of transition, and without the rite of separation from the original family, the next step, the formation of a couple bound together through marriage, would have been difficult if not impossible.⁴ Harlow and Laurence emphasize that the betrothal of daughters and sons also created a public symbol of the new status ascribed to the members of the less socially and economically advantaged family through verbal communication, especially that of naming the betrothed (*engyesis* in Greek, *sponsio* in Latin).⁵

The first connection between the families involved was generally made years before the formal betrothal took place, sometimes even before the son or daughter was born, or in their early childhood.⁶ In both Greece and Rome, girls were often betrothed at young ages, between the ages of seven and ten. Elite and upper-class families usually made marital arrangements earlier than those of lower social status. In Rome, girls could be legally married from the age of twelve, while boys tended to marry when they were several years older. In Athens, girls were likely to be married when slightly older, starting from the age of fourteen. Athenian men, however, usually married in their late twenties and girls in their late teens. The education of girls largely focused on readying them for marriage and the demands of domestic life. Preparations for the wedding ceremony customarily started as soon as the wedding date was set.⁷

MARRIAGE TIES: DOWRY AND PRESENTS

The bride and the groom prepared for the wedding through a series of offerings, dedications, and sacrifices. These prematrimonial practices ritually and preemptively purified the participants and propitiated the sacred forces, readying both spouses for their new roles as a married couple. Presents and dowries formed a concrete part of the new tie between the spouses.⁸ In Greece and the Hellenistic East, dowry practices varied among different cities. The size of a dowry depended, of course, on the prosperity of the family. When a father could not afford a dowry for his daughter, it was provided by close relatives, or even by the polis itself.⁹ In the Roman tradition, the giving of a dowry did not lend legal validity to a marriage, although it was still a common custom. The dowry was transferred from the bride's family to the groom's, and might contain jewelry, money, and slaves, and these items belonged to the husband for the duration of the marriage if the wife was married *cum manu*. In the case of divorce or the husband's death, and if the marriage was childless, the wife or her father could reclaim the dowry.¹⁰

Many important contracts and legal transactions, later inscribed in surviving historical documents, were originally made orally.[11] Antiquarians have asserted that in the Roman wedding ceremony, the bride pronounced the formula *ubi tu Gaius, ibi ego Gaia*, "where you are Gaius, I am Gaia," and this speech act helped to legitimize them as a couple.[12] In Athens, since the bride was not considered to be a legal agent, her presence was not even necessary for the act of *engye* (pledge), that is, of making a commitment to the marriage.[13]

While much evidence survives concerning nuptial rites and ceremonies celebrated by families, these ceremonies did not by themselves necessarily create a legal marriage.[14] Even if the giving of the dowry and a written marriage contract preceded the marriage, a marriage was only considered legal in Rome (*matrimonium iustum*) when it fulfilled certain conditions, preserved in extant legal sources, pertaining to the legal capacity to marry (*conubium*). Roman citizenship was a requirement demanded from both parties, as was legal age, and proof that the prospective spouses were not too closely related. The legal sources also maintain that the couple were required to live together with the mutual intention of forming a lasting union (*affectio maritalis*) and a shared purpose of producing offspring (*liberorum procreandorum causa*).[15]

Roman matrimony (*sine manu*) among elites of the late Republican and Imperial period, was characterized by a strict separation of property between husband and wife. What is more, a wife either stayed under the legal power of her father or, if her father had died, was placed under the tutelage of a guardian. This type of marriage solved one of the major problems resulting from the marriages of daughters to men outside their family: loss of property. When, therefore, a daughter stayed under her father's power, the property she inherited did not merge with her husband's. If the wife died without children, and if she had not drawn up a will, then her property reverted to her original (father's) family. As I have noted, the first marriage of a Roman daughter was customarily arranged by her family. When divorces became more frequent during the first century BCE, it became more possible for men and women to find more suitable or congenial partners for their second or third marriages on their own, without familial assistance.[16] Divorces were usually familial matters, and only the parties involved were notified.[17]

SPECIAL MARRIAGE BONDS AND THE MARRIAGE OF THE *FLAMEN* AND *FLAMINICA DIALIS*, PRIEST AND PRIESTESS OF JUPITER

The older and more traditional form of legally valid matrimony in Rome, the so-called cum manu marriage, was a relationship in which the wife fell under the jurisdiction of her husband (or his father, if the husband was not legally independent, or *sui iuris*). The wife then legally held the status of a daughter in relation to her husband (or his father) and could inherit his property if he died. There were three types of *manus*-marriages: *usus*, *coemptio*, and *confarreatio*. Usus was a practical marriage in which a transfer of the wife into the manus of the husband happened by default after they had been living together. The only requirement was that a man and a woman cohabitated for one full year. If the wife stayed away from her husband's home for three consecutive nights (the so-called usurpation of the *trinoctium*) she was no longer under her husband's power. Coemptio, in turn, means a "bride purchase": the groom paid a certain symbolic sum of money and received the bride in exchange.[18] It required five witnesses and included a simple wedding ceremony. Usually in cum manu marriage the wife possessed no property of her own, and she was entirely in the control of her husband.[19]

According to Roman tradition, the peculiar ceremony known as confarreatio (of which we know little but assume that a cake of spelt, *far*, was somehow used) was the oldest form of marriage, differing from both usus and coemptio in its arcane, elaborate religious rituals. This ceremony presided over by the Pontifex Maximus and the *Flamen Dialis* required at least ten witnesses.[20] It survived in its archaic form into the Imperial period because it was essential for the maintenance of state religion. Not only the principal priestly couples (*flamines* of Jupiter, Mars, and Quirinus) but also the *rex and regina sacrorum*, the so-called "king and queen of sacred things," had to be married by confarreatio, they also had to be born of parents married in confarreatio. It was for the most part a marriage confined to the old families of pure patrician origin. Confarreatio marriage was virtually indissoluble.[21]

When the Flamen Dialis, the head priest of Jupiter, attained his office, he was emancipated from the control of his father and became sui iuris.[22] He had several privileges: at banquets, for instance, he always occupied a special seat of honor and had a right to a *lictor*, bodyguard normally reserved for high-ranking magistrates.[23] Of paramount importance however was the assistance of his priestess-wife, the *Flaminica Dialis*, who was indispensable to her husband's office; she also enjoyed many privileges. Nevertheless, owing to their special priestly marriage, both priestess and priest of Jupiter were subject to a long list of ritual prohibitions that regulated their habits, diet, behavior, and even the private interactions between a husband and a wife.[24] Moreover, while the relationship between a married couple in confarreatio marriage was normally subject to the rules of *manus*-marriage (as a result of which the wife could usually not possess any property of her own and she was under the total economic control of her husband), the Flaminica Dialis enjoyed relative freedom from these marital restrictions.[25]

In his *Roman Questions*, Plutarch, an early second-century Greek writer, asks why the priest of Jupiter was required to resign his office when his wife died. Plutarch tries to answer the question by comparing the situation to a "conventional" marriage. He explains that the house of a married man was a complete house but was damaged and incomplete once his wife had died. Plutarch then analyzes the sacred bond between a priest and a priestess, and stresses the importance of the couple's working together, noting that the wife's assistance was essential in religious rites.[26]

The bond between a husband and wife in a confarreatio marriage was remarkably strong: the Flamen and Flaminica Dialis complemented each other in their marital as well as in their religious obligations. Plutarch even compared this couple with the most important public officers of Rome, the *censors*. According to him, "One might be less surprised at this resignation [of a priest of Jupiter if his wife died] if one should adduce also the fact that when one of the censors died, the other was obliged to resign his office."[27] The priest and priestess of Jupiter were considered a complete couple, and their home the "complete home" or *oikos teleios*.[28] The very raison d'etre of this unusual, dual priesthood was marriage.

In this marriage, the sacred order between the two genders was complementary.[29] Neither could fulfill their religious obligations, rites, and rituals without the other. By the standards of Roman culture, they were an ideal couple and an *exemplum* for others, and their special bond was visible in their social status and in their *habitus*.[30] The Flamen's dress was of central interest in the community, since he had to be easily recognizable, as did his wife. According to Festus, brides adopted the habit of using the veil from this particular priestess, as it was a symbol of the longevity of their marriage between Flamen and Flaminica—divorce was prohibited for this sacred couple.[31] Whatever the historical accuracy of this explanation, it documents how the marital bond between Flamen and Flaminica Dialis was publicly displayed as a model for others.

SPECIAL MARRIAGES INVOKED IN THE CONSTRUCTION OF ROMAN IDENTITY: AENEAS AND LAVINIA, THE SABINE WOMEN AND ROMAN MEN

The legendary history of Rome emphasizes the values of *matrimonium* as the strongest bond which unites a man and a woman, but at the same time also unites two peoples into one.[32] The Roman historian Livy claimed that the construction of a new Latin identity began centuries before the founding of Rome when, after the Trojan War, the leader of the Trojan refugees, Aeneas, came to Italy. The son of Anchises and the goddess Venus, Aeneas and his troops waged war with his troops against the Latins and their king Latinus. After fierce battles, the war ended with a public peace treaty, but the formal treaty did not suffice in this context and needed to be reinforced by a private one: consequently, Aeneas married king Latinus's daughter, Lavinia,[33] and their union was honored by the founding of the city of Lavinium, named for the bride. In this fashion, the name of the city preserved the memory of Lavinia's special role in Roman history.[34] The two peoples, the Latins and the Trojans, formed a new nation. Thus Livy emphasizes the significance of familial pacts and identifies marital contracts as the best guarantees for organized political and civic life.[35]

Perhaps the most significant marital bond in the legendary history of Rome is one linked to the founding legend of the city itself. Some have viewed the tale as a celebration of violence against women in Roman culture, but if we re-read the ancient sources, we will find, especially in the versions of Livy and Dionysius of Halicarnassus, that they also emphasize the value of the legal state of matrimony, and its potential for solving disputes and uniting people.[36]

Presumably all Romans knew the tale of how Romulus populated his new city: during the festival of Consus, organized by Romulus, Roman men abducted young Sabine women before their astonished families could rescue them.[37] This was an outrageous and violent act, but as soon as Romulus affirmed the status of these women as lawful wives and honorable matrons, the captured women started to accept their new position.[38] The story then describes how the famous Sabine women interrupted the battle between their Roman husbands and Sabine fathers, and ends with peace finally made between the two peoples.[39] The historical narrative emphasizes the importance of the successful intercession by the Sabine women, claiming that Romulus was so indebted to them that, when he divided the people into thirty *curiae*, he named these sections to honor the Sabine women.[40]

As we have seen, the institution of matrimony is of central importance in the foundation myths of Rome and the formation of its identity as a nation. In these two stories, what was united was greater than individual men and women. These unions forged a new community from the blending of two hostile ones. The basis of the union between the Romans and the Sabines was a contract of matrimony from which the roles, privileges, and obligations related to matrimony derived. These legendary stories testify to the central role of matrimony in Roman political and civic identity.

FROM LEGENDARY STORIES TO ORDINARY FAMILIES: MARRIAGE CONTRACTS

How then can we characterize the everyday experience of marriage among Greeks and Romans, and what kind of evidence do we have for marriage contracts? The ancient evidence points to one clear conclusion: that for most people, getting married was a life-changing experience, as it influenced the social status of each spouse and at the same time functioned as an important part of their families' strategies for negotiating their future. We have also seen that at ancient weddings, the material property belonging to the families of both spouses had immense importance. Most of the marriage contracts that survive, *tabulae nuptiales* or *dotales*, have been found in Egypt, due its dry climate conducive to the preservation of the papyri on which the contracts were written. Most of these documents were written in Greek and reflect Greek or local Egyptian marriage practices.[41]

Not surprisingly, these unique sources routinely mention certain parts of nuptial ceremonies. For example, many refer to the *ekdosis*, the giving away of the bride to the groom.[42] In addition to the dowry, which invariably was of central interest, the documents mention two different kinds of bridal marital property that remained with the wife during the marriage: smaller personal items that she used for her own adornment (*parapherna*), and larger forms of property, including land and slaves (*prosphora*). Some of the documents reveal even more detailed expectations for both spouses: in addition to the amount of property expected as contributions from each spouse, there are also remarks on marital duties: the husband was supposed to provide financial support to the family, and the wife was supposed to behave appropriately during the marriage. In the case of divorce or the death of a spouse, the documents even provide pre-arrangements for the future care of children that might be born to the couple.[43]

In addition to the wealth of Greek evidence, some fragmentary contracts in Latin and other languages have survived within these papyri.[44] Notably, Judith Evans Grubbs discusses a marriage contract of a Roman soldier from Dura Europos, written in Greek and dated in 232 CE. What we observe here is that these soldiers have acquired by this date the trappings of ordinary citizen weddings. That is, marriages were prohibited for Roman soldiers until the era of Claudius, after which they were tolerated to some extent. From the late second century onwards, soldiers had wives, but it took time until these unions were considered to be legal marriages. By the third century CE, soldiers were allowed to enter legally binding marriages while in service.[45] The soldier mentioned in the contract clearly wanted his wedding signed and sealed, in the fashion of many contemporary Romans.

An interesting papyrus from Oxyrhynchus, dated to 260 CE records the details of a union in which a bride was given in marriage by her mother.[46] Because this bride's case was not unique, we may guess that it reflects the variety and strong influence of local customs that are quite different from those adopted by Greeks living, for example, in Athens. These tabulae nuptiales, in general, emphasize how important it was to make a proper contract before the marriage and list all the property and dowry in detail. Like prenuptial agreements in the modern world, some ancient Greeks and Romans felt that it was necessary to prepare in advance for a possible divorce and for childbirth expenses. According to these documents, at least in Roman Egypt, a variety of different marriage customs were in use: the bride could be given away by her father, or a male relative, but also by her mother and in some cases even by herself (the self-*ekdosis*). Property held pride of place in these contracts, and the records of that property are very detailed and, as far as we know, accurate, revealing how desperately these ancient people wanted to prepare for the future.

THE TIES BETWEEN UPPER-CLASS MARITAL COUPLES

Marriage, of course, was an important part of the future strategies of families from different social strata for dealing with the future, but for families who held political power, marriage became central to their political activity, from the golden age of Athens of the fifth century BCE through the Imperial period in Rome. As Pauline Schmitt Pantel has pointed out, marriage was at the core of the citizens' civic duties: to become a successful politician, a man had to be married.[47] Therefore because marriage had a significant public and political dimension, a legal wife and a family were needed to construct a positive public image of a citizen in Athens as well as in Rome. Marriage guaranteed the continuity of the state and civic order. As Plutarch emphasizes in his "Advice to the Bride and Groom" (*Coniugalia Praecepta*), a man needed to have his household in proper harmony if he sought to harmonize the state, forum, and friends.[48]

Epistolary sources increase our knowledge about private bonds of affection, especially among the elite. We have, for instance, letters from Cicero and Pliny the Younger to their wives, attesting to their strong emotional ties and feelings toward their spouses during their absence.[49] In one letter, Pliny memorably expresses his emotional attachment to his wife Calpurnia vividly and concretely, by writing that even his feet bring him to Calpurnia's side of the house because he so deeply longs for her during her absence.[50]

Inscriptions too describe strong emotional ties between wife and husband and may even suggest a greater intellectual and marital compatibility between the spouses than we can detect in surviving literary works. One of the most interesting pieces of extant evidence about marriage is the so-called *Laudatio Turiae*, an epitaph from the late first century BCE. Attempts to identify the deceased woman as one and the same Turia mentioned by Valerius Maximus and Appian in their histories produced the inscription's current name.[51] Importantly, these historians claim that Turia saved her husband during the chaotic years of the late Republic, and the inscription records a similar story. The *Laudatio Turiae* is currently the longest surviving inscription about private lives in Roman antiquity.[52]

The inscription emphasizes the central role of the wife in her husband's private and public life, conduct also connected to the welfare of the family property, and the relationship between the happiness and mutual concern of spouses for one another is evident here. By taking care of family property, the spouses strengthened their bonds with one another. The traditional domestic virtues associated with Roman matrons—for example, loyalty toward their husbands, reasonable temperament, industry in working wool—are also mentioned here. The wife is described as a virtuous matron, even if she was not able to provide her husband with the thing that mattered most in a Roman marriage, namely a child.[53]

In fact her inability to bear children yields a tale of unexpected twists and turns. The wife is said to have suggested to her husband that he divorce her and find himself a new spouse with whom to have children. She was even willing to remain in the same house in the role of a sister or a mother-in-law—taking care of their mutual property (her husband was her guardian at the same time). In this eulogy the husband confesses that he was shocked by her suggestion, but he was clearly pleased by the great lengths to which she would go to benefit him in any way she could.[54]

Another seemingly unusual married couple, from the second century CE, comprises a famous philosopher, writer, and rhetorician from Northern Africa, "Lucius" Apuleius, and his newly wedded wife, a wealthy lady called Pudentilla. We know about their marriage in some detail because Pudentilla's family accused Apuleius of using magic to gain her attentions. To defend himself, Apuleius wrote a statement of self-defense, the *Apologia*, which reveals contemporary attitudes toward mature and rich women entering into second or third marriages. Pudentilla had been a widow for fourteen years before her marriage to the much younger and poorer Apuleius. Marriage, as we have already seen, was defined as an institution for producing offspring, which made a successful sexual relationship between husband and wife crucial. The family of Pudentilla did not believe she was able to perform satisfactorily in either of these areas. In his *Apologia*, Apuleius points out that Pudentilla had earlier suffered a physical illness caused by sexual abstinence and claims that she had decided to marry him in order to become healthier. In this way, Apuleius wanted to show that their marriage was "normal" and included an active sexual life.[55] Whatever the reality of their private life, Apuleius's speech documents just how powerful familial control could be, especially when a man had the temerity to woo a rich widow.

THE VOICE OF A WOMAN? THE MARRIAGE OF FABIA ACONIA PAULINA AND P. VETTIUS AGORIUS PRAETEXTATUS

A document worthy of mention comes to us from the fourth century CE, carved on the tombstone of Publius Vettius Agorius Praetextatus, an important imperial official and leader of the pagans in the fourth-century Senate. The background and the context of this inscription differs from that of the *Laudatio Turiae*, as this time it is the wife, Fabia Aconia Paulina, who lauds her husband and their marriage. They lived during the period of a violent schism between the pagan senators and the Christians, and Praetextatus figured prominently in this public debate, as a devout adherent of traditional Roman civic polytheism.

Paulina herself is also described in the tombstone: Her excellence is not defined as that embodied by the idealized, traditional wife of earlier Roman literature; rather, she endears herself to her husband through mutually shared religious and political participation in ceremonies, rites, and mysteries. In the tombstone, she is described vividly:

> Paulina, the partnership of our heart is the origin of your propriety; it is the bond of chastity and pure love and fidelity born in heaven. To this partnership I entrusted the hidden secrets of my mind; it was a gift of the gods, who bind our marriage couch with loving and chaste bonds. With a mother's devotion, with a wife's charm, with a sister's bond, with a daughter's modesty; with the great trust by which we are united with our friends, from the experience of our life together, by the alliance of our marriage, in pure, faithful, simple concord; you helped your husband, loved him, honored him, cared for him.[56]

The inscription informs us that they had lived together for forty years and thus shared their entire adult lives together. Paulina describes how she followed her husband as a priestess by performing the sacrificial rites of the *taurobolium* as well as serving in the cults of Hecate and Ceres. Here the husband and wife occupied substantially different roles from the ones we have observed earlier: this wife was drawn into mystery cults by her husband who was a priest. Accordingly, the inscription describes the services the husband rendered the community in combination with his religious duties.

Maijastina Kahlos has analyzed the political career of Praetextatus, emphasizing that he never converted to Christianity even though the Christianization of the Roman aristocracy was already in process during his lifetime. While analyzing the funerary poem and particularly Paulina's role in its composition, Kahlos stresses that the poem is especially significant because it illustrates late Roman ideas of female virtue and the ideals of marriage and marital love united by the practice of religion.[57]

MARRIAGE AS EDUCATION: PORPHYRY OF TYRE AND MARCELLA

We have seen already that in Plutarch's "Advice" to a married couple, an ideal wife was described as a loyal follower of her husband. It was important that she share the same friends and that she worship the same gods as her husband. In this context, Plutarch introduces the idea that the wife should study philosophy and discuss its lessons with her husband, along with striving to become more educated in all ways.[58] This notion becomes even more prominent in a letter written by Pomponius Porphyry to his wife Marcella in the third century where the idea of a married couple studying philosophy together is again represented as the highest good.[59] Porphyry himself was a pupil of Plotinus, the most famous philosopher of his time.[60]

Marcella was a wealthy widow of a friend of Porphyry's, with several daughters and sons. According to the letter, Porphyry's motivation to marry Marcella was not based on the hope of having new heirs: he presents himself more as a protector to Marcella. At this time Porphyry was the foremost opponent of Christianity, contributing several works to this debate, among them "Against Christians" and "The Philosophy from Oracles"—a defense of traditional Roman religious practices.

The letter to Marcella is not an intimate, private letter from a husband to his wife, but meant for public circulation. It is a didactic exposition of the Neoplatonic doctrine on salvation, and it introduces the practices of the Neoplatonic lifestyle. Therefore, Porphyry presents his new marriage in the context of a philosophical way of life, with his wife as his student.[61] The tie between a husband and wife in this particular case was education itself.

A considerable age difference between spouses ordinarily obtained in Greek and Roman marriages, resulting in the husband's assuming the role of an older partner and an adviser, but the relationship introduced by Porphyry, based on studying philosophy together and not on sexual interaction, was a new concept. We also encounter this kind of ideal relationship within the Christian communities.[62]

NEW TIES IN CHRISTIAN MARRIAGES

Christian influences especially from the fourth century CE onwards, injected new ideals about marital life into Roman culture. A fundamental Christian precept—that marriage was instituted and ordained by God, for the lifelong relationship between one husband and one wife—changed the character of marital life which had long been characterized, especially among the upper social classes, by divorces and remarriages. Christians fashioned marriage into a sacred institution. It was both a gift from God as well as the most important human relationship one could have. Yet many of the old Greek and Roman traditions and customs related to marriage and sex life remained untouched:[63] Augustine, for example, had several concubines.[64]

Nevertheless, a certain spiritualizing tendency related to marriage was also evident in non-Christian culture, as we have already seen. In the Christian period, asceticism offered an influential life model, posing new and different challenges to traditional family life as well as changes in attitudes toward the widowhood of young women.[65]

Even though Romans cherished the ideal of the *univira*, a matron who had only one husband during her entire lifetime, younger Roman widows were often compelled to remarry after the proper mourning period.[66] Christian culture introduced new models to follow: for example a widowed Christian woman, Melania the Elder, did not remarry but devoted her whole life to prayer and penitence at the tender age of twenty-two, after the death of her husband. Her granddaughter, Melania the Younger, married her cousin, Valerius Pinianus, as stipulated in the will of her father when she was still quite young. After she had produced two children, Melania requested that the couple live in celibacy together and in an ascetic manner. A marital couple living together like sister and brother was a Christian invention but not so far removed from the idea of Porphyry, as we have already seen. This new, Christian promotion of an ascetic lifestyle brought new challenges to the planning of future strategies for families. Nevertheless, even ascetic members of a family had the potential to bring recognition and honor to the household and the family name.[67]

In the process of forming this new Christian culture, interest in the education of young Christian women grew, as did the focus on who would educate these young women and with whom they would associate. Two of the most prominent early Christian authorities and teachers, Augustine and Jerome, emphasized the importance of Christian education in their letters. They, and other authorities, feared the corruptive influence of non-Christian members of families and even their staff, especially the household slaves.[68]

Therefore Christian innovations posed challenges to the Roman family in late antiquity. In a traditional Roman household, slaves could live in nonlegal committed unions (that often mirrored the marriages of free persons) if their patron agreed and even have children. Slave marriages and the children resulting from them existed at the whim of their owners.[69] From the fourth century onwards, wealthy Christian families preferred to have slaves from Christian families in their households. The novelty of this situation was that the slave family usually belonged to and participated in the same Christian community as its patron family. The situation exposed the conventional social order and could generate doubts and ideas which were even more revolutionary. Many Christian authors recognized slave marriages as lawful—provided that the owner of the slaves approved of these unions. Yet, to clarify the uneasy situation, John Chrysostom suggested that in a slave-holding Christian family the hierarchy should be clear: the patron of the house would hold authority over his wife, the wife over the enslaved staff, the enslaved men over their wives, and the wives over their children.[70]

The formation of a new Christian way of life required new solutions, and the Greek and Roman worlds now faced unprecedented challenges. Marriage and the ties between spouses were reformed while the idea that even the slaves could live as married couples and have certain family rights was recognized.[71]

CONCLUSION

This journey has taken us from the city-states to the universal metropolises, and from the private and humble sphere of the Egyptian papyri to the communities of upper-class Christians and slaves. From the very beginning, we have seen that the tie between a husband and wife also bound them to their families. Through marriage contracts, families documented their intent to invest in the future. The survival of the members of the family, the accumulation of family property as well as the creation of the next generation, were all bound together. One of the main purposes of this strategy for the future was to maintain the economic level, of the family. Yet there were also other pressing motivators, for example the continuity of the family name and legacy. The ties formed between families through marriages were of great importance, especially from an economic point of view. The contracts of tabulae nuptiales included detailed lists of the amount of property—expected from both parties—and gave detailed descriptions of the marital duties for both husband and wife equally. The prior arrangements made concerning the death of a spouse or a possible divorce were naturally of great interest and importance. Yet, there were differences between ethnic and social groups, the elite and the non-elite, though of the latter few first-hand accounts survive.

The purpose of a marriage was unquestionable: to produce lawful heirs, especially male ones. Nevertheless, the relative youth and the physiological problems of new mothers in the ancient world (caused by, for example, malnutrition) often caused negative reproductive outcomes. Fertility rates were low for young women, and babies were usually not conceived until mothers were in their late teens or older. Miscarriage as well as infant mortality rates were notably high.[72] A happy delivery of a healthy baby, preferably a boy, born into matrimony was the foremost desire of parents and their families.[73]

The cultural, ideological and religious meaning of marriage surfaces in legendary tales from the Roman mytho-historic tradition: the way in which the marriage of the sacred couple of the priest and priestess of Jupiter was celebrated, shows a more hidden part of the tie, strongly connected to the magical side of reproduction and gender complementarity.

Marriage as an institution that separated and united different ethnic groups was of special interest to classical writers, as was the central role of marriage in forming a new cultural entity and building an identity for the Roman people itself. Augustus's legislation highlighted the importance of marriage and the relationship between a man and wife in a manner that was unprecedented in the ancient world; he made every effort to increase the number of citizens through policy, emphasizing family and marriage. Therefore, it is not surprising that first-century writers, such as Livy and Dionysius of Halicarnassus, highlighted marriage as evidence for the integrity and the identity of the Roman people. Legendary Roman marriages, as represented in Latin historiography and literature, (Aeneas and Lavinia, Romans and Sabines) indicate that a pair of spouses was greater than the sum of their parts, as was, indeed, the whole Roman nation.

Some Roman antiquarians have insisted that the bride spoke words of consent at her wedding, yet the researchers still wrestle with questions of agency and the willingness of the spouses, especially the consent of the bride during this process.[74] The emotional tie between the spouses is clear from funerary inscriptions that provide testimony to warm relationships between the spouses as an ideal often celebrated in these private epitaphs.[75] Stereotypes of "happy" couples, looming large in classical literature, are visible in many funerary inscriptions.

A major change came in the second century when philosophical and Christian belief systems began to influence the ideas and ideals of matrimony. Plutarch represented marriage as a guarantee of the continuity of the state and civic order, equating the harmony of the state with that of the household.[76] An ideal wife was a loyal disciple of her husband; accordingly, Plutarch encouraged couples to discuss philosophical issues together.[77]

Plotinus's famous pupil, Porphyry of Tyre, introduced a new kind of model for marriage and the relationship between husband and wife: they were no longer meant to be one another's lovers but mutual lovers of philosophy. Porphyry's letter to Marcella, in which he outlines his ideas of matrimony, resembles a manifesto meant for public circulation rather than private communication.[78] The ideal bond between a husband and wife was more spiritual than sexual in this particular case.

The influences of Christianity on Roman culture, especially from the third and fourth centuries CE onwards, caused new ideals of marriage to emerge. Changes in attitudes toward divorce made choosing the right spouse even more crucial and, in fact, more difficult, as in the Christian noble circles this meant, in principle, that all brides had to be endowed with a proper Christian education. At the same time, the idea that ascetic marriage precluded a sexual relationship was introduced in some limited Christian circles. In addition, Christianity was open to all believers, even to slaves. For the first time, a slave family was recognized as a viable entity.[79]

In conclusion, we may therefore recognize at least four different ties of ancient marriage. The first is an emotional bond, the love between husband and wife, documented in funerary inscriptions as well as in romantic stories and letters. Second, there are ties between families that result from marriages: created by the social and economic motives behind the marriages, with the goal of future advancement of the families behind marriages. Third, we recognize legal bonds, which differ according to the status and the social class of the participants. The fourth class of ties between the spouses comprises spiritual dimensions. The complementary roles of the spouses in religion are recognizable, for example, in the confarreatio marriages of the most visible priests and priestesses in Rome. The marriage of the Flamen and Flaminica represented an ideal union and emphasized the need for both genders in the performance of sacred rituals on behalf of the whole community. The spiritual tie that bound Christian marriages together differed from earlier ideals: in these unions, both sides were expected to have their own particular agency and competence regarding religious and spiritual matters.

CHAPTER FIVE

The Family Economy

Consent and Consensuality in Ancient Greek and Roman Marriage

JUDITH P. HALLETT

My chapter reflects upon the relationship between ancient Greco-Roman marriage and two English nouns of Latin derivation: "consent," which dictionaries customarily define as agreement on a course of action by two or more individuals, and "consensuality," which I would define as the act of freely and mutually awarding consent, especially in the realm of sexual activity.[1] For example, the fifth edition of the *American Heritage Dictionary* defines the noun "consent" as "acceptance or approval of what is done by another, acquiescence," with "permission" as a synonym; and "agreement as to opinion or a course of action." This edition of the *AHD* does not include the noun "consensuality," merely the adjective "consensual" (and adverb "consensually"), which it defines, also on the same page, as "of or expressing a consensus," "(in a legal sense) existing or entered into by mutual consent without formalization by document or ceremony" and "involving the willing participation of both or all parties, especially in an illegal transaction or practice." Since 2011, however, feminist scholars and writers such as Wildfell (2015) have begun to employ the noun "consensuality" to describe mutual agreement to engage in sexual relations, and I have adopted this usage.

The first term, "consent," has long figured in discussions about marriage in the Anglophone world, most notably in the phrase "age of consent," used to specify the legally defined age at which a person is no longer required to obtain parental consent to get married; the second has only recently come into usage.[2] I will argue that both terms, and the concepts that they represent, have limited applicability in any discussion of how marriage operated in ancient Greek and Roman society. Although, as I have noted, "consensuality" is a new coinage; I employ it because it is the noun formed from "consensual," an adjective increasingly applied in the Anglophone world to sexual activities mutually agreed upon by the parties involved.[3]

As my discussion will emphasize, the "family economy"—in the form of acquiring, allocating, expending, and bequeathing material resources—played an important part in ancient Greek and Roman decisions about who was allowed to be married, and remain married, to whom, especially among the materially advantaged elite families about whom the most evidence survives. But my focus is on those involved with the decision-making itself, both the "deciders" and those who lived with the consequences of these decisions. For that reason, I have chosen to highlight how different notions of consent and consensuality obtained in ancient Greek and Roman marriage from those informing what is often regarded as "traditional Greek and Roman marriage" today; for the same reason I conclude with some observations about ancient Greek and Roman extramarital relationships in which what contemporary Westerners would regard as consent and consensuality loomed large.

I shared my first efforts to address the topic of consent and consensuality in ancient Greek and Roman marriage with a very different audience, and in a very different venue: at my local election polling station, on Tuesday, November 6, 2012. While I have been engaged in research and teaching on marriage, sexuality, and the family in the Greek and Roman worlds for several decades, that election day marked the first occasion when I began to reflect, in some depth, upon the major differences between ancient Greek and Roman marriage and marriage as it has evolved in my own twenty-first-century Western cultural milieu and on how these terms crystallize these differences.

To set the scene, I was performing in my official capacity as Democratic Party precinct chair in the 16th legislative district of the 8th congressional district of Maryland, the state where I reside. On that day, those eligible to vote in my precinct—Democrats, Republicans, and Independents—had the opportunity to cast ballots for the US president, the US senator from our state, and the member of the US House of Representatives from our congressional district. We were also voting on several special ballot initiatives. These included Question Six, a referendum to approve or reject the Civil Marriage Protection Act. This law, allowing marriage between members of the same sex to be recognized in our state, had been passed earlier that year by Maryland's bicameral state legislature and signed by Maryland's governor at the time, Martin J. O'Malley, a Democrat.[4]

Whatever the reason, on that election day, members of local churches descended in droves on the polling place in my precinct. This contingent sought to convince all voters to reject Question Six. Even more ambitiously, they were eager to persuade county Democratic Party officials, such as myself, to oppose the public position of our party, for which we had earlier voted and pledged to advocate publicly. As they swarmed in my direction outside the polling place, one member of this contingent, whose children had attended the local public schools with mine, went so far as to express her condolences to me for having a gay son. She remarked, to her mind reassuringly, that my son would still be able to "live in sin" in our state even if marriage equality was defeated.

This contingent, of what we would call *suasores* in Latin, had appointed a silver-haired attorney clad in an expensively tailored suit as their spokesperson.[5] He announced to me and my fellow Democrats at the polling place that he was solely seeking to protect and defend the time-honored traditions of ancient Greek and Roman marriage, since this tradition had served as a powerful moral stabilizing force in our lives as law-abiding American citizens. Proclaiming to all within earshot that he and his wife had been married for fifty years, he then hailed his own and every opposite-sex connubial union as the indispensable foundation of our nation's cherished Greek and Roman legacy: Western civilization.

I replied to his proclamation with a smile, and with approximately the following words, "Thanks for letting us know about your marriage! As it happens, I'm a professor of classics who researches the subject of the ancient Greek and Roman family. And I am eager to hear more about how you and your wife got and stayed married. But may I ask two questions. First, how long before your wedding day did your parents and her parents inform the two of you that they were planning to marry you to one another? Second, when and how did they introduce you to each another?"

"That's not how it happened at all," he responded. "My wife's parents never even met mine until the night before our wedding, when they took an immediate dislike to one another: I don't believe they spoke to each other more than five times after that. No surprises there, though. Her parents never thought I was good enough for their daughter. Although we're all Catholics, they're Germans from the country club set, and I'm Irish working class, the first in my family to attend college. My own parents referred to my wife and her folks as 'too rich for our blood.' So my wife and I had to wait to tie the knot until we were able to support ourselves on our own: three years after we both completed our undergraduate and professional degrees. Our wedding took place two weeks after I graduated from law school and three after she finished her social work training."

"How impressive," I remarked. "Your wife must have been a brilliant, precocious student to complete not only her undergraduate degree but also social work school by the time she was in her mid-teens."

"What are you talking about?" he retorted. "We were both twenty-five. In fact, she's six months older than I am."

"Sorry," I interjected. "Let's get back to her parents and their opposition to your marriage. How did you overcome it?"

"That's quite a story," he said, with a smile. "When we decided to get married, her grandmother, the mother of my wife's mother, had been controlling all the money in their family for decades. She threatened to disinherit my wife's mother and father if they placed any further obstacles in our path. Grossmutter (that's what they called her) had been forced by her own father to marry a man she didn't love She hoped to spare my wife her own heartaches."

"Fascinating," I replied. "But why did Grossmutter control all that money? How old was Grossmutter when she took hold of the family purse-strings?"

"Very good question," he rejoined. "She inherited it, on her twenty-first birthday, a few months after she gave birth to my wife's mother, from her own sadist of a father, who made a killing in real estate. He wed and outlived three wives but only managed to produce Grossmutter from all his marriages. While he did not have a high opinion of the female sex, Grossmutter was his only option as an heir. For one thing, Grossmutter's husband was a hopeless alcoholic, who dropped dead when my wife's mother was barely two. For another, Grossmutter's father didn't want to leave anything to his only brother and business partner, Onkel Adolf. For Onkel A. was what we call a confirmed bachelor. Sadly, Onkel A. could have used the funds, too, since he survived his brother by at least forty years."

My next question obviously startled him: " Then why didn't Grossmutter's father stipulate in his will that Grossmutter divorce the alcoholic husband he had chosen, marry Onkel Adolf, and—from the union of his own daughter and closest male biological relative—posthumously produce the closest thing to his own biological son, as a male heir to his own estate?"

The silver-haired *suasor* excitedly shook his head. "Wherever did you get that idea? Grossmutter and her husband already had a child of their own, my wife's mother, when he died. For Grossmutter, barely twenty, to have married her father's brother, who must have been close to sixty by then, would have been incest. Besides, Onkel Adolf wasn't interested in women. Let's grant that such men often marry women to produce children, and there's nothing wrong with those marriages, but I don't know how anyone could have forced old Adolf to do what it takes, if you understand my drift."

"Well, the obvious solution," I remarked, "was for Grossmutter's father to require in his will that Adolf fulfill his marital obligations to Grossmutter three times a month, even if their sexual efforts did not produce offspring, male or female."

My interrogatee seemed shocked by my suggestions, so, prudently returning to the topic of his parents-in-law, I asked "Was there anyone else whom your wife's parents would have preferred her to marry?"

"Odd you should ask me that particular question. After we had been married for about five years, right after my wife became pregnant for the third time, my father-in-law's own business partner, a wealthy, handsome fellow whom he adored like a son, lost his own young wife in an accident. And, from that day forward, whenever I would irritate my wife's father, he loudly let it be known that he wished my wife could be married to this man rather than me."

"So why, then, didn't he force you to divorce his daughter, and marry her to this other man?" I asked.

"Because," he uttered in an exasperated tone, "my wife and I loved one another. We were in our thirties, with two little children and a third on the way, and an expensive home we had just purchased, thanks to a gift from Grossmutter. And I thought I told you we're ALL Catholics. My wife and I chose to get and stay married. What right did her father have to force us to divorce? Where have you come up with these wild ideas and these ridiculous questions anyway? What are you trying to prove?"

My answer should not come as a surprise: "I have proven, conclusively, that you and your wife do not have anything resembling a traditional Greek or Roman marriage. And, that the kind of marriage you do have is what same-sex couples should be legally entitled to enjoy as well."

Later, I tried to explain, in some detail, to this man everything that was *not* "traditionally Greek and Roman" about his and his wife's twentieth-century American as well as Roman Catholic marriage. First, that he and his wife had freely chosen one another, as both sexual partners and life companions, when they were both mature adults of approximately the same age and (relatively high) educational level. Second, that what brought and kept them together as a couple were their own deep affection for one another, emotional compatibility, mutual sexual attraction, and, eventually, children: they were not joined in marriage as part of an agenda, imposed by their two sets of parents, that served shared parental socioeconomic needs rather than their own wishes as a marital couple. Third, that their marriage had in fact taken place and long endured despite initial parental disapproval of their proposed union, and, in their case, despite mutual, everlasting incompatibility between their two sets of parents. Fourth, that they had stayed together as a couple despite the apparent desire by at least one of their parents to end their marriage, so that this, male, parent might wed one of them to a different spouse, thereby arranging what he himself regarded as a currently more advantageous marital match in terms of his own needs and interests, even though his daughter's marriage had at this juncture resulted in two offspring and was soon slated to produce another.

Had I more time and endless patience at my disposal, I would also have commented on a striking feature of this man's distinctive personal circumstances. Namely, the exercise of financial control over her daughter, daughter's husband, and granddaughter by an older female family member who had inherited immense wealth from her own father as a young woman. Such conduct had enabled her granddaughter to marry the man of her choice in the first place and helped underwrite the couple's living expenses thereafter. Yet it would have been utterly unthinkable in fifth-century BCE Athens and not all that likely in republican and early imperial Rome.

Women could not inherit in their own right, or possess legal guardianship over a father's estate, in Athens at that time. After the passage, in 169 BCE, of the *Lex Voconia*, which prohibited a Roman man of the wealthiest census class from naming a woman as his heir, any Roman woman of that class who nonetheless managed to inherit her father's estate still needed the oversight of a guardian—at least until marital and moral legislation, passed by Emperor Augustus a century and a half later, allowed freeborn women with three offspring and freedwomen with four exemption from legal guardianship.[6] Even if elite Roman women wanted to invest their own financial resources in the marital happiness of male and female kin, they faced serious challenges in doing so. Most obviously, mothers and other female family members did not always have a say in selecting the marital partners of children ad other close relations.

Nor, in seeking to enlighten the silver-haired suasor about the differences between ancient Greek and Roman marriages and his own, did I deem it productive to delve into any more details of the Athenian legal and economic institution known as the *epiclerate*.[7] But I had been alluding to certain features of this compulsory marital union in my impudent inquiry about why the father of Grossmutter, his wife's grandmother, had not stipulated in his will that, if he were not survived by a son, his daughter was required to divorce her husband and marry her father's closest male relative on his father's side. The goal of the epiclerate was to produce a male heir who would be as biologically close as possible to a son that the deceased man would have sired in his lifetime. In fact, this child would have been biologically closer than one produced by the dead man and his wife, because even if his wife and he were kindred, she would not have been his own daughter.[8]

In such situations, not only the daughter—technically called an *epikleros*, which means "part of a paternal estate"—but also the man she now needed to marry, her father's closest male relative on his father's side, would be required to divorce their current spouses, tearing apart two households in the process. Scholarly discussions of the epiclerate often misrepresent its purpose and participants by translating epikleros as "heiress."[9] But, in fact, such a daughter could not inherit from her father in her own right: only a son of hers who had been fathered by her father's closest male relative enjoyed that privilege. It merits note that if an epikleros and this male relative did not produce a son, that male relative would have been next in line to inherit, creating a serious conflict of interest for him.

I also did not specifically call to the attention of the silver-haired suasor the high degree of governmental intervention into, and control over, ancient Greek and Roman marriage.[10] The epiclerate owed its existence to financially democratizing laws established by the legendary Athenian legislator Solon.[11] From the evidence provided by Xenophon in *Constitution of the Lacedaemonians* 1.7–9 and Plutarch in *Lycurgus* 15.6, one has reason to infer that marriages in Sparta—which paired brides in their late teens with grooms of more or less the same age—were arranged not only by the families of marital couples but also by government officials. Government officials also may have had a role in assigning married women whose husbands were away fighting as reproductive partners to other men, so as to insure a continual supply of male warriors and female warrior-bearers.[12] As for Rome, its legislation drastically restricted who could marry and stay married to whom. Augustus's aforementioned legislation may have offered incentives and rewards for marriage and child production. But it also compelled male family members to divorce and in some instances execute sexually misbehaving female relatives. In addition, it prohibited practitioners of certain professions, such as entertainers, from being the legitimate spouses of those belonging to Rome's most privileged and affluent classes.[13]

In the United States, our government has traditionally imposed relatively few legal restrictions on who could marry whom, and when they could marry. Even these have varied from state to state as well as evolved over the years. One such restriction is a minimum age for brides and grooms.[14] Another is the requirement that both partners not be married to other people at the time, although they can have been married to other people at earlier times, as long as they are widowed or legally divorced. For most of our country's history, certain southern states—such as Virginia, across the river from, and within sight of my home in, Maryland—did not allow blacks and whites to marry one another. Only a ruling by the US Supreme Court in 1967 brought that restriction to an end.[15] Needless to say, I was reluctant to furnish the silver-haired suasor with evidentiary ammunition to argue that governmental intervention in marital choice was a time-honored tradition among Greeks and Romans too, since this position was of course that assumed by opponents of marriage equality.

Nevertheless, with my question about how the wife of the silver-haired suasor was able to earn both an undergraduate degree and finish professional training in social work by the time she was in her mid-teens, I did acknowledge that elite Athenian and Roman women tended to marry by that age. But that was as far as I went. I did not, for example, share the information about ancient Greek marriage succinctly provided in a recent article on "Greek and Roman Marriage" by Alison Glazebrook and Kelly Olson:

> Marriage followed by childbirth, not menarche, marked the essential rite of passage from [girl to woman]. Menarche, in fact, was not necessary for marriage to take place in classical Athens. The Hippocratics prescribed marriage for premenstrual girls, who they believed were in a vulnerable state just before menarche and prone to violence, most frequently against themselves. [The Hippocratics claimed that] Menstrual blood unable to exit the body on account of a narrow opening pooled around the organs, causing erratic behavior. [They also asserted that] Sexual intercourse was the most effective way to bring release for young girls, since it widened the vagina and enabled the first menstrual flow. Marriage, more generally, was also seen [in Athens] as the most effective way to contain women and their sexuality.[16]

Glazebrook and Olson make the following remarks about the situation in Rome: "The legal age of marriage for girls was 12, the age at which the Romans thought menarche occurred; the girl was said then to be [capable of receiving a man]. But a betrothal ... could happen very early on, even when the couple were infants, although Augustus limited the length of a betrothal to two years."[17]

While I myself find these practices, and the rationales for them, utterly repellent, I have, in teaching courses on women and gender in classical antiquity, actually encountered various students who viewed them quite differently. Observing that many girls in Western countries today become sexually active by their mid-teens, some students have applauded the idea of "legally controlling" the sexual activity of females at the onset of adolescence through early, monogamous marriages, to men at least a decade older, arranged by the parents. Recognizing that compulsory, premenarchal vaginal penetration was bound to be painful and traumatic for young girls, others in my classes have opined that such experiences might discourage sexual experimentation, and reduce teenage pregnancy and sexually transmitted diseases, in that demographic group. Some students have insisted that forcing early adolescent girls to submit to vaginal penetration by much older men with whom they had little in common would foster more female, egalitarian homoerotic relationships.

Which brings us back to Question Six in Maryland. It passed on election day 2012, making same-sex marriage legal in our state.[18] Three years later, of course, the US Supreme Court made same-sex marriage legal throughout our entire land.[19] To me, one of the most important contrasts between opposite-sex marriage and same-sex marriage at the present moment in our planet's history is that whereas there is a time-honored, and by no means exclusively Greco-Roman, tradition pressuring, if not requiring, individuals to marry members of the opposite sex, there is no comparable tradition requiring, even encouraging marriage between members of the same sex. Same-sex unions are totally voluntary. We in the United States have long used the term "shotgun wedding" for nuptials arranged to avoid embarrassment to the families of a couple discovered to have engaged in premarital sexual relations, perhaps resulting in unintended pregnancy. The term derives from a putative scenario in which the father of the bride must resort to coercion, often by threatening the groom with a shotgun, to ensure that the groom "make an honest woman" of his daughter.[20] I have never heard of such a union between members of the same sex. For that reason same-sex marriages offer a more positive and salubrious model for all marriages. After all, they are predicated on both consent and consensuality.

Meanwhile, however, marriage in my own country, and among the Westernized residents of our planet generally, is increasingly a matter of choice. To return to my title and the topic of this discussion, consent and consensuality, marriage in Western society presumes consent by partners to the wishes of one another rather than consent to decisions of their parents. It also centers on consensuality, mutual erotic attraction between the partners, as a motivation for marriage, not a result that may or may not transpire from emotionally satisfying cohabitation. Marriage equality, involving marriages between partners of the same sex as well as the opposite sex, makes marriage in our Western society even more complicated than it has been in the past. But I, among others, welcome the complications.

From that dialogue at the polls on that election day, and my subsequent reflections on what I did and did not share in that dialogue, I have come to the conclusion that ancient Greek and Roman marriage chiefly differs from its contemporary Western counterpart in the severe limitations on consent and consensuality imposed on ancient Greek and Roman marital partners. Yes, marriage today, as in classical antiquity, is powerfully shaped and controlled by various sociocultural assumptions, even innovative forms of marriage such as those between members of the same sex. But numerous Greek and Roman practices attest that the main assumption about marriage was that the marital couple had very little say in, or control over, multiple aspects of their union, at least among the sociocultural elites.[21] In contrasting Greek and Roman marriage with the fifty-years of wedlock celebrated by the silver-haired suasor, I tried to highlight the most prominent among these practices, namely arranged marriages and forced divorces in the Athenian epiclerate as well as among the Roman elite. Some of the surviving evidence about Roman forced divorce powerfully attests to the emotional costs of tearing apart compatible marital partners, frequently already parents to one or more children. It includes Suetonius's life of the Roman emperor Tiberius, child as well as victim of a forced divorce, as well as the poetry of the Augustan elegist Lygdamus, who may or may not be Tiberius himself.[22]

But other practices that limit the consent and consensuality of married couples merit attention too. As Karen Klaiber Hersch has observed, the Roman wedding ritual itself dramatizes mental and physical assaults on the bride in the form of abduction, lament, and symbolic death, representing her as a unwilling victim of violence; this figurative violence then became corporeal reality in the bedchamber after the bride suffered violence at the hands of the groom.[23] As for the groom, it is also worth emphasizing the sexual performance pressures on married couples to produce children, even in cases where the wives were barely into their teens—and even in marriages where wives were not yet capable of child production.[24] Such pressures endeavor to create consensuality where it may not have actually existed. We should note, too, that while Athenian and Roman married men were allowed to engage in sexual relationships outside of their marriages, as long as they did not physically penetrate either freeborn boys or married and maritally-eligible women, often these extramarital sexual relationships involved the coercion of slaves; they, too, were anything but consensual.[25]

As it happens, the kind of consent and consensuality that obtained in the marriage of the silver-haired suasor were acknowledged and celebrated in Greco-Roman society itself, although I did not mention this to him. Our abundant evidence for such sentiments, and their social validation, ranges from the large body of surviving *epithalamia*, Greek and Latin poems composed to honor marrying couples, to innumerable Greek and Latin epitaphs commemorating mutually devoted husbands and wives.[26] However, accommodating the wishes of a partner, rather than those of a parent or partner's parent, in combination with mutual, reciprocal physical and emotional attraction are characteristically represented by various Greek and Roman sources as erotic passion rather than "connubial business as usual." Indeed, our sources, chief among them "love poets" representing "countercultural" sentiments, depict this kind of mutual consent and emotionally charged consensuality as occupying a central role in women's and men's adulterous liaisons as well as in men's relationships with the kinds of women portrayed as sexually desirable partners for more than a one-night stand, in the literary genres of Roman comedy, satire, lyric, and elegy.[27] By such women, I refer to free or freedwomen, rather than slaves, and to *meretrices*, a term which literally means females who deserve to be hired, and translated as "courtesans" rather than "prostitutes," and *mimae*, actresses in bawdy comic performances.[28] Yet for such women sexual activity glorified as love was in fact their paid profession and may not have been entirely consensual either.

In this connection, I would spotlight the literary genres of Roman erotic lyric and Latin love elegy in particular, because they furnish valuable testimony to Greek and Roman attitudes and practices involving consent and consensuality outside of marriage. Strikingly, Roman lyric and elegy characterize the *domina*, best defined as a female in erotic control of the male poet, as simultaneously an adulterous married woman and a paid *meretrix*.[29] Significantly, too, such lyric and elegiac poets as Catullus and "Lygdamus" represent themselves as simultaneously rejecting basic Roman marital conventions while elevating marriage as a monogamous relational ideal for those engaged in consenting, consensual illicit liaisons.[30] To be sure, Greek and Roman marriage may differ in many respects from its modern counterpart as a sociocultural institution. Yet marriage in classical antiquity had its attractions and appeal in its own day, even for those seeking a powerful human bond differing from marriage itself.[31]

CHAPTER SIX

Love, Sex, and Sexuality

Marriage: The Myth of Intimate Strangers

VERED LEV KENAAN

THE BOND BETWEEN COSMIC AND HUMAN MARRIAGES

Therefore a man shall leave his father and his mother and hold fast to his wife, and they shall become one flesh. (Genesis 2:24)

I will surely multiply your pain in childbearing;
in pain you shall bring forth children.
Your desire shall be contrary to your husband,
but he shall rule over you. (Genesis 3:16)

As we see in the quotes above from the book of Genesis, the union of feminine and masculine elements is a common motif in cosmological narratives across cultures. Mythological accounts of the beginning of the world often imagine the production of things and concepts through sexual and erotic images. In Hesiod's *Theogony,* a Greek epic poem from the end of the eighth century BCE, the cosmological role of sexuality is represented by the inclusion of Eros as one of the universe's first four beings. Eros appears as a primary cosmic force, an abstract divinity whose distinctive beauty is associated with irresistible power: he is "the most beautiful among the immortal gods, the limb-melter" (*Th.* 120–121).

And yet, Eros's defining characteristics are absent from the primordial stage of the world's development. His absence is emphasized by the narrator's use of negative phrases that mark his noninvolvement in the act of procreation, which, it should be noted, is either a fatherless, or a motherless, act of reproduction. Gaia (Earth), for example, who is the mother and sole progenitor of Ouranos, the sky, the mountains, and the sea, gives birth without delightful love, *ater philotetos ephimerou* (*Th.* 132). Similarly, Nyx, Night, gives birth through parthenogenesis, *ou tini koimetheisa theon* (*Th.* 213). The negative phrase, "sleeping with none of the gods," is indicative of the problems that the narrator faces when he attempts to describe the genesis of the cosmos. For the narrator, the order of things is maintained through procreation, an act that, as he understands it, demands two participants, a male and a female who come together and procreate in an erotic encounter. However, the initial act of creation in the Hesiodic narrative involves just a single progenitor, and it is therefore presented as exceptional and unlike the prevailing mode of sexual procreation.

FIGURE 6.1 The birth of Aphrodite from a shell. Eros or Himeros flutters by her side. A detail from an Attic red-figure pelike, fourth century BCE. The Archeological Museum of Thessaloniki. Alamy Stock Photo.

Hesiod's version of the beginning of the world presents a heterogeneous picture of giving birth. It rejects the hegemony of oneness, instead, stressing the plurality of existence. The divine genealogy displays multiple modes of creation: the first four beings have no parents at all; others are born to only one parent. Among the Olympian gods, the example of the motherless goddess Athena emerging from Zeus's head indicates that in the Olympian realm the production of offspring does not necessarily require marriage or copulation. And yet the Olympian generation of gods adopts sexual reproduction as a norm.[1]

The first sexual union mentioned in the *Theogony* takes place in the chthonic family. Chaos, the first of the four cosmic elements, is the sole parent of two children: Erebos and Nyx. Darkness and Night are brother and sister whose kinship is reflected in their conceptual affinity. Together they are associated with embryonic and dark dimensions and mark an important space in Greek mythology and thought.[2] Their union produces two children. Mingling in love (*philoteti migeista*) with Erebos, Nyx gives birth to Aether and Day. Although their children's relation to the realm of light places these offspring in opposition to their parents, conceptually they remain akin to them. Through Hesiod's poetry we recognize the cosmic marriage of Erebos and Nyx whenever we experience the sunrise, the moment when the darkness of night recedes giving way to the brightness of day.

Cosmological unions between natural and conceptual elements reflect familiar scenes from everyday life. Images of cosmological unions are imported specifically from the human sphere and are modeled on intimate encounters between lovers as well as the emotional life of married couples. Thus, even the highest cosmic event uniting the earth and the heavens carries striking analogies to human marriage. In the *Theogony,* Hesiod refers only briefly to sexual intercourse between Mother Earth, Gaia, and her heavenly son, Ouranos, but its significance is multifaceted. First of all, the union between Earth and Heaven manifests a *hieros gamos,* a sacred marriage between the two primal gods. Their marriage leads to the foundation of the most central branch of the divine genealogy. Gaia and Ouranos are the formidable ancestors from whom the two main generations of gods descend: the older Titans and their offspring—the younger Olympian gods, who ultimately become the rulers of the universe. Gaia is said to give birth to the Titans after having bedded with Heaven: "Ourano eunetheisa tek' Okeanon bathudinen" (*Th.* 133). The reference to Gaia as *Ourano eunetheisa,* "having bedded with Ouranos," evokes the important image of *eune,* the matrimonial bed. In connoting the act of sexual intercourse, the verb *eunao* also metonymically resonates the idea of marriage through its relation to the bed.[3] Marriage is consummated in *thalamos,* an intimate inner chamber where the marital bed is located and the bride and the groom are invited to mate.

Hesiod represents cosmic intercourse by drawing an analogy to the human sphere. With the evocation of the marital bed, the poet mixes the divine with the human. Thus, the cosmic intercourse of Gaia and Ouranos imitates the human example. While the sexual function of the marriage bed is common to both cosmic and human bonds, its ethical significance as a respectful site of loyalty and chastity is specifically related to human couples.

These marital values of loyalty and chastity are reflected in a scene from Homer's *Odyssey* in which the Greek chieftain Menelaus responds to the news Telemachus brings from Ithaca. When Telemachus visits the Spartan palace, he confides his fears to his host, telling Menelaus how anxious he is about his status at home: the family property, the house (*oikos* 4.318; *domos* 4.319), is being shattered by Penelope's suitors. Menelaus's response shows great concern for Odysseus's son's complaints. And yet, Menelaus's concerns do not focus on the property of Telemachus's family but, rather, on the safety of a particular object in Odysseus's palace. Menelaus's disconcertment is directed specifically at the fate of the marital bed of Odysseus and Penelope. From Menelaus's perspective, its possible violation symbolizes the ruin of the whole house:

> ho popoi, he mala de kraterophronos andros eune
> ethelon eunethenai analkidies autoi eontes. (Hom. *Od.* 4.333–334)
> (What a disgrace! The cowards wish to sleep
> in the dauntless man's bed.)

Indeed, Menelaus is less attuned to Telemachus's worries than he is sensitive to Odysseus's marital interests. Menelaus's dismay concentrates specifically on the marital bed, the object that unites a husband and his wife. It is an object that represents interiority and the safety of the house. The suitors' intrusion into Odysseus's palace alarms Menelaus who identifies their violation as sexual. Their constant intimidation lies in their intention to sleep in the bed of the absent husband. The suitors' greediness is a manifestation of their sexual desire, and hence their target is to sexually violate the sacred wedlock of Odysseus and Penelope. It is therefore the vulnerability of eune, and the marriage itself, that concerns Menelaus the most.[4]

Marriage beds are supposed to be the sites of intimate moments that married couples experience without interference from others. In the *Odyssey*, the marriage bed is the site where the reliability of the marital connection is tested. After twenty years of separation, Penelope and Odysseus are finally united. But they cannot completely overcome their mutual suspicions. Penelope is not sure whether the old beggar is indeed her missing husband; meanwhile Odysseus is uncertain about his wife's fidelity.[5] Both husband and wife meet as strangers, and request signs in order to prove the truthful essence of their marital bond and thereby to re-establish their previous intimacy. It is only through shared memories that they can be certain of the other's true identity. The history of their marriage bed including its construction and its exact location in the palace is evoked to verify the husband's real identity as well as his wife's chastity.[6] Penelope designs a recognition test. She craftily asks Eurycleia in front of Odysseus to "move for him the firm bed's framework (*pukinon lechos*) outside of the well-built bedchamber (*ektos eustatheos thalamou*) which he made himself." There, she orders the old maid to "place the firm bed's framework and throw upon it the mattress (*eunen*)" (Hom. *Od*. 23. 177–179). Penelope's orders are impossible to carry out since, as she and Odysseus well know, the bed, which was skillfully built by Odysseus many years ago, is fixed to a sturdy tree trunk. Odysseus's indignant response to Penelope's request reveals his true identity and Penelope satisfyingly concludes:

> But now, since you have now spoken signs easy to recognize
> Of our bed (*eunes hemeteres*), that no other mortal man has seen,
> But only you and I – and only one handmaiden,
> Actoris, whom my father gave to me when I came here,
> Who guarded the door of our firm chamber (*pukinou thalamoio*)
> You indeed persuade my heart, though it is an unchangeable heart. (Hom. *Od*. 23.225–230)

The dialogue between the two provides a rare example of a scene of recognition in ancient literature. Whereas typical recognition scenes aim at revealing the truthful identity of a character, this scene also entails the re-establishment of the ostensible strangers' past familiarity. Time is responsible for their estrangement, they have not seen each other for twenty years. By identifying each other, they also recover their old connection, and they begin to recall the history of their marriage.

Penelope's speech does a most remarkable thing: it brings to life a sense of the marital dyad that had disappeared. Her speech employs language as a means to restore the intimate rapport between husband and wife. As the two strangers re-establish their shared intimate language, they once again become an intimate pair. After Odysseus passes the recognition test, Penelope addresses him with more personal indexical pronouns. Her language, thus, once again declares them husband and wife: "you and I," *su t' ego* (Hom. *Od*. 23.227).[7]

The dialogic relationship between husband and wife needs to be defined topographically. The marital space is located inside; it is enclosed and protected from the rest of the world.[8] In the *Odyssey* Book 23, the marital bed signifies a locus of intimacy inside the "firm chamber."[9] The fact that only Odysseus and Penelope are allowed in the chamber is essential for appreciating the significance of this archaic picture of the secret room in the history of marriage.[10] The married couple's room retains an aura of a sacred space. Their nuptial chamber is a sort of a shrine dedicated to matrimonial privacy. The Homeric description of the nuptial room is a literary transgression that lets the reader see what was otherwise forbidden to outsiders.[11]

The humanization of cosmic marriages is tied to the sexualization of nature. The fundamental principle unifying both cosmic and human marriages is teleological. Marriage as an institution is directed toward the purpose of reproduction and procreation. The union between Heaven and Earth produces, according to Hesiod, a set of twelve Titans and two sets of three monstrous children.[12] The association between the union of Gaia and Ouranos and human marriage is established by sexualizing their copulation and by naming their offspring *paides* and *tekna*.[13] A fragment of the last play of Aeschylus's Danaid trilogy provides a detailed picture of cosmic intercourse. This fragment from the fifth century intensifies the erotic connotation of the earlier Hesiodic account. The speaker is the goddess Aphrodite who describes the marriage between Heaven and Earth:[14]

> Now the holy Heaven desires to penetrate (*trosai*) the Earth, now desire (*eros*) takes hold of the Earth for her marriage (*gamou*) with Heaven. The rain falls from the brimming Heaven and impregnates the Earth, and for mortals she brings forth grazing for their flocks, cereals to sustain life, and the fruit of trees. And from this moist wedding (*gamou*) she comes to her fulfillment. Of these things, I am the cause. (Aeschylus frag. 44 Radt)

The fragment is different from Hesiod's genealogical account in two ways. Unlike the Hesiodic account that focuses on cosmic intercourse as a singular primal event leading to the birth of new divinities, the cosmic marriage between Earth and Sky in Aeschylus represents a modus operandi, a regulative figure in the natural order of things. In contrast to the Hesiodic account of cosmic marriage, Aeschylus's description has strong erotic undertones, which link the religious and the pornographic. The divine speaker, Aphrodite, describes the work of Eros. Her rhetoric of sexual arousal is effective as it sexually stimulates her listeners. The intercourse between Earth and Sky is a manifestation of an asymmetrical, yet mutual desire: Heaven desires to penetrate Earth, while Earth desires to be united with Heaven. "The sexual difference," Froma Zeitlin writes, "is acknowledged in the two forms this desire takes: for the male, a desire to "wound" the female,[15] and for the female, a desire for sexual union in the interests of procreation."[16] Though the dichotomous relation between masculine activity and feminine passivity is apparent in this cosmic union, the source of the pair's sexual desire is external and puts both of them under its spell. The primal cause of the desire is Aphrodite and her divine executor, Eros, who equally inflames Heaven and Earth. In this sense, the fragment presents marriage as a divine dictum, a cosmic principle and a fundamental order of nature, which gods,[17] humans, and animals obey. Moreover, the erotic core of marriage is contagious. The primal couple's mutual desire spreads and infects the whole universe with a desire for procreation.[18] The universal usefulness of marriage demonstrates that for mankind marriage is a categorical imperative. Any resistance to the natural law of *hieros gamos*, the sacred marriage of Earth and Sky, results in drought and sterility and is therefore a threat to human existence. Cosmic marriage provides a paradigmatic act that should be imitated by humans. In *Totem and Taboo*, Freud explains the sexualization of nature through Frazer's "imitative" and "homoeopathic" relation between the human and the cosmic:[19]

Rain is produced magically by imitating it or the clouds and storms which give rise to it, by "playing at rain," one might almost say ... In the same way, the fertility of the earth is magically promoted by a dramatic representation of human intercourse. Thus, to take one from a countless number of instances, "in some parts of Java, at the season when the bloom will soon be on the rice, the husbandman and his wife visit their field by night and there engage in sexual intercourse"[20] to encourage the fertility of the rice by their example.[21]

As a fundamental institution in the life of the community in general and the Greek polis in particular, marriage establishes a necessary sympathy between nature and culture. It also establishes the necessary harmony between the divine and human spheres, which is so important for the city's fecundity. The fragment of the last play of the Danaid trilogy quoted above is a vivid expression of the synergy between the cosmic and the human spheres. It ordains a relationship between cosmic reproduction and human fertility, and it does so by sexually stimulating the listeners. Aphrodite's speech, as various scholars believe, is delivered at the courtroom where the forty-nine Danaids who vehemently resist the idea of marriage are probably being prosecuted for killing their forty-nine grooms on their wedding night.[22] The scene of the trial seems to be a defense of the institution of marriage and an attempt to establish its significance in the city. Marriage, according to the symbolic order of the polis, is "a microcosmic reflection of the *hieros gamos,*" argues Zeitlin and, furthermore, "Aphrodite's paradigm in the fragment of the last play sacralizes the act of sexual penetration, the prelude to fertility, and teaches the female to imitate the earth."[23] It has been suggested that in the trilogy the Danaids's trial eventually led to the foundation of the Thesmophoria.[24]

Zeitlin explains that the festival established the dignified status of the institution of marriage in the Greek city. In honoring the institution of marriage, the Thesmophoria reflects the exalted status of marriage in the city, and Aeschylus expresses this ideology through the myth of the Danaids. Aeschylus is interested in the re-education of the resisting virgins. The Danaids cease to see marriage as "a form of enslavement and degradation" and learn to re-evaluate matrimony.[25] The ritual of the Thesmophoria provided Aeschylus, as Zeitlin argues, with an opportunity to establish the foundational status of the myth of the Danaids, and through the festival he could commemorate the re-education of the virgins.[26] Aphrodite alludes to the connection between the Danaids and the Thesmophoria in her speech.[27] The Danaids learn about their sexuality, whose beneficial power the Thesmophoria translates into the political life of the community from Aphrodite. The Thesmophoria centers on the valuable blessing that the women's rite of passage confers on the city. It concerns, therefore, the virgin's political transformation and raises her political self-consciousness. The ideology behind the festival of Thesmophoria presents marriage as a rite for incorporating women into the community of the city as wives and mothers. Hence, the festival in which women celebrate their contribution to the life of the city also politicizes fertilization:

> The Thesmophoria sacralizes female fertility to suggest conversely that the earth imitates the women. Each model is a counterpart to the other. Together they affirm the symbiosis of human and divine spheres as a dependable law of nature in a hierarchical system that allots to each a socially designated place and role but which, through analogy, coordinates the terms into a coherent ideological whole.[28]

In accepting marriage, the Greek woman imitates the earth, but in her vocation as a citizen she concomitantly offers a model of imitation for the earth.[29]

The civic ideology uses marriage as a means to integrate woman into a community dominated by a male hierarchy. The ideological framework presents marriage as the key to the social transformation of woman. In the polis, marriage offers a solution for the woman's existential otherness. Paradoxically the hierarchical order that marriage preserves between the sexes offers women a certain sense of liberation and independence. According to the ideology of the polis, marriage begins to undermine the traditional segregation of women by emphasizing the wife's contribution to her family and her community. Initially, however, the woman is the other: "In political terms," as Froma Zeitlin explains in reference to the role of women in the Thesmophoria "the woman is first an *astoxenos* (resident alien), then a *metoikos*, and finally a citizen-wife of the Thesmophoria."[30]

Let us now turn to an investigation of the feminine experience of marriage and specifically attempts to explore the perspective of the woman as an *astoxenos*. The idea of the origins of women as resident aliens can be traced to the fractures that disrupt the harmonious picture of marriage between Earth and Sky. Although the image of the cosmic marriage cannot be erased from the memories of women, the ideology of the civic wedding is designed to conceal the very fact of female otherness. And as we shall see, the cosmological union, the *hieros gamos* is itself a painful reminder for the bride of the inequality and oppression at the core of marriage.

MARRIAGE AS RAPE: THE FEMININE PERSEPCTIVE

In Hesiod's *Theogony,* natural phenomena are gendered and the cosmological evolution often reflects the features of a gender struggle. Hesiod presents the first marital conflict as a wife's resistance to the husband's oppression. This conflict signals a critical moment in the beginning of the world, when the primal marriage of Gaia and Ouranos leads to an important cosmological development. Following their sexual union, an irrevocable tension between the divine couple explodes. Gaia, we should remember, is not a virginal figure. Her marriage with Ouranos deviates in many respects from the conventional pattern of Greek weddings. Her marriage does not unite a virgin bride and a groom. Gaia is already a mother when she is first united with her husband. Moreover, she is the mother of her husband, Ouranos. Their marital conflict, like so many in the *Theogony,* is connected to giving birth, which is the ultimate goal of marriage.[31]

The *Theogony* distinguishes the shared act of giving birth to a child conceived by two parents from the act of giving birth to a child conceived by a single parent. Gaia's shared parenthood with Ouranos marks a turning point in her status as a primal element. While Gaia's prior experience as a single mother conveys her supremacy, her shared parenthood reflects a decrease in her power. As one of the first four elements, Gaia's single-motherhood expresses freedom and independence. She is unruly and autonomous in giving birth alone to Sky, the Mountains, and the Sea. However, once she shares parenthood with one of her sons, the one whom Hesiod describes as "equal to herself,"[32] Gaia loses her secure autonomy:

> For all these, who came forth from Earth and Sky as the most terrible of their children were hated by their own father from the beginning. And as soon as any of them was born, Sky put them away out of sight in a hiding-place in Earth and did not let them come up the light, and he rejoiced in his evil deed. But huge Earth groaned within (*entos stonachizeto*), for she was constricted, and she devised a tricky, evil stratagem. At once she created an element (*genos*), of gray adamant, and she fashioned a big sickle and showed it to her dear sons. (Hes. *Th.* 154–163)

Ouranos refuses to separate himself from Gaia, and thus the couple remains in a continuous state of intercourse. The enforced intercourse derives from Ouranos's wish to obstruct the natural emergence of the children from their mother. The father hates his own children (*sphetero d'echthonto toke*; Hes. *Th.* 155) while the mother cannot tolerate him and groans within. Gaia protests inside, but she does not disclose her dissatisfaction to her consort. She prefers instead to confer with her children and only to them she discloses her resentment toward the deeds of their father. From her point of view, the children are an integral part of the mother and hence should side with her against the father. The mother's autonomy depends on the emancipation of her children. The father's pathological behavior betrays, however, just the opposite perception. From his point of view, the children's deliverance threatens to bring an end to his new supremacy. The obstinate father remembers what it means to be his wife's son and therefore is intimidated by his children-siblings whom he considers to be potential rivals. This paradigmatic conflict between a wife and her husband welcomes a psychoanalytically oriented interpretation that points, as Richard Caldwell does, to its Oedipal core:

> If he married his mother, his sons will also want to marry theirs. Ouranos, by virtue of his Oedipal success, figures that his sons will want to do the same, and the continuous intercourse that represents this success serves also to eliminate the threat potentially posed by his children.[33]

The focus on the rivalry between the father and the children brackets the mother's interests. Ouranos considers Gaia to be nothing more than a receptacle. And yet, at the same time, his exclusive position as the Earth's mate is an important source of power for him which he struggles to preserve at all costs. Gaia's address to her children boldly expresses her position toward their father and his behavior: he is a wicked father (*pater atasthalos*; Hes. *Th.* 164), and his behavior is nothing but "an evil outrage" (*kake lobe*; Hes. *Th.* 165). More specifically, it is the husband's sexual behavior which she detests most, since the husband's desire is nothing more than a reflection of pure will to power. Thus, the erotic description of their intercourse is abruptly disrupted by the wife's act of resistance. She creates a big sickle and persuades the youngest son, Chronus, to castrate his father with it. Hence, the scene of cosmic lovemaking becomes violent:

> And great Sky came, bringing night with him; and spreading himself out around Earth in his desire for love he lay outstretched in all directions. Then his son reached out from his ambush with his left hand, and with his right hand he grasped the monstrous sickle, long and jagged, and eagerly he reaped the genitals from his dear father. (Hes. *Th.* 176–180)

Although the above passage does not underscore the active role that Gaia plays in the familial scandal, she nevertheless is the leading agent behind the scenes. Gaia's reaction to the marriage designates a prevailing attitude in the mythic conception of marital relationships.

The marriage subdues Gaia and leads to a new cosmic order that gives Heaven precedence. Heaven with its association with light and reason constitutes the domain of the future ruling gods, the Olympians, the grandchildren of Gaia and Ouranus. These Olympian offspring are the antithesis of the dark materiality of the great Mother Earth.[34] Thus although Gaia retains her primal status as a cosmic ancestor, she specifies a chthonic domain of otherness. From below, Gaia's resistance continues to reverberate in the collective memory of divine and human virgins.

A virgin's resistance to marriage stems first of all from her desire to preserve a life of unrestrained freedom, which was the condition of the great Mother Earth before her matrimonial union. In the Olympian domain there are three goddesses who insist upon remaining outside the constraints of marriage: Athena, Artemis, and Hestia.[35] These goddesses give up the duties of wife and mother for other responsibilities in the human and cosmic spheres. Feminine resistance to marriage is translated into the specific request with which virgins appeal to their fathers. In the *Hymn to Aphrodite*, Hestia's resistance to marriage reverberates with the legacy of her grandmother Earth:

> Nor yet do the doings of Aphrodite appeal to the modest maiden Hestia ... lady courted by Poseidon and Apollo, but she was not willing, she refused them firmly, and swore a great oath (which she has, indeed, kept), touching the head of father Zeus, goat-rider Zeus, that she would be a virgin for all time, the noble goddess.[36]

The father of the Olympian gods, Zeus, exceptionally consents to Hestia's irregular request and grants her "a fine privilege instead of marriage" (*kalos geras anti gamou* (H. Aph. 29). The image of the resisting virgin goddess who hates the idea of marriage remains central to the mythological attempt to decipher feminine experience.[37] The Danaids and Daphne provide striking examples of maidens who refuse marriage. Daphne hates matrimony as if it were a crime, says the Roman poet Ovid,[38] and embraces her transformation into a tree as a means of escaping Apollo's sexual assault. The fifty Danaids detest so vehemently the idea of marrying their fifty Egyptian cousins that they would rather die:

> This evil could no longer be avoided
> My heart is trembling and darkened.
> My father's lookout has caught me; I'm overwhelmed by fear.
> I would rather meet my doom
> In the noose.[39]

The Danaides' resistance to marriage involves revulsion against men, whom they experience as threatening aliens. Their fear of their grooms is typical of mythic virgins who will shortly encounter their first erotic experience. In various myths concerning virgins, feminine resistance is provoked by the danger of rape or, alternatively, marriage, which is often perceived as a sublimated form of rape. This tradition, resting primarily on the myth of Demeter and Persephone, connects the first public expression of the female voice with the act of rape. Myth constructs the rape of virgins as the moment when the feminine voice is heard for the first time within the public (male) sphere. She speaks out, she screams, she cries. Thus, Persephone, Demeter's daughter protests:

> Snatching her against her will, Hades led her crying
> Into his golden chariot. She screamed with a loud voice ...
> Her father's brother was carrying her by force by Zeus' plan.[40]

Persephone's rape in the *Hymn to Demeter* is accorded the metonymic meaning of marriage and death. Her resistance to marriage is a response to an act of violence directed at her that separates her from her mother. The mythic daughter is expelled from the sheltered world under the tutelage of her mother. Young women do not wish to part from their parents. Weddings are usually forced upon them, as is the first night of love.[41] Ancient Greek

FIGURE 6.2 *Apollo and Daphne*, 1908, John William Waterhouse (1849–1917). Private Collection. Wikimedia Commons.

and Roman nuptial poems reveal that the ceremonies include an element of abduction. This is also the source of the traditional custom of carrying the bride over the threshold of the young couple's new home. Plutarch anchors this custom in Roman culture and interprets it as a memorial gesture to the abduction of the Sabine women in ancient Rome:

FIGURE 6.3 The abduction of Persephone by Hades, detail from Amphipolis mosaic, Macedonia, fourth century BCE. Alamy Stock Photo.

And it continues to be the custom down to the present time that the bride shall not of herself cross the threshold into her new home, but be lifted up and carried in, because the Sabine women were carried in by force, and did not go in of their own accord.[42]

Plutarch's reflection on one of the customs of the wedding ceremony uncovers the history behind the ritual gestures. For the Romans the lifting of the bride on the threshold into her new home might have been a gesture of cheerfulness celebrating the happy event of the wedding. And yet, Plutarch's remark demonstrates that the history of the ceremonial convention is no longer accessible and must be uncovered and elucidated. By the same token, a modern spectator would not connect conventional romantic photos of brides dressed in white being held by their elegant grooms as commemorating a mythological rape. The cultural erasing of the primal violence that mythological brides suffer from marriage is undone however, not only by reconnecting it to a certain historic event as Plutarch does but also by attending to the bride's mythic experience of alienation and estrangement from the ritual passage of marriage.

For virgins marriage is far from being a symbol of harmony and transparency. Marriage represents an abrupt cut from nature through a separation from childhood, or an intervention in the symbiotic mother-daughter relationship, or through the bride's disconnection from her parental home. Marriage introduces the bride to a principle of otherness that shapes her new sense of subjectivity. A new dimension of self-consciousness transforms the bride. She now has a past; she remembers a different time. She knows

FIGURE 6.4 *The Abduction of the Sabine Women*, 1634–1635, Nicolas Poussin (1594–1665). Metropolitan Museum of Art. Wikimedia Commons.

that she has left behind a life of natural harmony in which the principle of negation was completely alien. Now, indeed, she is forcefully cut off from her primary nature, but through this transition a new horizon of meaning opens for her and within it she experiences a new sense of freedom.

In Greek mythology, the bride's melancholic perspective on marriage that emphasizes the cultural significance of the rite corresponds to a tragic male perspective on marriage dominant in the ancient mythological imagination. Mythic constructions of the male point of view on marriage emphasize anxieties and fears, which the recognition of marriage as an irreversible pact brings about. The most antagonistic reflection of marriage comes from the Hesiodic myth of the first woman that centers on her introducing the tricky idea of marriage into the life of innocent men.

MARRIAGE AS TRAP: THE MALE PERSPECTIVE

Hesiod begins the episode of the first woman "then," during a distant past that is disconnected from the present "now."[43] The "then" is indexical, and it refers to a mythological point of departure in the history of humanity. In the Hesiodic imagination, the first woman signals the end of a blissful mythic past. More specifically, she marks the drastic end of a golden age in which gods and men mingled and shared meals together. Furthermore, she brought an end to the Hesiodic fantasy of sameness: paradise is literally a world without women. Men are impeccably happy because they live under the illusion that they are identical to the gods and, moreover, they live under the assumption that they are identical to themselves.[44] Thus, in the Hesiodic version of the Edenic beginning, men were part of a homogenous race in which men and gods were inseparable, and men were sexually indistinguishable.

Men lost their sameness as soon as the distinction between the human and the divine began to surface. A series of transformative events brought on by the conflict between Zeus and Prometheus finalized the process of separating human life from the life of gods. Following these events, men became different from the gods. They became responsible for their own nourishment through hard work and the cultivation of the earth. In "The Myth of Prometheus," Jean-Pierre Vernant analyzes the sequence of events that are mentioned in both Hesiod's *Theogony* and his *Works and Days*.[45] Vernant presents a network of correspondences between the different episodes through which Zeus and Prometheus determine the deterioration of the human condition: the sacrifice of the ox, the hidden celestial fire, the hidden grain, and finally the creation of first woman that introduces humanity to the new idea of gender difference. Vernant explains that Pandora "is a part of the human species, but at the same time she founds a *genos gunaikos*, a race of women that is not exactly the same as the race of men but at the same time is not altogether different from it."[46] Pandora is taken to be the mark of the idea of gender difference. Woman, as Nicole Loraux puts it in *The Children of Athena*, "separates men from gods. Better yet, she separates them from themselves, since she introduces sexuality, that asymmetry of self and other."[47] The creation of the first woman comes as a punishment and retribution on behalf of Zeus. She is a great damage, a source for a great grief, *mega pema* (Hes. W&D 56; Hes. Th. 592), a gift, *doron* (Hes. W&D 85), and a deceptive trap, *dolon amechanon*, (Hes. W&D 83; Hes. Th. 589) whose threatening duality is famously coined by Hesiod through the oxymoron: *kalon kakon* (Hes. Th. 585), namely, beautiful evil.

The two Hesiodic descriptions of the creation of the first woman share many similarities and above all provide an archetypical setting for the paradigmatic appearance of the first bride. The first woman appears as a veiled *parthenos* fully dressed and adorned as a virgin bride ready to be given to marriage. Thus, the creation of woman foreshadows the institutionalization of marriage. Moreover, the compound origin of Pandora makes her a symbolic figure of marriage. She is a mixture of earth and water. By blending the opposite states of wet and dry, she introduces through the act of mixing, *phurein* (Hes. W&D 61), the main purpose of marriage: coupling man and woman together.

The French structuralist interpretation represented by Vernant's seminal work on the Hesiodic myth of the first woman considers the institutionalization of marriage as a foundational myth for ancient Greek society. At the concluding part of "The Myth of Prometheus," Vernant emphasizes the contribution of marriage to the ambiguity of human existence:

> There can be no happiness without unhappiness, no birth without death, no abundance without toil, no Prometheus without Epimetheus – in a word, no Man without Pandora.[48]

Vernant's decision to conclude his essay with the maxim that there is no man without woman indicates the central role of marriage in a myth that attempts to decipher the meaning of life. The union of man and woman, according to Vernant, entails all the ambiguities that human life contains. Marriage, as an act of coupling and merging, thematizes mixing as a general principle of the human condition. It is a mixture of happiness and unhappiness, birth and death, abundance and toil, foreknowledge and

FIGURE 6.5 The birth/creation of Pandora, Attic red-figure krater, fifth century BCE. Ashmolean Museum. Alamy Stock Photo.

afterthought. This set of ambiguities captures Hesiod's famous diatribe against marrying a woman:

> And he [Zeus] bestowed another evil thing in exchange for that good one: whoever flees marriage and the dire works of women and chooses not to marry arrives at deadly old age deprived of assistance; while he lives he does not lack means of sustenance, but when he has died his distant relatives divide up his substance. On the other hand, that man to whom the portion of marriage falls as a share, and who acquires a cherished wife, well-fitted in her thoughts, for him evil is balanced continually with good during his whole life. But he who obtains the baneful species lives with incessant woe in his breast, in his spirit and heart, and his evil is incurable.[49]

The inevitable fate of marriage befalls men alone. There is no doubt that Hesiod is blind to the common fate that both men and women share in regards to marriage. The narrator's lament on the inexorable doom that marriage brings with it adopts the husband's point of view. The woman, according to this point of view, is not identified as an equal victim who suffers from the mixed qualities of marriage but, rather, she represents the very cause through which man finds himself locked in wedlock. Thus, man's archetypical resentment of marriage disregards the woman's vehement resistance to the same phenomenon. From the perspectives of both the bride and the groom, marriage is fundamentally a union between two strangers.

The Greek mythological framework defies any romantic conception of marriage of two identical soul mates. And yet, by acknowledging the primary significance of difference in marriage, the man and woman who are initially strangers, can, as time passes, eventually become partners who deeply know each other. This is the basic movement that characterizes the reunion between Penelope and Odysseus. As the reader of the *Odyssey* recognizes, intimacy in marriage is not an immediate and spontaneous outcome of the marital encounter. Married couples, such as Odysseus and Penelope, experience their separation with great difficulty. They share a feeling of mutual estrangement. The twenty-year period of separation is not the only way to explain the source of this estrangement. The lapse of time is definitely important, but rather than function as the root of their feelings, it might be a way of reminding the elderly couple of the initial structure of their marriage, the union of two strangers.

CHAPTER SEVEN

Breaking Vows

EVA CANTARELLA

In classical antiquity, breaking vows—even though this is a modern idea, since neither Greeks nor Romans "vowed" anything during their marriage ceremonies—was a gendered behavior. In both Greece and Rome, the legal and social rules imposed on women alone the obligation of being sexually faithful to their husbands. Men, instead, were allowed to have sexual intercourse (both hetero- and homosexual) when married. However, different rules concerning sexuality were imposed by each culture.

We begin in Greece. In the classical period, each of the Greek poleis was regulated by its own laws according to its different ethnic origins. Therefore, the rules concerning sexual behavior were different in the Ionic and the Doric states. From the Doric world we possess documentation sufficient to reconstruct the laws of only two cities: the well-known Peloponnesian Sparta and the Cretan Gortyn. However, they both pose several methodological problems. Evidence on Sparta comes in some cases from Athenian-educated authors ideologically biased in favor of the Spartan ideologies and customs, such as Xenophon and Plutarch; in other cases from authors biased against it, such as Aristotle. In contrast the evidence from Gortyn is contained in an important, well-preserved and still readable text known as the Law Code of Gortyn inscribed on stone by the city's public authorities, yet it is unfortunately the only document containing relevant information on the local institutions and rules. These circumstances prevent us from knowing how far removed these laws were from lived social practices. which was the distance, always and wherever existing, between the law and social behavior. But we will return later on to this problem when we investigate the Law Code's content.

Evidence from Ionic cities comes to us in the main from Athens. Given the fact that Athens is the only Greek polis whose institutions may be reconstructed with near completeness, we will start with an exposition of Athenian marriage laws and customs, recalling that Athenian authors claimed that their wives were constrained by their customs to observe the strictest sexual fidelity, while Athenian men were allowed almost complete sexual freedom. For example, as we read in the famous speech *Against Neaira* attributed to Demosthenes, all men were, at a minimum, allowed or even expected to have sexual relations with three types of women, each of them with a different role: a wife (*damar*) "for the birth of legitimate children"; a concubine (*pallake*) "for the care of the body" (meaning the possibility of having regular sexual relations); and a companion "for the pleasure" (called *hetaira*), a prostitute, albeit very different (and evaluated differently by society) from the sex workers, called *pornai*, who plied their trade in the streets or in the brothels. The *hetairai* received a professional education that gave them the capacity to participate with men in social occasions such as the famous banquets (*symposia*) where wives were not allowed. They had sexual relations with their clients that were usually not exclusive and often frequent.

In addition, Athenian men maintained long-lasting, intense emotional and sexual relationships with young men (thirteen to seventeen years old, as a rule) with whom they were bound by the conventions of so-called "pederastic love" (from the word *pais*, meaning "boy" or "child"), these ties were accorded social and cultural acceptance because of their perceived fundamental importance to the *paideia* of the young Athenians, in that they facilitated the process of transmitting the social and educational values and the proper behavior believed to make good citizens.

Therefore Athenian husbands enjoyed an abundant and explicitly articulated sexual freedom, while their wives were bound to a strict sexual fidelity. Any transgression of that rule by a wife was punished as a crime called *moicheia*, a term (and a crime) whose interpretation has been the object of a long dispute in the last decades of the twentieth century. Traditionally, scholars had defined as moicheia any sexual intercourse between a male Athenian citizen and the wife, the daughter, the sister, the mother, or the free concubine of another citizen (unless this woman was a prostitute).[1] In an influential article from 1984, however, David Cohen argued for a different and much more restricted meaning of the word. In his opinion moicheia signified only the behavior today called "adultery," that is to say the sexual betrayal of a married unfaithful wife.[2] However few scholars accepted this claim and in the following years roundly criticized his interpretation, resurrecting the old theory that any sexual relationship between a married or unmarried woman with a man who was not her husband fell under the rubric moicheia, citing in support of this view the texts I will discuss below that confirmed a wider meaning of that word.

The first is the famous foundational Athenian law, enacted in 621–620 BCE, from the time when the legislator Draco decided to prohibit the old precivic practice of revenge and imposed on the Athenians the new civic "rule of law," stating that voluntary homicide was a crime that must be punished by death. However, the change from an ancient revenge culture to a new culture instituting a "political" legal system proved difficult, and Draco very wisely, in order to ensure the law's observance, stated that in some exceptional cases homicide would be considered as a *phonos dikaios* (lawful homicide) and would remain an unpunishable act. Among those exceptional cases was the homicide committed by the man who had killed another man caught in his house while having sexual intercourse with his wife, his mother, his daughter, his sister, and his free concubine. In other words, with any woman belonging de jure or de facto to the family group.

We turn next to Aristotle's claims. Whereas the above mentioned law, quoted by Demosthenes (23.53), does not qualify with the word *moichos* the man that could be killed with impunity, Aristotle, referring to the same law, lists among others the case of a moichos caught in the act (*Ath. Pol.* 57.3). Hence, he confirms that moichos was the lover not only of a married woman but also of a (not yet married) daughter or sister, or of a (no longer married) mother.

Further elements in favor of the wider interpretation of *moicheia* come from the pseudo-Demosthenic speech *Against Neaera* (Dem. 59). Although it may not be a totally reliable source, it recounts the story about a charge of moicheia leveled against a man who had intercourse with Phano, an unmarried woman, daughter of Neaira. The scandals provoked by the two women are certainly exaggerated by the unknown author of the speech, who seems to amplify the details of Neaera's life and presents her entire story as a sort of soap opera. Nonetheless, it seems highly improbable that, whoever this author was, he could define as moicheia sexual intercourse with an unmarried woman, such as Phano, if moicheia was committed only with married women.

An additional question raised by the possible interpretations of moicheia concerns the possibility of killing with impunity both the woman whose behavior had dishonored the family and her accomplice. One of the reasons quoted in favor of the existence of this "right to kill," not mentioned in the law, is the claim that it would have been superfluous to mention it: according to this hypothesis the right to kill one's own children would have been included in the personal powers of the Greek head of the family. According to some scholars, however, this power would have existed only in the most ancient period predating our extant literary sources, when in the Greek cities a father's power did not end at the time that his son reached the age of majority; rather, paternal power would have been everlasting, in effect existing whatever the age of the living man's children (as was true later in Rome). But this hypothesis has no support in the sources and evidently arose from the old nineteenth-century tendency to reconstruct the Greek legal principles on the basis of those adopted in Rome, a tendency quelled many years ago by the teaching of Hans Julius Wolff, the father of modern Greek legal science.

Nevertheless, at times scholars have resurrected a timeworn argument for the existence of an ancient paternal power of life and death over children. This unreliable theory invokes the speech *Against Timarchus* (1.182). Here Aeschines, in order to convince the jury to condemn Timarchus for sexual misbehavior, laments the loss of the morally upstanding "good old days" by citing the example of a father who decided to punish a daughter who had lost her virginity by enclosing her with a horse in a room, leaving her to be killed by the animal (although he provides no explanation of how this imaginary murder was to occur).[3] But the penalty for women who had enjoyed illicit sexual relations was not death. As we read in a law recorded in the pseudo-Demosthenic speech *Against Neaira* (87) the woman surprised while committing moicheia was prohibited from appearing in public cult ceremonies and, if she attempted to participate, would "suffer whatever may happen to her, apart from death."[4] Moreover neither her husband nor her father were accorded the right to inflict on her the penalty of their choice (except death). As explicitly stated in section 86 of the speech, it was *ho boulomenos* (whoever wanted to do it).

Finally (except for the unreliable quotation above in Aeschines), in the sources we cannot find a single reference to fathers who had exercised this (supposed) power of life and death over their children. However, in spite of these considerations that argue for limited or expanded definitions of moicheia, the question is still open to debate. What is universally accepted, instead, is the fact that (even if she could not be killed with impunity if caught in the act) an adulteress could anyhow risk her life: moicheia was a public crime and as such was prosecuted with a *graphe*, i.e., a public action that any citizen could propose, the penalty for which could also be death (Aristot. *Ath. Pol.* 59.3).

DORIC CITIES

Sparta

In spite of the scarcity of material and the ideological biases of the authors who report about it, the information we possess about Sparta is nevertheless sufficient to offer an overview of a political and familial organization in which the relationship between the public and the private sphere was radically different from that of the Ionic cities.

According to tradition, the first rules governing these relationships were imposed by Lycurgus, the earliest Spartan legislator, who established the educational system of the young Spartiates, frequently called "the equals" (*homoioi*), those citizens who at the age of majority would enjoy full rights. At birth, the future homoioi were examined by the *gerontes* (older male citizens) in charge, to check if their physical fitness was sufficient to make them strong and capable soldiers as adults (*Lyc.* 16). If because of some illness or deformity they were judged unfit, they were abandoned on a mountain (Mount Taigetus); if they were strong and well formed, they were allowed to live with their natal families until they were seven years old. At that age they began a new phase of life in the *agelai*, bands of boys their own age, where they exercised under the guidance of an older boy in order to become brave soldiers. Once they reached their twentieth year, an age when they were called *eirenes*, they started to train the younger men for war. As Plutarch writes in Sparta the sons "were not a private good of their fathers, but a common good of the State" (*Lyc.* 15.8), and Xenophon confirms this claim, recording that "In Sparta Lycurgus gave every man the power to his son and over the sons of his citizens" (*Lac. Pol.* 6.1).

According to Plutarch, the state also always controlled the conjugal life of the Spartiates, not only by punishing those who did not marry *(Lyc.* 15.1–2) but by imposing on all men between thirty and sixty years of age participation every night in the public banquet for adult men, called *syssitia*. According to Xenophon, Lycurgus imposed restrictions even on the sexual life of young married couples. He was convinced that sons conceived during passionate sexual intercourse were stronger than those conceived during distracted or undesired sex (*Lac. Pol.* 14), and Plutarch says that in order to increase their sexual desire for their wives, the new married young men, before sleeping with them, had to spend the night with friends (*Lyc.* 15.3–5).

Further evidence about the nature of Spartan marriage and the relationship between spouses comes from a controversial statement by Plutarch, who in his biographies of Lycurgus and Numa writes that both kings, the Spartan and the Roman, convinced their citizens to abandon their old and egoistic jealousies and to trade their wives in order to increase the number of citizens (Lyc., *Numa*, 3.1). However, as Plutarch adds, the Spartan and the Roman methods of reaching this goal were different: a Roman who did not have children could convince a friend who had already generated a sufficient number of heirs to lend him his wife (for all time, or only for a certain period). A Spartan husband instead could allow another man to share his own wife without interrupting his own marriage. The reliability of this statement has been questioned, especially as far as the Roman custom was concerned.[5] Only the evidence concerning Sparta confirmed by Xenophon[6] is commonly considered by modern scholarship as reliable and reflective of real historical practice.[7]

Further controversies about Spartan marriage arose because of Plutarch's statement that neither adultery nor sexual violence existed in Sparta (*Lyc.* 15.9–10): did he mean that in Sparta the laws did not consider these behaviors punishable or that nobody committed those crimes? In all probability, Lycurgus's assertion was intended as an idealization crafted as a rebuttal to the Athenian cliché endorsed by Aristotle (*Pol.* II, 1269 b), who describes Spartan women as sexually out of control, and suggests that their behavior, caused by the absence of male discipline, was the reason for an imbalance in the constitution of the city that had increased the material greed of their inhabitants.

To conclude, we have seen that the paucity of evidence about Sparta, in combination with the problems posed by the biases of our ancient sources, impose many caveats on interpreters. Nevertheless, keeping all that in mind, the surviving pieces of information

Gortyn

Evidence from Gortyn, carved into the inscription known as *"The Law Code of Gortyn,"* has been (and still is) the object of important scholarly debate. Some scholars maintain that the Code was enacted by a local legislator, while others argue that it was deliberated in a popular assembly by the Gortynian citizens. When the so-called "oriental" documents, the *Codes of the Ancient Near East,* were decrypted, new scholarship gave birth to further dissent, forcing scholars to re-evaluate their very nature and significance.[8] According to the great majority of the specialists of that field the Near Eastern Codes were not "codes" in the modern sense of the word but jurisprudential treaties, and this opinion in turn influenced some of the scholars working on the Gortynian Law Code, who started to look at them as a collection of legal principles that would not necessarily influence judgments in court.[9]

But other scholars formulated different and, in my opinion, more convincing ideas. Among them, Michael Gagarin, one of the leading specialists in Gortynian studies, observed that the nature of the Law Code of Gortyn was different from that of the "Oriental Codes": while those (namely that of Hammurabi) were "instructive and educative in the judicial order," the Law Code of Gortyn was "true legislation."[10] An important and convincing opinion, confirmed by the content of the *Great Inscription*, consisted of an organic formulation of the entire normative system of the city, content that makes the Law Code of Gortyn a fundamental and unique document, among those concerning the Doric cities. Despite the lack of other sources coming from Gortyn preventing us from knowing how long the legal principles (or rules) were respected in that city, the *Great Inscription* is the only document that allows us to compare in detail Doric and Ionic institutions. And of particular interest to the present discussion, the inscription contains detailed information on the problem of breaking vows, testifying to unexpected peculiarities in the local sexual behaviors and, indeed, the entire matrimonial system.

Perhaps the more surprising of these peculiarities is the fact that legal marriage in Gortyn (monogamous, as in all the other Greek cities) was defined, not only as a union between two free persons but also between two slaves (*douloi* or *oikeis*, without apparent distinction). No less surprising is the fact that a free woman could marry a slave and be tied to him in a marital union that was, by its very nature, uxorilocal and not, as was the usual practice, virilocal (col. VII, 1 ff.).

Furthermore, the law stated that if a woman gave birth to a child after divorcing her husband, she had to present the baby to her former husband, who would decide if he wanted to raise the child in his house. If he did not want it, the woman could decide to raise the baby herself (in her father's house, where she would have to return after the divorce) (III, 44–52).

Gortynian women, then, enjoyed more freedom and rights than other Greek women, as is additionally confirmed by the rules concerning the consequences of moicheia, a behavior that in Gortyn encompassed even more sexual acts than the ones indicated by the sources concerning Athens. As marriage was not limited to the union of free persons, in Gortyn moicheia could also be committed by, and with, slaves. A further difference between the Gortynian and the Ionic concept of moicheia consisted in the consequences proceeding from the crime. As we read in the *Great Inscription*, the persons who committed that crime, even if caught in the act, did not risk their lives. The penalty consisted of a fine, the value of which was greater according to the status of the woman involved, of her accomplice, and of the house in which they were caught. As we read in the text of the inscription, column II, lines 20–45:

> If a person will be caught committing *moicheia* with a free woman in the house of the woman's father, brother or husband, he will pay 100 staters. If [will be caught] in the house of a different person he will pay 50 staters. If [will be caught] with the woman of an *apetairos* [i.e. a person belonging to a socially inferior status] he will pay 10 staters. But a slave [if caught] with a free woman will pay the double. If [caught] with the woman of another slave he will pay 5 staters. Within three days the relatives of the *moichos* will solemnly invite his relatives to redeem him within five days. If the *moichos* will be a slave the invitation will be made to the slave's master in front of two witnesses. If nobody will redeem him, the persons who caught him may treat him as they want. If he says that he was drawn in a trap, if the penalty for his case is higher than 50 staters, the person who caught him must swear that he did not trap him and caught him in the act invoking a curse against himself if he lies. Four persons must be present; if he is an *apetairos* two persons and if he is a slave his master and one other person.[11]

ROME

In Rome women who broke their marital "vow" of fidelity—remember, as we have already said, that there was no technical vow during the wedding ceremony—could be punished by death. The rule was reportedly instituted by Romulus, the mythical founder of the city, who gave their husbands the right to execute them. Women's sexual behavior was a family matter, but Romans viewed drinking as part and parcel of sexual behavior and so made women's drinking of wine punishable by death (Dion. Halic. *Roman. Antiquit.* 2.25.6). Ancient writers quibbled over the reasons for this prohibition against women's consumption of wine: according to some, it was because of the abortive properties of wine (although in fact Roman law punished a woman seeking an abortion without her husband's consent with divorce, not death: Plut. *Quaest. Rom.* 22). Moreover, the Romans, as did other ancient peoples, believed that wine contained a life force: therefore the woman who drank wine admitted into her body an external force, by which act she became an adulteress. Whichever one of these ancient hypotheses is most convincing has been and is still discussed by modern scholars, but aside from questions about the theoretical basis of the law one circumstance is indisputable: the law was created to control the female sector of the population. We read that "The woman fond of drinking wine closes the door to virtue and opens it to vice."[12] That is, drinking wine could induce women to forget their duties and commit adultery.[13] This outsized fear of women's drinking led to rigorous enforcement of the law, with terrible results. Valerius Maximus[14] claimed that a certain Egnatius Metellus beat his wife to death because she drank some wine, a case that was cited because, incredibly, Egnatius was acquitted: his fault was that he killed her in an improper way. Women found guilty of drinking were condemned to death by starvation, as we will see later, buried alive in the family cellar. Thus Egnatius's fault was his method of killing his wife, not the killing itself. A comment from Cato, some centuries later, illustrates how some Roman men were convinced of the justice of their laws on adultery. Cato boasted, "if you [meaning 'you, husband'] were to catch your wife in adultery you can kill her; if she catches you, she could not even touch you with a finger" (Gell. *Noct. Att.* 10.23.5).

However, according to the sources, for many centuries women's obedience to the principle of chastity and fidelity to their husbands was not codified in a law. Ancient Roman writers asserted that their wives did not need the threat of punishment to respect their duties and their public and private chaste personae; they were thought to embody spontaneously a model of behavior taught them by a series of *exempla*, the traditional anecdotes that the Romans, with educational intent, repeated *ad infinitum*. Perhaps the best-known exemplum was the famous Lucretia, Collatinus's perfect wife.

Seduced by the beauty and the virtue of Lucretia, the young Sextus, son of the Etruscan king Tarquinius (nicknamed Superbus), profited from a moment when she was alone, entered her bedroom and declared her his love. Lucretia of course rejected his offers, but the young and arrogant youth told her that if she did not give in to his lust, he would kill her and put near her body the naked body of a slave. Thus all would believe that Lucretia had been killed justly by Sextus while committing this most shameful act of adultery. Lucretia did not have any other choice but to submit her body to the rape. But as soon as Tarquinius left she summoned her husband and her father, told them what had happened and informed them of her decision to commit suicide "so that never ever a Roman woman will be exposed to such a shameful crime," as she proclaimed (Livy 1.58–60). Her father's plea "only her body had been violated, not her soul," as he tried to convince her not to punish herself, was totally irrelevant: in Roman culture, a woman whose body had been violated was expected to commit suicide. These were the unwritten rules, and the duty of the men of the family was to revenge the offense, in order to redeem the honor of the group. Women's chastity (meaning virginity for unmarried women and sexual fidelity for the married ones) was one of the pillars on which the honor of Roman families was based. Any real or suspected instance of sexual misbehavior by a woman shamed her entire family, and the male members of the clan were expected to re-establish its damaged social and political respectability by a public demonstration of their capacity to react to the offense with the same (or with an even stronger) physical and moral retaliation. Indeed, taking revenge was the only means of erasing the stain that had sullied their honor. But Lucretia's rape was not only a family matter. She was a symbol, for she represented women's perfection. The violation of her body imposed on all Romans the duty to avenge their collective offended honor, as they did in rising up against the Etruscan kings, who were expelled from Rome. The offense against Lucretia, as the Romans framed it, made possible a change in government from monarchy to Republic. Some centuries later, again, another (imaginary) affront to women's bodily integrity determined another crucial event in Roman history, when the decemvirs were driven out because the infamous decemvir Appius Claudius attempted to violate the virgin Virginia (Livy 3.44–48)

Having investigated the most famous accounts of wives' private and public conduct as well as the prevailing ideologies concerning sexuality during the centuries of the Republic, we turn to the very beginnings of empire with the new legislation of Augustus. These laws brought a startling change to Roman customs, introducing the idea that women's sexual behavior was not a totally private matter. One of the most significant pieces of legislation was the *lex Iulia de adulteriis*, a milestone in the history of Roman family relationships and sexual ethics.

In the Augustan era, women had achieved such a degree of personal and economic freedom that modern scholars began to speak of Roman women's emancipation in this period. While these same scholars noted the danger in applying modern terminology to the ancient world, they also argued that the radical changes in women's lives in this era actually justify the use of the term.

In the first centuries of the city, women at marriage departed from their natal home and family and entered into that of their husbands, who controlled their wives with a power (similar to *patria potestas*) called *manus*. As the centuries went by, this kind of marriage (called by modern Roman legal scholars *cum manu*) fell into increasing disfavor, and in the Augustan Age it was almost obsolete. Marriage had started to be viewed as the union of two persons who cohabited together in order to give birth to legitimate offspring, and indeed this committed union ceased to exist if both or one of the spouses lacked this intention (called *maritalis affectio*). A revolutionary change in the nature of marriage had taken place: a young person's marriage and divorce was no longer subject to the will of his or her *paterfamilias*—as it had been for centuries—but became a personal choice, nearly unparalleled in Western history for the liberty it allowed.

Not surprisingly, Roman imperialism itself increased women's liberty and complicated relations between genders. In the course of the last two centuries of the Republic, the succession of wars (most notably the second Punic War in the late third century BCE) had decimated the masculine population. Many women had lost fathers and husbands, and the male guardianship of many women (which, according to the law, lasted for their entire lives) in fact did not exist in actual practice. In addition, since male mortality in war was very high, patrimonies were increasingly inherited by women, both as daughters and as wives. Women's freedoms had increased to such an extent that some detect in the surviving literature a new and deep male unease. For centuries, men had asserted that the basis of the force of the state was the respect of "family values" that they themselves had invented, and they continued to hold that conviction.

For example, paraphrasing Plato, Scipio (in Cicero, *Res Publica* 1.43) says that women's and slaves' disobedience leads to anarchy, and we have reason to infer that the majority of male Romans were indeed consumed by a similar paranoia, because the various literary works of the late Republic reveal the tensions of men facing women's consciousness of their new capabilities and rights. A cultural transition was in place and relationships between men and women were more complicated than ever before; Juvenal, for example, complains that women are now "in control" (*dominae*) of men (Juv. *Sat.* 6.29–30).

Augustus, apparently anxious over an ongoing, serious decrease in birth rates among the aristocracy, believed that this demographic development was in some way connected to women's emancipation and, like the majority of contemporary Romans, attributed this development to the loss of traditional moral values. He therefore decided to encourage elite Romans to get married and to have children, passing two laws: the *lex Iulia de maritandis ordinibus* (18 BCE) and the *lex Papia Poppaea nuptialis* (9 BCE), which later merged into a single text (*lex Iulia et Papia*). The two laws required men between twenty-five and sixty, and women between twenty-five and fifty, to marry persons of the appropriate social class (or remarry if divorced or widowed).[15] In order to increase the birth rate, infertile marriages were punished with limitations on inheritance, and fertile couples were promised rewards, the most important of which was the *ius liberorum*, which was the right of especially fertile mothers to be freed from male guardianship.

But the most important of his laws was the *lex Iulia de adulteriis*, in which the word *adulterium* did not refer in the strict sense to intercourse between a married woman and anyone other than her husband. It also included *stuprum*, a term defined as any disgraceful sexual congress of, or with, a virgin or a widow.[16]

It seems that Augustus's intent was for the law to reintroduce into Roman family life ancestral and all but forgotten ideals. But while the legislation confirmed old principles, it also introduced a radically new principle. Sexual crimes became criminal, that is to say, illicit behaviors that could be prosecuted in a public trial upon denunciation of any citizen and were given a criminal penalty: exile on an island (*relegatio in insula*) for both members of the adulterous couple (needless to say, exiled on two different islands). In addition, the law stipulated that, with exception of relationships with prostitutes and between persons cohabiting as husband and wife, all extramarital sexual relations were crimes to be punished by a special standing court (a *quaestio perpetua*, specifically a *questio de adulteriis*), which continued to function until the age of the Severans (in the late second century CE). When the *quaestio de adulteriis* fell out of use, the crime was then punished with a trial known as *cognitio extra ordinem,* and as such judged by the emperor or an imperial officer. Significantly, then, with the passage of the *lex Iulia*, punishment of *adulterium* in the broader sense passed from the private to the public sphere.[17] As rightly noted by D. Cohen, "the Augustan marital legislation represents a massive and deliberate appropriation by the state of a new regulatory sphere: marriage, divorce and sexuality."[18]

However, there were exceptions to the principle that sexual crimes concerned the entire state, and in these cases adultery was conceived of in the strictest sense; therefore special rules were established that reconciled the new principles with the old ones. These concerned fathers and husbands, who retained the old right to kill or *ius occidendi* (although this right was granted only in special cases and circumstances). In other words, the law did not abrogate the right to kill traditionally granted to fathers and husbands, it only limited it.

After the passage of the *lex Iulia,* a father could kill with impunity his daughter and her lover only if he had caught them engaged in sexual activity in his, or in his son-in-law's, house. In addition he had to kill them immediately, as the jurist Ulpian writes, "by one blow and one attack, with equal anger against both" (D. 48.5.42.4), in other words, he was required to kill them in a fit of rage caused by the discovery of their illicit relationship.

Thus a husband retained the right to kill the male accomplice caught *in flagrante delicto* in his house (or if he was a slave or an "infamous" person such as a gladiator, a dancer, or even a freedman) but he no longer had the right to kill the adulterous wife and was required only to repudiate her. If he did not, he could be accused of pandering.

But Augustus's faith in the effects of his law was destined to be disappointed. A law proposing that any citizen could accuse any woman of sexual misbehavior led to unacceptable or downright disastrous results. Besides any consideration of the morality of such a decree, Romans for purely selfish reasons realized that if they accused the wife of a political enemy of adultery, how could they be certain that a similar unfortunate and dishonorable situation would not happen to them? Reflecting perhaps the anxieties of many Romans, one century after the law was passed Tacitus wrote "every house was upset by the intrigues of the informers. Once the cause of disasters was crimes, now the cause is the informers."[19]

Many factors contributed to the unpopularity of *lex Iulia de adulteriis*. Both women and men were dissatisfied with it, and made a public display of this dissatisfaction with an interesting, all too often ignored episode. To show what they thought of the Augustus's legislation, many Roman women made a point of registering themselves in the list of the prostitutes, who, as we know, were prohibited from marrying the elite whom the law was meant to affect. The historical proof of the event is bolstered by the accounts of Suetonius[20] and Tacitus[21] and confirmed by Papinianus in a text included in Justinian's

Digest.[22] But what was the impetus for such an incredible initiative? Its organizers and participants were surely members of the upper classes, therefore perfectly aware of the fact that nobody would have ever denounced them. The reason for the protest was certainly not fear; it was rather a way to ridicule Augustus. It was an unprecedented, almost unthinkable behavior that has been identified as an act of civic disobedience by D. Daube[23] and was the first women's protest of its kind recorded in classical history. And it was not performed only on a few occasions for a few days or weeks; the protest continued for years, even after Augustus's death. Under his successor, Tiberius, a scandal arose centering on a certain Vistilia who belonged to the rank of the *equites* (knights) and had registered in the list. According to Tacitus, Tiberius, to avoid the repetition of a similar uprising, prohibited the matrons of that class from entering into the profession of prostitution.[24] According to Suetonius he also exiled from Rome the matrons who had registered in the list and proposed that in the absence of public accusers, the old system would be reapplied.[25] But any effort to impose observance of the law failed: the *lex Iulia* was not obeyed. In a famous invective poem Juvenal, accusing women of all possible vices, calls down upon them application of the law: "Where are you, *lex Iulia*," he asks, "Are you sleeping?"[26] Juvenal's suspected misogyny coupled with the excesses of satire (in which genre Juvenal's poems are perhaps the best known) encourages us to approach his work with great caution, but as far as the *lex Iulia* is concerned, he was probably right: the *lex Iulia* does seem to have been sleeping, for the women condemned for adultery, in the course of one century, amounted to no more than twelve.

Augustus's attempt to solve the problem of sexual morality had failed, but it was destined to produce important effects in the following centuries. As D. Cohen has rightly noted, the *lex Iulia* concerned "far more then ensuring the chastity of Roman women, far more than checking the moral corruption of the age. The appropriation of the family, sexuality and reproduction for the purposes of state policy was not entirely successful, but it established a principle that, when adopted by a Christianized Empire would have far-reaching consequences."[27]

Limiting ourselves to the most relevant, let us recall that under the Christian emperors the penalties for adultery were made harsher. Constantine's sons, Constantius and Constans, in 339 CE, decreed that an adulteress and her accomplice had to be put to death with the terrible *poena cullei*, that until that moment had been reserved for parricides and consisted of drowning the condemned person in a bag (*culleus*) with a dog, a monkey, a rooster, and a viper.[28]

Some of Augustus's limitations on killing (with impunity) unfaithful wives caught in the act were re-established. The first step in this direction was made by Antoninus Pius, followed by Marcus Aurelius and Commodus, who stated that the husband who killed his adulterous wife would be punished less severely than a common murderer, because it "is very difficult (for him) to moderate his righteous grief (*iustus dolor*)."[29] The sentence for this husband was hard labor if he was of lower status, and relegation or exile to an island if he was of higher status. Marcus Aurelius and Commodus also established less severe penalties for the husband who had killed his wife's lover,[30] even if the aforementioned conditions of place and person were not met (D. 48.5.39[38].8); moreover, Alexander Severus decreed in 213 and 223 CE that this penalty should be exile (Cod. Iust. 9.9.4).

These changes reached a culmination in 506 CE with the *lex Romana Visigothorum* aimed at the Romans who lived under the Visigoths, a law that granted to the husband an almost complete impunity.[31] In the mid-fifth century the law was introduced into the imperial legislation and was applied to the entire empire by the constitution of the emperor Majorianus. Only under Justinian were the limits of impunity again tightened; he stated that the law demanded only the killing of the lover, not of the wife, and decreed that the husband enjoyed impunity only if he killed his wife's frequent lover and not only an occasional one.[32]

Finally, in 556 Justinian established that a guilty wife could avoid the death penalty by being shut up in a convent and allowed to leave only if the husband forgave her within two years. If not, or if the husband died during that period, she would spend the rest of her life in the convent.[33] And so female adultery was punished with a sort of life imprisonment. As at the beginning of Roman history, women's sexual fidelity was considered the fundamental and absolute duty of women. This concept is further confirmed by a sacred institution, the college of the Vestals, the priestesses of the Goddess Vesta, women who were at once specially privileged and also burdened with the responsibility of the safety of the state, the lives of the Vestals are the best indicators of the consequences of breaking vows for all women.

Selected from among the noblest Roman families at an age between six and ten years old, at the moment of their consecration, the Vestals pronounced a vow that bound them to chastity for thirty years, the tenure of their priesthood. During that period they were subject to the absolute control of the most powerful of the religious Roman authorities, the *Pontifex Maximus*, whose powers over them included the right to put them to death if they had, or were merely suspected of having had, sexual intercourse. This power the Pontifices exercised throughout the centuries with impressive continuity: the first Vestal put to death, as far as we know, was Pinaria, under the Etruscan king Tarquinius Priscus;[34] during the fifth century BCE there were two executions: in 483 the victim was Oppia, in 472 Orbinia; in the following century,[35] in 337, Minucia.[36] In the third century BCE the victims were four: in 273 *Sestilia*[37] and in 214–213 Emilia, Licinia, and Marcia.[38] The executions continued into the Imperial period: under Domitian's reign (in 91 CE, Cornelia)[39]; in the third century under Caracalla in 231 CE, Aurelia Severa, Clodia Laeta, and Pomponia Rufina were executed,[40] and perhaps the last condemnation took place in the fourth century.[41]

In the dreadful history of these executions, what is striking more than the number of victims is the way in which the Vestals were put to death. In a solemn public ceremony, the condemned Vestal, in a closed litter, crossed the city directed to a site called the "wicked field," in which an underground room had been excavated. Into this room were placed a bed, a torch, a piece of bread, water, milk, and some oil, and finally the Vestal was placed inside as well and locked in, probably dying of suffocation before starvation.[42] When they broke their vows, the Vestals committed a *sacrilegium* that required expiations and the special, theatrical publicity of their death. But we note that Vestals died in the same way as all the women who had broken theirs vows.

Both in Greece and in Rome, death was gendered, and executions differed according to the crime committed and the status of the criminal. In Rome, if the criminal was free he might be burned or flogged to death (a death also reserved for the accomplice of the guilty Vestal), hurled from a rock or thrown into the sea, or might suffer the penalty of being sewn in to the sack with animals and drowned; if he was a slave, he would be crucified. But these executions were reserved for men. Women were executed in their own houses, in silence, with no publicity: they were closed in the family storeroom (usually a cellar) and abandoned to their fate. They died starving, or suffocating, in exactly the same way as the Vestals. The analogy is evident and certainly not accidental. A Vestal's vows were the sacral projection of an average woman's most important duty, just as their secular tasks were the projection of domestic feminine tasks. The first of these homely tasks consisted in performing every year on June 15, the rite called *stercoratio* (or *delatio stercoris*), the removing of filth from the temple of the Goddess; their second duty consisted of the preparation of *mola salsa*, the salted meal that, in an animal sacrifice, had to be spread on the victim's body, on the altar and on the knife of the person who celebrated the ritual. A Vestal's daily tasks, then, consisted of cleaning and preparing food, the same tasks of every woman in her own house for her own family. On a civic level, the symbolic value of the Vestal's role made it inevitable that they would be executed in the same manner as the average Roman wife. The record of Vestal execution is perhaps the best indicator of the civic importance of chastity for every Roman member of the female sex.

CHAPTER EIGHT

Representation

NOELLE ZEINER-CARMICHAEL

To my Tim, whose final breath lives within me.
Timothy Douglas Carmichael, May 2, 1969 – February 9, 2018

Previous chapters in this volume have explored various aspects of marriage in culture, governance, and daily lived realities. This chapter focuses on how representations of marriage in antiquity played an integral role in maintaining and reinforcing gendered ideologies. The goal is to offer a panoramic view of how Greeks and Romans transferred marriage from a daily social practice into written contexts that expressed symbolic meanings by reinforcing cultural values and ideologies. Any analysis involving different civilizations and spanning nearly three milennia presents challenges: perspectives on non-elite or marginalized groups are underrepresented, and the prevalence of male voices obfuscates and even distorts the reality of ancient married life.[1] The approach is therefore thematic, tracing representations of marriage through its "life cycle," from betrothal to death. Attitudes and representations of marriage were by no means homogenous for the Greeks and Romans, of course, but recurring patterns do emerge, so the examples echo many of the sources and topics explored in the preceding chapters, and interrogate the complex intersectionalities between marriage and related social institutions dominated by patriarchal mores such as politics and literary production. The translation of ephemeral experiences into enduring written genres complicates how we "read" representations of (un)married men and women, and it highlights the profound role of marriage in promulgating cultural values and gender ideologies. The examples included in this chapter attempt to synthesize, both diachronically and cross-culturally, recurring images and themes, and to underscore the diversity of sources that reproduced them. The division between reality and ideal could be large: representations of marriage reproduce social codes of conduct and normative assumptions about gender roles, but may not replicate the actual experiences otherwise viewed within written discourse as aberrations or transgressions.[2]

This chapter, then, considers "re-presentations" more than "representations." The images of marriage found in written sources result from negotiations carried out between the producer (e.g., author) and consumer (e.g., the reader or viewer). It is in the gap between "re" and "presentation" where new meanings are created or existing ideals are reinforced. In comprising an interactive process that involves a medium (e.g., author), a mode of transference (e.g., genre), and a recipient (e.g., audience),[3] "re-presentation" is inherently political; repeated images, transferred through varied forms of discourse, create "dominant meanings" that ultimately contribute to the creation and reinforcement of ideology.[4] It is this process and outcome, then, to which I refer when using the term "representation" throughout this chapter. In the case of ancient Greece and Rome, representations of marriage reified ideologies based on heteronormative behavior and patriarchal values, even if social practices rarely aligned. The repetitive idealizations of brides and wives, especially, are structured around binary opposites based on established gender ideals and normative assumptions, which themselves were formulated and regulated by men and often, if we believe our sources, wholeheartedly adopted by women, attempting to survive as captives in a system they did not invent. Thus, depictions of idealized marriage (or, transgressions against it) frequently functioned as symbolic "codes," facilitating translation between the language of representation and intended meanings.[5] The complex dynamic between inside–outside/private–public, that is, the "spatial politics" of ancient Greece and Rome, moreover, appears prominently in the representations (= "re-presentations") of marriage for expressing persisting gender structures and cultural values.[6] When audiences and readers engaged with idealized (or transgressive) representations of marriage, they participated in a self-reflective and introspective process, sympathizing with or rejecting an image, and sometimes both.

PART ONE: GETTING MARRIED

The betrothal

The process of marriage began with betrothal, and its depiction is found in a variety of sources, such as epic, drama, and historical narrative. Since prematrimonial and wedding ceremonies played an essential role in affirming the legitimacy of a union and transference of property, in many cases the betrothal comprised a public formulaic pledge. Throughout Greek history, the wedding (*gamos*) was typically preceded by the engagement, or *engyē* (lit. "in the hand"), comprising a contract between a bride's father and her future groom. This was typically fulfilled verbally and confirmed symbolically through a handshake between the two males.[7] In the Roman world, a formal engagement (*sponsalia*) generally occurred only with *manus*-marriages and involved a formulaic verbal pledge (*stipulatio*) between the father and future son-in-law. The frequency of this type of formal engagement, however, declined by the first century BCE, and was replaced by simple consent.[8]

Betrothals fulfilled a practical function in everyday life, and their representations provided opportunities for literary and symbolic purposes. The genre of comedy re-performed marriage betrothals and in so doing reinforced, through humor, normative attitudes and practices.[9] Marriage is a common theme in comedic drama, reflecting how the social institution of theatre, both in its performative and written context, perpetuated cultural ideals. A stock plot of both Greek New Comedy in Athens and Roman comedy involved star-crossed lovers who were prohibited from marrying due to incompatible class status; betrothal scenes are frequently employed to resolve this tension. Menander's *Perikeiromene* (*The Rape of Locks*, c. 302 BCE), for instance, revolves around a lover's quarrel between the unmarried Athenian citizen Polemon and his beloved Glykera; thanks to her mistaken identity as a non-freeborn, Glykera was excluded from the polis and the institution of marriage, forced to be content as Polemon's concubine (*pallake*) rather than wife (*gynaika*).[10] When, however, Glykera is discovered to be the freeborn daughter of Pataecus, a citizen from Corinth, her new status immediately makes her eligible for marriage, and the conflict is resolved. Accordingly, the play concludes with a re-presentation of the *engye* (betrothal) and the formulaic promise between father and son-in-law: "Pataecus (Pataikos) pledges his daughter to Polemon for cultivating future children" (1013–1014).[11] In classical Athens, marriage between an Athenian citizen and the freeborn daughter of a citizen affirmed the political ties between polis and *oikos*.[12] Following Athens' defeat in the Peloponnesian War, however, this political landscape changed: contemporary issues related to democracy, egalitarianism, and the individual arose, while the status of women improved and they acquired more rights, such as owning property.[13] Thus, the engagement scene in Menander's play is not a straightforward reproduction of long-standing marital ideology; while the engagement reflects the continued pragmatic purpose of marriage (procreation), it also legitimizes a relationship that had originated out of mutual attraction—and not kinship economic interests—and one that involved a non-Athenian citizen.

In resolving the plot, the betrothal responds to the new social milieu, simultaneously reaffirming heteronormative traditions. Thus, Glykera's former independence and assertive role as *pallake* dissipates through the betrothal; her proclamations at the beginning of the play (e.g., "I know what's best for me," 148) are silenced as her father authoritatively pledges her transfer. This merging of independence and passivity mirrors the intersection between traditional social practices (e.g., marriage based on an economic exchange between families) and emerging fourth-century sensibilities that refocused attention inward, from the state to the individual.[14] Glykera and Polemon's marriage is romantic and sexual, not economic- or kinship-based; reproduced on stage, the betrothal legitimized a union that originated from self-will, thereby affirming the continued function of marriage for reinforcing a gender hierarchy that was deeply entrenched in long-standing cultural values.[15]

During the Roman Republic, *manus*-marriages involving a bride's passive transference from her father's home (and guardianship) to her husband's often began with engagement (*sponsalia*). Marriage as a theme appears regularly in the comedies of the Roman playwright Plautus (second–third century BCE), who was influenced by Menander. Betrothal scenes occur often, sometimes reproducing the formulaic *stipulatio* (pledge): the groom poses the question ("*Spondesne?*" "Will you pledge her?") and the bride's father affirms ("*Spondeo*," "Yes, I pledge her.").[16] In some comedies the (future) bride is a freeborn virgin (*puella*), whose idealized qualities are described but never enacted on stage by the bride herself.[17] It is paradoxically through her absence and silence that the bride affirms the social practice and gender ideology of Roman *manus*-marriages. Kept off-stage, the puella embodies the chastity and modesty of the ideal bride, while her silent "role" ultimately resolves the plot through an engagement scene at which she is not present. In other comedies, the bride resembles Menander's Glykera and represents two Roman feminine "types," the freeborn virgin bride (*puella*) and the sexually charged *meretrix* (mistress). Here, she does appear on stage, as we find in Plautus's *Curculio*, which follows a plotline similar to the *Perikeiromene*. Planesium is a *meretrix* and thus prohibited from marriage, but is later discovered to be freeborn (635–658); a betrothal takes place (at which she is present), and the formulaic *stipulatio* (674) transforms her from the sexually provocative mistress into the demure, ideal *nupta* (bride). Marriage status established the gap between these two feminine types; this is underscored by a spatial analogy offered by another character: the mistress is like a highway (*publica via*), publicly accessible, while the bride remains safeguarded, like a private, fenced piece of property (33–38).[18] The representation of Planesium—on stage—reflects Roman cultural values concerning actresses, who were associated with excessive pleasure and immoderation (and thus also assumed to be prostitutes). The actress appears on stage to be "consumed" for entertainment by the public; she served as a foil to the respectable bride, whose role in the public wedding ceremony, like the behind-the-scenes puella, was carefully controlled by rituals and the engendered expectations imposed upon her.[19]

The wedding

The ideals of marriage that were reinforced through comedy on stage were also reproduced in wedding ceremonies and literary representations of them. While the groom occupied center stage in comedy, the bride was the main focus of a wedding. Its customs and rituals made her the object of the public gaze, a symbol of the engendered ideals associated with the institution of marriage. The wedding procession (*komos/deductio in domum mariti*), which led a bride to her new home, celebrated her transition from girl to wife with a parade full of sights, sounds, and smells. Literary sources recreate the public spectacle and the overall sensory experience, as we find in Sappho's description of Hector and Andromache's wedding which enumerates mule-drawn wheeled carts, throngs of women and men, chariots, the "sweet-sounding" *aulos* and castanets, loudly sung hymns, perfumes and incense, and the shouts of attendees invoking Apollo (Fr. 44) (see Figures 8.1 and 8.2).[20] The representation is surely hyperbolic but aptly communicates the impact of the public setting for validating weddings, which was reinforced by their weekly, or even daily, performance, visible to bystanders from all social classes.[21]

FIGURE 8.1 Black-figure hydria depicting a wedding procession, Lysippides-Andokides Group, Greek, *c.* 520 BCE. Walters Art Museum. Wikimedia Commons.

FIGURE 8.2 Detail from an Attic red-figure pyxis, Marlay Painter, 440–430 BCE. British Museum. Wikimedia Commons.

The public setting of the wedding ceremony was a legitimizing force even when transferred from its original ephemeral context into a new (written) one. A courtroom speech by the fourth-century orator Hyperides, for example, employs the representation of a wedding procession to defend his client Lycophron against charges of adultery. The participants and vehicles of the parade, he argues, would have blocked Lycophron's access to the bride, making it impossible to seduce her, as the prosecution had charged (5). Similarly, a speech by Isaeus (fourth century BCE) exploits the public wedding feast (*gamos*) as evidence for proving a mother's freeborn status that formed the evidentiary basis in an inheritance case. Had she not been freeborn, it is argued, the wedding feast would not have been celebrated publicly (8.18–20), but concealed. Clearly, the re-presentations of a public wedding as legal proof in the performative context of the courtroom might result in significant economic ramifications for the individual or family.[22] Similarly, when it came to Roman weddings, the public ceremony confirmed marital *consensus*, a legal requirement for marriage, which likewise might have implications for property or inheritance disputes involving the couple.[23]

The translation of the wedding ceremony into written discourse was fully realized in the Greek and Roman *epithalamium*. The epithalamium began as a hymn performed during the bridal procession or outside the wedding chamber and evolved into a distinct literary genre.[24] *Epithalamia* reproduced ceremonial aspects of the wedding and, more symbolically, reinforced engendered ideals: the transformation of a young virgin bride to wife is mirrored in the poem's structural and narrative progression. Intersections among the ephemeral, ceremonial, literary, and performative are revealed through recurring images and literary conventions that merge reality with the imagined, as in the attendance of deities who validate the marriage (e.g., Hymenaios or Venus) or through epic motifs. Above all, epithalamia idealized the unions between bride and groom, often presenting both as youthful and at similar life stages, even though in reality the disparity between the young virgin bride and her older, more (sexually) experienced groom could be quite pronounced. The regular practice of such idealization is further supported by epithalamia involving famous mythological gods or heroes and visual representations such as vase paintings (see Figures 8.1 and 8.2) and sarcophagi, where the groom might be depicted as much younger than the customary marriage age for Greek males.[25] Examples of Greek epithalamia from the Archaic and Hellenistic periods, such as those of Sappho (sixth century BCE) and Theocritus (fourth century BCE), established many of the literary conventions that were later adapted by Roman authors to suit their own contexts or authorial purposes. The long Greco-Roman tradition of the epithalamium, moreover, reveals a continuance of traditional ideals and literary conventions, despite changes in cultural values and social practices over time.

Marriage was an abrupt life adjustment for Greek and Roman girls, a reality reflected in the epithalamium. Marriage brought a plethora of new responsibilities, duties, and social expectations; given this sudden symbolic and pragmatic change from girl to wife, it is no surprise that representations in a variety of sources often entailed motifs involving the bride's imagined state of mind, such as verbal lamentations, separation, and even death.[26] For instance, the female speaker in a fourth-century BCE Greek poem by Erinna nostalgically recalls girlhood activities shared with her friend Baucis, like doll-playing; these interactions came to an abrupt halt with Baucis's wedding, a separation now more profoundly felt because of her premature death.[27] A bride's reluctance to marry, represented by descriptions of her comportment or lamentations, may have reflected reality but also symbolized idealized virtues, such as her chastity and modesty, and was thus a common topos applied even to second-time brides. The bride's anxious, abrupt departure from girlhood resembled a kind of death; indeed, weddings and funerals shared similar customs, such as processions and lit torches,[28] and might thematically overlap in written discourse. Epitaphs honoring deceased virgins (i.e., girls of marriageable age) often bemoan their lost wedding day and unfulfilled status as wife and mother. These expressions also stressed temporality and the intersection of present and future time: recent suitors will never be chosen as the groom, and the bride's beauty (i.e., fertility) is now wasted. The theme of "replacement" is prominent, whereby bridal beds, dowries, and wedding ceremonies are replaced with tombs, pyres, and funeral rites.

Not surprisingly, representations of grooms contrast those of the bride and align with masculine ideals: the groom is confident, virulent, and sexually experienced, sometimes likened to Ares or Mars.[29] For him marriage was a less sudden transformation, although it required, at least ideologically, a behavioral shift, namely abandoning previous sexual affairs and habits in exchange for the marital sex that would produce legitimate children.[30] The first-time bride, however, was a potential mother; her fertility was a main focus of the epithalamic encomium, usually translated by idealized images representing her beauty and comportment. Specific details communicated larger symbolic meanings that ultimately reinforced patriarchal values. A bride's complexion, eyes, and hair, for example, were conventional objects of praise communicating her beauty and symbolizing her fertility. Sappho (103 b) describes a "bride with beautiful feet," and in Theocritus's epithalamium (*Idyll* 8) Helen's "fair face" is lauded. "Beauty" was one of several conventional virtues contributing to the idealized Greek and Roman bride,[31] and was connected to fertility as well as desirability. Yet the ideal bride was also demure and modest, expressed through descriptions of her comportment during the wedding ceremony, such as her downcast eyes and blushing cheeks. Although in reality these aspects of her appearance or demeanor may not have been visible to wedding spectators, the epithalamium provides a space for these representations. The many images appearing in the epithalamium symbolizing a bride's beauty, fertility, and modesty together reinforced engendered ideals that expected the (Athenian) wife to be *sophron*; under the guardianship of her husband (*kyrios*), she lived secluded in her husband's house, prohibited from interacting with non-kin males.[32] In contrast, the elite Roman wife enjoyed greater movement outside the house, which allowed her to enjoy certain freedoms and a status inaccessible to unmarried girls and women; still, her physical presence within public contexts and spaces were ideologically (and sometimes physically) controlled. She was expected to embody the ideal of *pudicitia* (modesty) and thus follow an unwritten social code of conduct involving her appearance and behavior. The similarities in Greek and Roman representations of a bride's beauty and modesty attest to a shared cultural ideology that espoused marriage for the purposes of procreation and maintaining male dominance.

A bride's beauty and fertility were also represented through references to nature, including fruits and flowers. Sappho (105 a) compares the bride to an apple and in another, clearly sexual, metaphor, to a hyacinth trampled underfoot (105 c). In Theocritus's *Epithalamium for Helen and Menelaus* (*Idyll* 18), hyacinths are woven into the hair of the bridal entourage, and Helen is likened to a cypress tree and Thessalian horse (29–31). Such comparisons symbolize the bride's desirability and "ripeness," anticipating her wedding-night "deflowering."[33] Untamed sexuality required "domestication" through the ritual of marriage and the fulfillment of gender expectations.[34] Within patriarchal societies, a woman's fertility, i.e., her ability to produce legitimate, or illegitimate children as the case may be, was recognized as a powerful force in either confirming or disrupting gendered norms and political structures, and thus, from the male perspective, required formal and informal regulation through laws and cultural expectations, both reinforced through visual and literary representations. The epithalamium translated male fears about a woman's biological potential into a cultural ideology that promoted marriage as a mediating force and the vehicle for producing legitimate children.

Since Greek and Roman wives functioned as transferors of citizenship,[35] procreation within marriage assured the state's viability; therefore, a bride's fertility (manifest through her idealized beauty) was invested with significant cultural value. Images of ceremonial decorations or wedding rituals appearing in epithalamia were themselves imbued with meaning, requiring interpretation by both spectators of the real event and readers of text.[36] The bride's veil, processional torches, and household items (e.g., baskets and spindles) were emblematic of engendered marital ideals involving expected conduct and duties, such as chastity (veil), tending to the hearth (torches), and wool-working (spindle).[37] The repetition of such iconography created dominant meanings that were easily "translatable" by onlookers and readers. Showering the couple with fruit, flowers, or nuts (e.g., Semonides 187 PMG; Catullus 61.119–125), or poetic invocations of Hymenaeus, were also reproduced in the epithalamium, symbolizing marriage's pragmatic purpose, which was reinforced by the poem's conventional closing prayer for the swift arrival of children.

Roman authors frequently adapted the literary conventions of the epithalamium to suit their individual purposes or contexts. However, Catullus, in his poem (61) celebrating the real-life marriage of Junia and Manlius Torquatus, likens the bride's beauty to a hyacinth; unlike Sappho's flower, which grows wild in the mountains and is trampled by shepherds, here it is cultivated and protected within a wealthy man's elegant, cultivated garden (61.88–90). The revised metaphor echoes Plautus's comparison between freeborn brides and fenced-off land (*Curculio* 33–38, noted above), and aptly reflects Junia's aristocratic status. Scholarly analysis of the poem has revealed how Catullus's adaptations of conventional comparisons challenge the Roman ideal of conjugal parity (*par coniubium*) and examine the theme of marital unification by uncovering contradictions between the joining of two disparate entities, the bride and groom.[38]

The epithalamium underwent further development during the first century CE. In his poem celebrating the marriage of Stella and Violentilla, Statius utilizes his portrayal of Violentilla and images of her beauty to refocus attention on the groom. By merging conventional epithalamic images of beauty with those of erotic elegy, Statius enhances Stella's status as an elegiac poet.[39] Violentilla's literary persona as Stella's elegiac mistress (*domina*) is playfully interwoven throughout the poem. On the one hand, she appears as the idealized chaste and modest bride with fair complexion (1.2.110–111), downcast eyes, and blushing face (1.2.12); elsewhere, she becomes the conventional domina of elegy, with pale skin and snow-white arms (23), capable of alluring mythological gods away from their female consorts and rendering her lover/groom powerless (77). Statius's epithalamium is a significant departure from earlier Greek and Roman examples; his innovative reworking of the idealized beauty associated with two feminine binaries, the traditional (epithalamic) nupta and the (elegiac) domina, reflect tradition and reality.[40] Roman imperial women like Violentilla enjoyed economic and marital independence; her representation simultaneously conforms to long-standing gender norms and marital ideals, but reflects her present-day political context. The emperor Domitian's moral reforms restored those of Augustus and reinvigorated traditional idealizations of marital chastity and modesty. Statius's adaptation of the epithalamium reflects literary and political self-consciousness. By relocating attention from the bride to the groom, he enhances Stella's prominence as a poet; but he also affirms the imperial ideology of Domitianic Rome and, in so doing, asserts his own literary authority and status.

Statius's innovations influenced subsequent authors, who likewise adapted the epithalamium to fit their cultural context and authorial intent.[41] Of particular note are the epithalamia written by Claudian (late fourth–early fifth centuries CE, *Carm.* 9–14), which celebrate the wedding of the Roman emperor Honorius to his wife Maria, the daughter of Stilicho (Honorius's guard and military general of the western armies). Claudian employs the familiar epithalamic conventions; through new motifs and contemporary allusions, however, his representation of Honorius and Maria's idealized wedding symbolizes the necessary unification and assuagement required to ease existing tensions between the Roman East and West.[42] His epithalamia thus merge literary convention with political propaganda. In a similar way, Paulinus of Nola (fourth century) adapts the pagan epithalamium for communicating Christian ideals and content, creating a new version that contributed to the ongoing development of Christian literature.[43] Such adaptations over time illustrate how representations of marriage perpetuated long-standing gender ideals while addressing contemporary literary, cultural, and political interests.

PART TWO: MARRIED LIFE

Entering the house

The ceremonial rites and ideals associated with the wedding anticipated a wife's household responsibilities and expected conduct, including overseeing the management of the household (for example, child-rearing, housework, finances). A wife's lived experience was informed by her domestic environment, both in the architecture of the house and by her symbolic (and physical) position within it.[44] The inevitability of marriage for most girls meant that preparations for married life would have begun from early childhood, through instruction by her mother and other female members, and through observation of family roles, wedding ceremonies, and idealized visual representations depicted in art and on objects (for example, vase painting, Roman wall paintings).[45] Despite the training she received in her natal home, many sources represent the new wife as inexperienced, requiring "domestication" upon entering her new house. These sentiments certainly reflect the common age disparity between a husband and first-time bride,[46] but also reveal assumptions about gender hierarchy and the influence of a wife's conduct on her husband's status. "Training" encompassed instruction about the workings of the house and responsibilities related to its management, but was implicitly aimed at establishing a power dynamic that ensured her subordination and compliance—in the form of fidelity—toward her husband. It is likely, in fact, that husbands preferred a first-time wife precisely because her young age and marital inexperience may have facilitated her subordination or, in idealized terms, fidelity.[47] Accordingly, representations of inexperienced wives needing oversight from their paternalistic husbands aligned with the cultural values and gender ideals associated with both wives and husbands. Her reliance upon him as a "teacher" reinforced power dynamics both within the walls of the Greek *oikos* and Roman *domus*, and in the public sphere, whether she was physically there or not.[48]

Even if a wife enjoyed some freedom in public, as in the case of Roman women, ideologically a woman's place was in the home; it was in the house that she received her "training" as a girl and as a wife. An especially notable example comes from the Greek Archaic poet Hesiod whose didactic poem, the *Works and Days* offers practical instruction on farm management and moralizing advice on the value and necessity of hard work. Marriage provides a wife, and the resulting division of labor between the husband's agricultural tasks outside and a wife's household duties inside, ensure the estate's economic success. To this end, Hesiod recommends "bringing a wife home," at age thirty (695–697) and choosing an eighteen-year-old "virgin" (*parthenos*) in order to teach her "good habits" (698–699). He also advises taking time to search carefully for a suitable wife so that the marriage does not become a source of derision among neighbors: "For a man possesses nothing better than a wife, if she is good; but nothing worse, if she is a bad wife" (701–705). Hesiod's comments reflect a more general misogynistic attitude,[49] but his correlation between the recommended age of a bride (and her "trainability") and the symbolic role of marriage in the community is especially striking. Concern for selecting a young, and thus compliant, "trainable" wife reflects gendered ideals: the wife's fulfillment of expected marital duties and conduct had a bearing on her husband's reputation as head of the household-family (*oikos*) and guardian (*kyrios*).[50] This notion would attain full expression for Romans who recognized—and exploited—the idealized wife's symbolic potential through her display in carefully controlled public contexts.[51] The theme of marital pedagogy is intimately connected with power and marital ideals: the perceived need to train and control a new wife—and a husband's claims about doing so successfully—corresponds to long-standing assumptions about the "untamed" nature of girls and their innate lack of self-control (*sophrosyne*).

The necessity of "training" a new wife is reflected in another didactic text from the second century CE, which recontextualizes Hesiod's marital pedagogy. In his treatise, *Regimen for Young Girls*, the Greek physician Rufus of Ephesus provides instruction on gynecological healthcare for virgins (i.e., young girls of marriageable age, twelve to eighteen years old); although Rufus focuses on future brides, and not wives, his work offers a comparable parallel from a medical perspective. Using Hesiod's *Works and Days* to support his argument, Rufus explains that, contrary to contemporary social practice, eighteen was the ideal age for girls to marry. If this age seems too late in light of current practices, he notes, they should recall Hesiod's context, when "females toiled equally with males," and thus would appreciate the validity of his age recommendation.[52] The intervening eight centuries between the two authors indicates a continuity, and persistent endurance, of these cultural expectations even while evidence suggests that social practices had changed. The passage reveals Rufus's careful negotiation in mediating an emerging conflict between medical interests and ongoing customs that pressured girls to marry at a young age.[53]

While Hesiod's age recommendation focused on a wife's potential trainability, Rufus appropriates this advice to fulfill his own literary purpose, which outlines a diet and exercise regimen that will prepare a girl for marriage and control her desires while her body became sexually mature enough for marriage. Hesiod's original agricultural context is also exploited, despite the cosmopolitan context of imperial Rome: Rufus links the physical activity of Hesiod's wives with his own medical recommendation for exercise in order to prepare a girl's body for childbearing or for controlling sexual desire.[54] Rufus's exploitation of Hesiod "as an authorizing figure" exhibits a continuation of male attempts to subordinate women and control their bodies through the institution of marriage and the expected roles of brides and wives.[55]

Good health is represented as a significant influence on a wife's ability to carry out her duties, both physically, sexually, and morally. Rufus's diet and exercise regimen for the future bride was precipitated by Xenophon's *Treatise on Estate Management* (*Oikonomikos*, fourth century), a Socratic dialogue in which the main character Isomachos describes the inexperience of his fifteen-year-old-wife, who required initial instruction in the organization and management of the estate. Part of this "education" concerns her health: certain household tasks such as kneading dough and folding clothes, provide physical exercise that in turn would promote a healthy appetite and enhance her complexion (10.11–12). Notably, Isomachos characterizes the outcome of her housework in sexual terms: her improved appearance will increase her attractiveness and desirability. This domestic power dynamic is also evident in Isomachos's explication of a division of labor based on gender and space: outdoor (agricultural) work belongs to the husband and indoor work falls to the wife (7.21). Isomachos's pedagogical objective in teaching his wife how to manage the house is to facilitate his own leisure time outside of it (6.17). The husband's paternalistic and authoritative self-positioning is largely represented through his wife's depiction as inexperienced and compliant.

While Xenophon's advice is transmitted through the voice of Isomachos and the Socratic dialogue, it asserts his own masculine identity. A parallel can be found with the first-century Roman author Pliny the Younger, who uses letters to (and about) his young wife Calpurnia for the purposes of self-fashioning. A letter to her grandfather, for example, attributes her recent miscarriage to youth and inexperience: she did not realize she was pregnant and thus did not properly attend to her health (*Epistle* 8.1). Her "mistake" threatened her health (and frustrated Pliny's ongoing efforts to father a child and heir), but he finds comfort in her "proven fertility." Taken together, representations of marital pedagogy expose recurring ideas that idealized the young, inexperienced wife as a receptacle for the husband's knowledge and guidance; moreover, they suggest how written discourse might publicize an author's own idealized status as husband by reproducing images that highlight his wife's compliance, inexperience, and her subordinate position with the physical and symbolic boundaries of the house.[56]

Living in the house

Among the many household duties which Xenophon assigns to his wife, textile production is prominent. Although slaves were responsible for much of the labor, she was required to oversee the production of clothing, from the sorting of the wool, to its spinning and weaving, distinctly indoor tasks (*Oec.* 7.35–36). The estate, its farm and physical structure, Xenophon notes, are conducive to textile production as the place which facilitates "making clothing from wool" (7.21). Xenophon's comments reflect more than a simple economic interest or social practice. Textile production is a prominent theme in literary and non-literary sources, where it is generally associated with positive images of women (see, for example, Figure 8.3).[57] Weaving in particular was traditionally associated with the responsibilities of a wife; Hesiod, for example, advises the best days of the month for a woman to set up her loom (*W&D* 779–780). In Homer's *Iliad*, Andromache is the last to learn of her husband's death and when the discovery scene unfolds, we find her in one of the innermost rooms of the palace, completely oblivious and entirely focused on her weaving. The representation of Andromache's industrious activity within the inner walls of the palace reflects Greek social values concerning gender and domestic space, and symbolizes her modesty and chastity. Yet the image also expresses spousal fidelity and devotion, manifest by her frantic departure from the loom in search of news and her subsequent lamentations upon hearing of Hector's death (*Iliad* 440–41).

Similarly, in the *Odyssey* Helen appears sitting next to her husband at home, restored to him after her adventure, a basket of wool and spindle by her side (4.120–135). Perhaps most iconographic among the Homeric sisterhood is Penelope, who utilizes weaving as a tactic to put off her suitors; despite the cunningness associated with her textile production, the image contributed to Penelope's paradigmatic status within Greco-Roman tradition as the archetypal faithful wife. She, like other wives engaged in wool-working, embodied *sophrosyne*, an idealization that could encompass various feminine virtues such as chastity, silence, or moral restraint.[58] Although the term "*sophrosyne*" is not applied to the Homeric Andromache or Penelope, by the fifth century it was regularly used to define the ideal wife by virtue of her chastity and fidelity. In Euripides, Andromache defines her reputation vis-à-vis *sophrosyne*, explaining that her esteemed reputation among the Greeks was due to her remaining in the house (despite wanting otherwise) (*Trojan Women*, 643–658) and because she put aside her own jealousy about Hector's extramarital affairs to nurse his children born out of wedlock (*Andromache* 205–227).[59] Spinning and weaving demanded time and effort, and were a manifestation of a wife's industriousness and domestic diligence. These productive activities required staying inside the home, thereby limiting opportunities for engaging in non-productive (i.e., consumptive) activities or illicit interactions outside of it.

FIGURE 8.3 Woman spinning, detail from an Attic white-ground oinochoe, Byrgos Painter, *c.* 490 BCE. British Museum. Wikimedia Commons.

The symbolic role of textile production was also a topos in Roman representations of marriage, as funerary inscriptions and monuments attest. Among the conventional ideals honoring deceased wives on epitaphs (modesty, chastity, frugality), "wool-working" appears frequently. A well-known funeral monument dedicated to Claudia by her husband, for example, describes how she loved her husband, bore two sons, was a pleasant conversationalist, and graceful. The inscription concludes simply: "She managed the house and worked wool" (CIL 6.14346, second century BCE).[60] Thus, references to *lanifica* (wool-worker) or *lanam fecit* (she made wool) became coded funerary language that idealized a wife's industry and, by association, her fidelity.[61] The virtue of wool-working also characterized the legendary women of Rome's history. Livy's (first century BCE) "Rape of Lucretia" (*From the Founding of the City*, 1.57–60) illustrates how representations of women engaged in textile work offered opportunities for idealizing a wife and, in turn, could serve additional literary purposes. Livy's story is set in Rome's early history (sixth century BCE) during the last king's reign. A hyper-masculine competition between the king's sons and a respectable Roman military officer, Collatinus, who each claim his own wife as the most virtuous, ends with a test: the men make surprise visits to each of their houses late at night. While the royal wives are found "surrounded by luxury," eating and drinking with friends, Collatinus's wife Lucretia is discovered in the house's atrium, spinning wool by lamplight. She wins the contest, but her beauty and industriousness inspire the king's son to return to her house, where he then "conquers" Lucretia's "steadfast chastity." Her husband and father absolve Lucretia of her guilt, but, driven by thoughts of her posthumous reputation, she commits suicide in an effort to preserve her, and her family's, name.

On the one hand, Livy's Lucretia resembles Penelope and Andromache: her diligence at the loom long into the night proves her modesty (*pudicitia*). However, Lucretia works in the *atrium*, a formal reception area open to visitors. Her location reflects the difference between Greek and Roman housing and spatial boundaries, but it also symbolically links her to the idealized Roman household, since the atrium was used for displaying the family's ancestral funeral masks (*imagines*) and performing daily offerings to the household gods, both a sign of religious devotion.[62] Livy's positioning of Lucretia's wool-working in the atrium symbolically connects her chastity with the idealized domestic space. When she, and her space, are subsequently penetrated by Sextus Tarquinius, the violation sets in motion a series of events that ultimately lead to the king's dethronement and the establishment of the Roman Republic.

The story of Lucretia must be read against the larger cultural and political backdrop; Livy's appropriation of the wool-working motif contributes to Lucretia's representation as the ideal Roman wife, since it implicitly signals her fidelity and devotion. Within the larger context, Lucretia's textile production and self-sacrificing death embody the type of woman whom Augustus's moral reforms and marriage legislation attempted to fashion.[63] The laws he instituted rewarded those who produced children and established illicit sexual acts (such as adultery) a public state concern rather than a private family matter. The idealized, virtuous wife who diligently attended her loom thus reflected imperial ideology.[64] According to Suetonius (*Life of Augustus* 74), Augustus claims to have worn only wool clothes produced by the women of his household, including his wife Livia; given the common practice among elite Romans of sourcing ready-made clothes from external producers outside the house, Augustus's claim appears highly unlikely in reality; rather, it reflects one small aspect of a larger propaganda program that aimed at restoring traditional Roman social practices through engendered ideology and within the institution of marriage. Distinction between knowledge of wool-working and actual practice had long ago been acknowledged by Xenophon, who noted that elite households bought ready-made clothes as a matter of convenience, even though the household's women had knowledge of, and experience in, textile production (*Memorabilia* 2.7.6). Thus, even by the time of Xenophon's writing, wool-working had become obsolete for elite women but was vigorously maintained as a literary trope.

Representations of idealized wives performing household tasks symbolized, in profoundly spatial ways, expected gender roles and virtues: indoor versus outside, private versus public, housework versus agriculture/politics.[65] The story of Lucretia functions as an important narrative transition in Livy's history, marking Rome's shift from monarchy to republic; the details of his version (for example, time, location), however, address broader thematic and literary concerns. Livy's account links uncontrolled female sexuality with potential moral and political decline; as a narrative catalyst, Lucretia's rape and sacrificial suicide free Rome from monarchical oppression; her story thematically reinforced the connection between traditional (feminine) virtue and political stability—as did the ideology and moral reforms of the Augustan principacy following the turbulent collapse of the Roman Republic.[66]

Domestic diligence manifested through wool-working or household tasks signaled a wife's diligence and devotion to husband and home; it was through her conduct that she proved her virtue. Lucretia's death represents the ultimate act of spousal fidelity. The topos of sacrifice occurs in many literary sources that address gender roles and ideals. A wife's willingness to undertake risks—or even death—on behalf of her husband confirmed the established gender hierarchy within marriage.[67] Euripides' *Alcestis* perhaps best illustrates this highest form of spousal fidelity (see Figure 8.4); her husband, King Admetus of Thessaly, was destined to die for offending the gods but convinced Apollo that he be allowed to find a replacement. Admetus's mother and father refuse, although Admetus cites their advanced age as a rational basis for compliance.[68] Only his wife Alcestis proves willing. As Alcestis dies in his arms, Admetus proclaims her the "best of all wives," and his subsequent grief signals his affection; and yet his conjugal love appears to result directly out of her martyrdom. Admetus's willingness to let his wife die in his stead raises questions about the inherent, perceived values of gender roles and the value of a wife's life versus that of a husband. Alcestis's self-sacrificing action made her a quintessential model of spousal fidelity;[69] she is later used as a measure of comparison, as, for example, for Callicratia, who proclaims herself a "new Alcestis," after sacrificing her life for Zeno, her husband, an act that earned her reverence from "all men" (*Greek Anthology* 7.691). Other later references occur, appropriately enough, on funerary epitaphs, which invoke Alcestis as the pinnacle of marital fidelity.[70]

In addition to these Greek women, Romans also developed their own non-mythological exempla to represent marital fidelity. Notably, these idealized women are historical, such as Arria, whose self-sacrificing fidelity had become famous by the late first century CE and is recorded by several authors.[71] When her philosopher husband, Paetus, could not summon the courage to commit suicide (on order of the emperor Claudius, 42 CE), she is said to have grabbed the dagger from his hands, stabbed herself and returned it, uttering the famous last words, "It doesn't hurt, Paetus!" (see Figure 8.5). Her courage and, most of all, her unwillingness to live without her husband, earned her the reputation as a more contemporary paradigm of marital fidelity.

The longest version of Arria's story appears in a letter by Pliny the Younger (*Epistle* 3.16) where he expands her story to argue that the least familiar anecdotes are often the ones most worthy of being recorded. While others had specifically celebrated Arria's final act and last words, Pliny's focus lies in other anecdotes related first-hand by Arria's granddaughter, Fannia, ones that are "far less known but no less significant" (2). These accounts serve to enhance her marital fidelity, normally exemplified by her suicide; for example, she insists on accompanying her husband back to Rome following his arrest in Dalmatia; when refused, she hires a small fishing boat to follow him. The anecdote

FIGURE 8.4 *Admetus and Alcestis*, Roman painting, first century CE. Pompeii, Naples National Archaeological Museum. Wikimedia Commons.

echoes a common topos of marital devotion, that is, wives following their husbands into battle or exile. Additionally, while her husband was gravely ill, Arria concealed their son's death, arranging the funeral and hiding her own grief through feigned smiles—all in an effort to spare him discomfort or anxiety. Pliny implies that these mundane acts are in fact more self-sacrificing than her famous suicide since they did not offer the promise of posthumous fame.

FIGURE 8.5 *Arria and Paetus*, Pierre Lepautre (1659–1744). Louvre. Wikimedia Commons.

Pliny's epistolary representation of the legendary Arria confirms the cultural value attached to wifely fidelity. His historical account within the epistolary context, however, indicates authorial self-fashioning.[72] Pliny's emphasis on—and publication of—the unfamiliar aspects of Arria's history that he acquired first-hand, enhances his own status as an authoritative source that supplements the already existing historical record; through his portrayal of Arria, Pliny presents himself as a historian, a thematic strain that is woven throughout the collection. His "biography" of Arria solidifies her as an exemplum *par excellence* of spousal fidelity and fulfills the epistolary purpose implied by the letter's opening, where he introduces Arria as a wife who, "at her husband's death gave not just comfort, but an example" (*exemplum* 1).[73] In serving as a model of courage for her husband, Arria also becomes a model of spousal fidelity. Her virtue, moreover, is echoed by Calpurnia, whose spousal fidelity is portrayed in terms of her avid interest in Pliny's literary and litigation activities, a (self-)representation that enhances his own status as author and husband.[74]

Additional examples from the Roman period reveal the role of exile and proscription as an impetus for a wife's spousal fidelity. In many cases, these images also contribute to the author's larger thematic or literary goals. Other sources narrate stories involving historical wives whose husbands had been proscribed following Caesar's assassination in 44 BCE. Valerius Maximus (first century CE) recounts how Turia bravely concealed her husband in the bedroom rafters, a "singular loyalty" (*singularique fide*) that ensured Lucretius avoided exile and remained "safe in his wife's arms" (*Memorable Doings and Sayings* 6.7.2). Sulpicia exhibited similar fidelity when she disguised herself as a slave and secretly followed her exiled husband to Sicily against his wishes (6.7.3). In Appian's history (second century CE), we find a passage containing a sequence of devoted wives; for instance, Lentulus's wife resolutely follows him into exile even after he refused her, while Antius's wife hides him in a bag and hires porters to transport him to the nearest harbor (*Roman History* 39–40). A pattern emerges: these wives either help their husbands escape proscribed death through concealment or secure their well-being by stealthily following them into (self-imposed) exile. Notably, these women attained fame for acting outside traditional gender expectations, through their atypical—even extreme—courage, self-initiative, or altruism. In all cases, moreover, the wives' devotion ensures their husbands' comfort and good health during the ordeal. The representation of a wife who undertake risks, or even death, on her husband's behalf reinforces ideals about marriage; in reality, however, a husband's disgraced status and economic ruin could leave his wife vulnerable, financially and socially: a glorious, memorable suicide that earned her legendary fame may have seemed preferable. In many cases, it is masculine identity that is reified by the representation of a wife's self-sacrificing fidelity. Conspicuously, Appian's devoted wives are nameless: their actions, not their personalities, were thematically important to his history. As symbolic ideals, they serve as a literary device to underscore the ramifications of political turmoil that leads to divided loyalties—and civil war.[75] Their sacrificial acts reaffirm the value of marriage (and the family) as a stabilizing force, providing models of allegiance amidst extreme political unrest.

For most Greek and Roman wives, everyday life involved mundane tasks that never won them posthumous fame or literary immortality. Expectations about their roles both inside and outside the house demanded certain responsibilities that maintained firm gender boundaries between "women's work" and "men's work." Positive representations reinforce this hierarchy through images that are often spatially symbolic, such as the dutiful wife busy at her loom inside the house or cleverly concealing her husband at her own risk. Her conduct thus became identified with virtues that could be used to assert her husband's status in the public context from which she was symbolically, and even physically, excluded.

CONCLUSION: DEATH AND THE IDEAL MARRIAGE

Death and marriage were ideologically linked and aligned with a cultural belief that one should be present for his or her spouse's final breath.[76] Both death and marriage were viewed as significant points on one's life timeline and thus celebrated by public, standardized rituals that acknowledged status transformations (for example, bride to wife, wife to widow).⁷⁷ Like weddings, funerals also overlapped with written discourse, as in epitaphs, consolation letters, and epicedia; these funerary texts, like epithalamia, merged the real with the ideal, social practice with literary conventions.

In occupying public space, funeral monuments represented proof of a spouse's devotion and the harmony of their marriage; a consciousness of the potential passerby no doubt influenced the development of conventions for funerary inscriptions as well as the construction of elaborate sarcophagi. Themes of temporality and "replacement" appear on epitaphs honoring deceased wives, as explained above in the case of unmarried virgins. Sometimes, it is the deceased wife who herself speaks from the grave in the present tense, as with Baucis, who laments the torches once used in her wedding-day procession, and now carried by her father-in-law in her funeral (*Greek Anthology* 7.712). Similarly, the same virtues that idealize the bride in the epithalamium (for example, chastity, modesty, and beauty) appear as ideological language in written funerary discourses and remain fairly consistent, even when the cultural contexts might change. For instance, a second- to third-century CE epigram honoring Marcia Helike praises her beauty in conventional terms, comparing her to Aphrodite; yet, Marcia was a Christian and is thus also celebrated for her devotion to "God's laws." Such intersectionality between pagan and Christian attests to the syncretic, enduring role of convention and idealization in representations of marriage.

The merging of lived reality with idealization is particularly noteworthy in the *Laudatio Turiae* (Dessau, ILS 8393), an epitaph honoring Turia and erected by her husband in the late first century BCE (see Figure 8.6).⁷⁸ Spousal fidelity emerges as a particularly prominent theme, both as an idealized virtue extolled by her husband and, reciprocally,

FIGURE 8.6 *Laudatio Turiae*, marble, late first century BCE. Epigraphic Museum of the Baths of Diocletian, Rome. Wikimedia Commons.

proof of his devotion to her. Specific details highlight evidence of Turia's loyalty, for example, to her parents, whose deaths she avenged (7). It is her marital fidelity to her husband, however, that justifies the exceptionally long inscription. During the political turmoil leading up to her husband's eventual exile (49 BCE), Turia prepared him a hiding place (4) and defended their house during an attempted break-in (9a). While she did not follow him into exile, like other wives, she secretly sent money and resources by boldly deceiving her husband's watchful adversaries (2a). The topoi of risk, concealment, and deception that appear in literary contexts, such as those discussed above, reappear here in the funerary inscriptional context; moreover, it was through her "courageous" efforts back in Rome that Turia secured her husband's recall (6a). The specific details of Turia's self-sacrificing acts merge real with ideal, proving her embodiment of the idealized virtues ascribed to her elsewhere in the inscription (for example, loyalty, wool-working, and modesty; 30). Turia's fidelity was "reciprocated" by her husband, but not only through the funerary monument: although she was unable to bear children he refused to divorce her (41) and they remained married for forty years "in harmony" (27).

A marriage's longevity was one proof of its "success" and was reinforced by the ideal of conjugal accord, which was also celebrated in epitaphs. The wife–husband relationship was inherently asymmetrical, and exactly what constituted "harmony" was certainly individual for each relationship. As an ideal, a marriage's perceived harmony was open to public scrutiny, and what really went on in a marriage "behind closed doors" could not always be controlled by the publication of idealized representations. Correspondence between Cicero and Atticus, for example, illustrates the real-life discord that might occur in a marriage, here between Quintus and Pomponia, Cicero's brother and Atticus's sister. Their letters reveal attempts by Cicero and Atticus to mediate and preserve the complex interfamilial dynamics,[79] but clearly Quintus and Pomponia did not enjoy a harmonious union. Such dissonance may have resulted from the reduced age gap between husband and wife, whereby the traditional engendered power dynamic existing between a very young wife and her older husband was not present.[80]

Disharmony might imply a husband's inability to control the stability and cohesion of his household, and consequent susceptibility to derision or criticism by his peers, as we saw with Hesiod. Similarly, a wife's potential "negative power" in adversely affecting her husband's status (and her own reputation), was often translated into misogynistic or skeptical sentiments. In Aeschylus's *Seven Against Thebes* (fifth century), King Eteocles rants against the city's married women who had attempted to impede preparations for war, reminding them that public space was the domain of men, and women belonged inside the house avoiding trouble (181–202). A similar idea is reiterated by Cato who denounces the Roman women who had taken to Rome's public spaces in demonstration against the Oppian Law, which had restricted their use of luxury items (Livy, *History of Rome* 34.1). Cato decries the loss of domestic authority by husbands over their wives, warning that, if not checked, such "untamed" amoral women will begin meddling in the Forum, inserting themselves into political affairs. The articulation of gender roles and ideals through spatial distinctions reveals how marriage might disrupt imagined boundary lines between public and private, domestic and political.[81] Recurring male invective against women who transgressed these spatial and symbolic borders reveals deep-seated anxieties about how a wife's conduct might dislocate the public image of marital accord and, in turn, adversely affect her, and her husband's, reputation.[82] When, for example, Julius Caesar (praetor and Pontifex Maximus, 61 BCE) learned that Clodius had snuck into his house while his wife Pompeia was hosting a women's-only ritual (the *Bona Dea*), he immediately divorced her.[83] The right to host the rites was given only to the wife of a leading magistrate (like praetor), and constituted a significant honor for her and the family. Pompeia's compromising situation and her (presumed) culpability made her status as "Caesar's wife" a political liability. Thus, clearly, a woman's symbolic presence in public as "wife" invested her with the capability of influencing her husband's image. Similarly, in a letter to Quintilianus, Pliny the Younger offers his less affluent friend the funds to purchase clothing and other accoutrements for his daughter, who was engaged to "the very distinguished Nonius Celer," who required "a certain elegance."[84] Pliny delicately praises the bride's excellent upbringing but suggests his donation will enhance her inner worth through external symbols (i.e., clothing and jewelry). These visible manifestations will appropriately reflect her future husband's status—and political ambitions. This need to balance the dichotomy between inner (virtue) and outer (appearance) reflects also the concern for conjugal harmony, which was best achieved by making sure the bride and groom were a suitably "matched" pair (*par coniugium*), if not in actual economic or class terms, then at least in appearances.

The equality of a match might thus encourage accord between husband and wife. This notion found its fullest expression in Roman literary and material sources. "Conjugal harmony," or *concordia*, is listed among other canonical virtues on funerary epitaphs, while various literary representations, by way of anecdote, narrative, or imagery, provided examples of the kinds of (asymmetrical) interactions that created or illustrated marital accord.[85] Personified Concordia, moreover, was frequently represented as the deity overseeing Roman weddings and, thus too, the whole course of the marriage; consequently, she often appears in epithalamia and funerary discourses. In fact, concordia and spousal fidelity often go hand-in-hand; we see this in the *epicedion* to Abascantus on the death of his wife Priscilla,[86] where Statius combines idealized imagery and personalized details to represent the conjugal fidelity and harmony shared and reciprocated by each. At the time of the poem's composition, Abascantus was serving in the imperial court as secretary *ab epistulis*, but it appears his job may have been in jeopardy (indeed, he was subsequently dismissed). Statius deftly extends the spousal fidelity and accord demonstrated within the private space of marriage to the public realm.[87] He transfers the traditional marital ideals ascribed to Abascantus's spousal persona to his political one, a skillful literary maneuver designed to prove Abascantus's devotion to the emperor Domitian and thus revalidate his position within the imperial court. Statius's poem illustrates how the representation of marital ideals within a funerary context could be exploited for expressing meanings that extended well beyond the bonds of marriage.

The appropriation of concordia for ideological, political purposes is illustrated by the *dextrarum iunctio*, an image depicting a married couple holding hands, commonly appearing on funerary monuments to symbolize conjugal harmony (see Figure 8.7).[88] This visual image was eventually adopted for political purposes, not unlike the virtue of woolworking. For example, during the period of the Antonines in the second century CE, the *dextrarum iunctio* was reinvested with new meaning through a different discourse: coin issues from the period use the image to communicate marital harmony, and thus the dynasty's stability, but could also be decoded as a political message about the harmonious governance of the newly instituted joint ruler-ship, i.e., the *Concordia Augustorum* (see Figure 8.8).[89] In addition, such images of concordia communicated the emperor's cooperation with the Senate, if only on a symbolic level.[90] Thus, while Roman concordia (and its iconography) represented the pinnacle of marital success on the level of the private citizen, it attained new ideological value at the level of the emperor.

FIGURE 8.7 Scene of a *dextrarum iunctio, Sarcophagus of the Brothers, c.* 250 CE. Naples National Archaeological Museum. Wikimedia Commons.

FIGURE 8.8 Sestertius showing betrothal of Marcus Aurelius to Faustina the Younger, 139 CE.

Greek and Roman marriage was a state institution;[91] as the vehicle for legitimate procreation, it also reinforced engendered standards of behavior for husbands and wives through public performative or written contexts. While ceremonies did not legalize marriages,[92] they proved the legitimacy of the (sexual) union (and its future children) through the enactment of established rituals involving communal participation.[93] Genuine affection naturally existed between some husbands and wives, however, literary sources transmit ideals rather than realities. In general, Greek and Roman representations of marriage emphasize the gender hierarchy between wife and husband and utilize coded images to reaffirm heteronormative behavior. The transference of ritualized, ephemeral practices related to marriage (like weddings or deaths) into written discourses helped perpetuate traditional cultural values and, in many cases, generated additional meanings with profound political and ideological implications.

NOTES

INTRODUCTION

1. This volume would not have been possible without the unfailing generosity of two great scholars, Claude Emmanuelle Centlivres Challet and Judith P. Hallett.
2. Austen 2008: 22, 60.
3. Recently Cavalier 1996; Hersch 2010a; Treggiari 1991; Vérilhac and Vial 1998.
4. Zeus bore Athena, while Hera bore Hephaestus.
5. See Cantarella in this volume.
6. At the time of writing, a lawsuit concerning a wedding cake, "Masterpiece Cakeshop v. Colorado Civil Rights Commission," has reached the Supreme Court of the United States.
7. Generally speaking, for even some Romans chose "quiet" weddings (see Apuleius's *Apologia* 88).
8. For example, a coming-of-age ceremony, an entrance into a religious community, accession to high office (coronation, inauguration).
9. This ideal was not cherished by all or most Romans, as I noted above, for while the *univira* was celebrated, divorce and remarriage were not uncommon in the Roman world. However, a woman might be mocked for remarrying too often (see Juv. 6.224–226).
10. See Hersch (2010a), passim. Importantly, Greek and Roman families were virilocal.
11. Oakley and Sinos (1993), passim.
12. Although the beauty, lineage, or fine clothes of the groom are highlighted in literary depictions of the wedding.
13. In Greek and Roman mythology, the often miserable, wronged Hera and Juno wrong other women in turn, for both are frequently depicted in art and literature hunting down and punishing Zeus's and Jupiter's rape victims.
14. Conflicting standards for wifely behavior could exist in the selfsame text. See the discussion on Helen in Homer's *Odyssey*, below. Legendary Roman wives too were commemorated for meekness or temerity or both in the first book of Livy's *History*.
15. The lifetime unions of slaves, for example. See Treggiari (1991) and Hersch (2010).
16. Herodotus 2.53.
17. Nowhere more obviously than in Book Six, in which Hector visits his brother Paris and finds him with the married Helen; he then escapes the stench of adultery to head straight to his own wife and son.
18. The king and queen of Troy, Hecuba and Priam, seem happy together, but their marital relationship is given little space. She appears chiefly in the role of Hector's mother rather than wife to Priam.
19. Her agony most famously recounted in Euripides' *Troades* and *Andromache*.
20. She appears before her husband and his guest as both a comely, chaste, contented wife, surrounded by female chaperones who aid her in the matronly art of weaving; yet at the same time, she shames herself before the men, invoking her shameful liaison at the end of the two speeches she gives (*Od.* 4.138–146, 4.235–264).

21. For example, in Book 24 of the *Odyssey*, the miserable shades of famous Greek warriors in the underworld compare wives, noting Odysseus's felicity in having Penelope as a wife. (See Felson-Rubin 1994.)
22. *Od.* 1.13. Interestingly, Pandarus the Trojan wishes to get back to "country and wife and house" (*Il.* 5.213).
23. Odysseus and his human comrades were not alone in their sexual adventures; in both the *Iliad* and *Odyssey*, we learn that the gods too seek pleasures outside of marriage. But when one of those gods is a wife, punishment may follow, as we see in the tale Demodocus sings (*Od.* 8. 266–366) of Hephaistos's ingenious and very public capture of his beautiful wife Aphrodite with the war-god Ares *in flagrante delicto*.
24. See Gaca (2010, 2012, 2014, 2015) on sexual violence in epic, and Hallett in this volume.
25. Interestingly, while Agamemnon and Odysseus share beds with women they are not married to, we note that Agamemnon has sex with (presumably) unwilling slaves, while Odysseus accepts amorous invitations from free, independent, powerful women. And we note that while Agamemnon met a violent end, Odysseus returned home safely and lived happily ever after. It seems then that from these earliest glimmerings of Greek literature, our sympathies are being steered toward the man who remains in love with his wife.
26. Traditionally dated to 700 BCE.
27. Hes., *Works and Days*, 590–607.
28. See Lev Kenaan (2008) and in this volume.
29. Putting a stamp on a person's sexuality in antiquity is notoriously difficult, as ancient terms do not always coincide with modern ideas. See Campanile, Carlà-Uhink, and Facella 2017; Corbeill 2014; Foxhall 2013; Hubbard 2014; Loraux 1995; Masterson, Rabinowitz, and Robson 2015; Orrells 2015.
30. For example, poems 44 (for Hector and Andromache), 103–117 (these are shorter fragments quoted by later authors as exemplary epithalamic turns of phrase).
31. See Zeiner-Carmichael in this volume.
32. Notably explored by Rehm (1994).
33. Frg. 128c, 6–8.
34. See Dillon, Wasdin, and Zeiner-Carmichael in this volume.
35. We learn in the *Agamemnon* (1590ff) that adultery ran in the family. Aegisthus's father Thyestes dallied with Agamemnon's mother Aerope, so Agamemnon's father Atreus, in turn, killed two of Thyestes's sons, cooked them, and served them as a meal to their unwitting father, who ate their flesh. The curse continued as Aegisthus, Thyestes's one remaining son, slept with Atreus's son's wife Klytemnestra, and then both killed Agamemnon.
36. A non-Greek, a powerful witch, possessed of great intellect, a victim, a murderer.
37. Eur., *Med.* 231–254.
38. Eur., *Hippol.* 678–733.
39. Importantly, because marriage is certainly not her domain, Aphrodite notes that Hippolytus refuses sex *and* marriage.
40. *Lysis.* 530–538.
41. Treggiari 1991: 8–13.
42. Discussed in every chapter of this volume.
43. Ovid, *Fasti* 6.637–640. On the shrine of Concord, see Flory 1984.
44. At *Aen.* 3.475 Helenus hails Anchises as one worthy of being married to Venus, but we notice that she does not attend his funeral in Book 5.
45. It may be said that Aeneas is the "anti-Midas of relationships," for everyone he touches shrivels and dies: Creusa, Anchises, Dido, Turnus, and he provides little comfort as a

father when he tells his son Iulius to learn from him hard work, not good fortune (*Aen.* 12.595–596).
46. The deaths of all she held dear, followed by living as a slave to Pyrrhus, the hateful son of Achilles.
47. *Aeneid* 4.160–172. For example, Caldwell 2008; Heinze 1957; Hersch 2018; Monti 1981; Muecke 1983; Pöschl 1950; Quinn 1968; Spence 1999; Williams 1996.
48. *Aen.* 4.356–361.
49. In the first programmatic line of the *Aeneid* Vergil informs his readers *arma virumque cano*: he will sing both the *Odyssey* (*virum*: the man) and the *Iliad* (*arma*: weapons).
50. My speculation.
51. She promises she will not kill the hated Trojan refugees, and in return accepts that they have a name change and henceforth be Romans (*Aen.* 12.819–828).
52. Antiquity was divided (as it was over Helen's putative complicity in her abduction) over Rhea Silvia's culpability. At least Livy (1.4.1) says she was *compressa vi* (taken by force).
53. Hersch 2018: 5–8.
54. See Hersch 2010a.
55. Ovid, *Fasti* 2.139: *tu rapis, hic castas duce se iubet esse maritas*.
56. So hostile were the women's families to the unions that they all returned to fight Rome after the abduction.
57. Son or grandson of Tanaquil and L. Tarquinius Priscus; sources diverge.
58. She notably put his successor, Servius, on the throne.
59. Famously Livy 1.57–60 and Dionysius *AR* 4. 64–85. By the time of the reign of Nero her rape is lampooned in Petronius's *Satyrica* 9.
60. See Perry in this volume.
61. Dionysius *AR* 2.25; Plutarch, *Rom.* 22.3–4.
62. On Romulus's wife Hersilia and his possible children see the investigation of Wiseman (1983).
63. Accounts vary of Numa's marriage to the woodland goddess Egeria and possible children. See, for example, Livy 1.21, Dionysius *AR* 2.61–2, Ovid *Fasti* 3.154; 259–93; Plutarch *Numa* 4.
64. Livy 1.40.
65. Livy and Dionysius were writing under Augustus, and we saw how Ovid damned Romulus to praise Augustus, above.
66. See Boëls-Janssen 2005; Zipes 2012.
67. Children and sexes Plin., *HN* 7.57, mother of Gracchi Plut., *TG* 8.7. Snake story: Cic., *Div.* I.36, Val. Max. 4.6.1, Plin., *HN* 7.122, Plut., *TG* 1.2–3.
68. Pliny, *HN* 34.31.
69. See Mustakallio and Zeiner-Carmichael in this volume.
70. Hersch 2010b; Larsson Lovén 1998.
71. Dionysius *AR* 2.25.7; Plutarch *QR* 14, *Rom.* 35, *Numa* 25; Valerius Maximus *Mem.* 2.1.4; Aulus Gellius *NA* 4.3.1, claim that his was the first divorce (although the Twelve Tables had a provision for divorce, which makes this "first divorce" seem the stuff of legend).
72. Valerius Maximus, *Mem.* 6.3.9–12.
73. Plutarch *Caesar* 9–10.
74. As well as widows and freeborn youths: see Plautus, *Curc.* 1.33–8. See Plautus 2011; Fantham 1991.
75. Suetonius, *Galba* 22.
76. Tacitus, *Ann.* 15.37; Suetonius Nero 28, 29. See Hersch 2010a: 33–39.

77. Letter 3.16 (Arria).
78. Letters 3.11, 7.19 and 9.13 (Arria Younger and Fannia).
79. Tacitus, *Ger.* 19–20.
80. Petronius, *Sat.* 37.
81. The worship of Christ, Isis, and Mithras figure prominently.
82. Family portraits were already long a feature in funerary art of the Republic. See Davies 1985; Reekmans 1958 and Reinsberg 2006.
83. Hersch 2010a: 208–212.
84. The meaning of this sculptured marital handclasp has provoked considerable debate. A number of scholars have argued that this gesture, called the *dextrarum iunctio*, represents an act that was indispensable to—and indeed was the high point of—a Roman wedding: the point at which the couple could be considered legally married. Others disagree, citing the lack of literary evidence and calling the handclasp in art rather than a gesture of eternal marital concord. See Hersch 2010a: 199–212.
85. In fact C. Iulius Hermes is given here in the nominative rather than the expected dative.
86. Suggested by Dr. Centlivres Challet in personal correspondence, who adds, "the freedman who commemorates his friend decides to have his friend represented the way the deceased would have wanted it: like all other people, in the usual, popular pose of a man being a husband, having achieved domestic bliss. Indeed, nothing disproves the fact that the deceased was not married; his monied friend might have decided to represent him in the most expected pose of the day: with his wife. This would then not be an exception to the rule, but would on the contrary confirm all we understand about the importance of marriage, including in death, and the importance, for the deceased, of its commemoration."

CHAPTER 1

1. The title of the chapter is something of a misnomer, since courtship, at least in the common modern sense of the groom's wooing of a bride, was not especially common in the ancient world. Rather, the father or guardian of the bride would typically be responsible for selecting her husband and arranging the marriage.
2. Pollux, a third-century CE scholar, wrote a treatise on words, the *Onomasticon*, which provides many terms for different elements of the Greek wedding. A similar source for Latin terminology is Festus, a late second-century CE compiler of the works of the Augustan Verrius Flaccus.
3. Oakley and Sinos (1993) analyze wedding imagery on Greek vases; Hersch (2010a) contains some images of Roman wedding iconography.
4. Morales (2004) provides a nuanced treatment of sexuality in Achilles Tatius. Harper (2013) also uses the novels as background for marriage in late antiquity.
5. See Hallett in this volume.
6. Athenian women were veiled and most often visible to those outside their family at religious festivals. Protagonists in the novels by Chariton and Xenophon of Ephesus encounter each other at religious festivals; elsewhere in *Leucippe and Clitophon*, a suitor attempts to abduct Leucippe based on the reputation of her beauty alone.
7. Importantly, scholars can find no description of the dress of an unmarried, adult woman in Roman society (Sebesta 1994: 50; Hersch 2010a: 62).
8. Hes. (*Theog.* 600–612) presents marriage as a necessary evil: women are a drain on resources but required to produce heirs. For philosophical discussions of marriage, see Musonius Rufus fr. 12 and 13.

9. Noy (1990) argues that matchmakers were more commonly used in Greece than in Rome.
10. See Rudd 1981, along with the chapter by Hallett in this volume.
11. Ulpian (*D.* 23.1.12) claims that the Roman bride could dissent only if the groom was shameful or unworthy.
12. See *D.* 23.1.13 and 23.2.21–22.
13. Perry, in this volume, treats in detail the legal restrictions on partners.
14. [Aristotle], *A.P.* 26.3; Plut., *Per.* 37.2–4. See Ogden 1996: 59–69, for a discussion of the evidence.
15. See below and Miles 1995: 179–219, on the ideological importance of the myth of the Sabine women.
16. For Greek slave families, see Golden 2011; for Rome, see Hersch 2010a: 29–33; Rawson 1974; and Treggiari 1981. The law code of Gortyn does seem to regulate legitimate marriages between slaves. Latin funerary inscriptions attest that those not able to marry legally might still refer to each other as husband and wife.
17. Similar joke at Mart., *Ep.* 8.12. For a cynical expression of the dowry as a means of purchasing a husband, see the speech of Medea at Eur., *Med.* 230–251. Related remarks occur in Roman comedy. See, for example, Plautus, *Asin.* 87.
18. Evans Grubbs 2002: 83–87; and Treggiari 1991: 60–80.
19. Evans Grubbs 2010: 92–94.
20. An older bride marries young man in Plutarch's *Amatorius*, sparking intense debate.
21. In Xenophon, *Oec.* 7.5, Ischomachus reports that his bride was fourteen years old when they married. For more on the couples' ages, see Vérilhac and Vial 1998: 214–218.
22. See Shaw (1987) and Scheidel (2007) on the age of marriage as recorded on tombstones.
23. Aristotle, *Pol.* 7.1335a warns against marrying too young and suggests that women should marry at eighteen and men at thirty-seven. See Caldwell 2015: 94–104, for discussion of medical writers.
24. Vérilhac and Vial (1998: 93–95) show that marriage between half-siblings who share a father was infrequent, as was marriage between uncles and nieces. Most Greeks did not permit marriage between siblings who shared a mother, although it did occur in Sparta. See Leduc 1992: 254.
25. Leduc 1992: 282–285, Patterson 1998: 91–106.
26. See Ager (2005) on Ptolemaic sibling marriages, and Strong (2005) on Roman tolerance of sibling marriage among non-elites in the province of Egypt.
27. The *Odyssey*'s Penelope illustrates virtuous fidelity in refusing to choose a new husband, primarily because Odysseus eventually returns home. In fact, remarriage was normal and non-stigmatized in antiquity. See also the experiences of Apuleius and Pudentilla, described in Apuleius, *Apologia*.
28. For details on the engagement, see Treggiari (2007), who thinks that Tullia was charmed by the seductive attentions of Dolabella; Jeppesen-Wigelsworth (2013) argues that Tullia acted out of political, not romantic, motivations.
29. Stat., *Silvae* 1.2. See Hersch (2007: 203) on Violentilla's parentless existence.
30. Carlon 2009: 148–159. See also Pliny, *Ep.* 1.14, on the selection of a groom.
31. See Diod. Sic. 9.10.4 on the pervasiveness of the term *engye*. Herod 6.57.4 also uses the terminology of *engye* for Spartan engagements.
32. An engagement handshake between two men has been identified on a vase by Oakley and Sinos (1993: 9).
33. Caldwell (2015: 117) raises the possibility that in the Imperial period, fiancées could cohabit until the bride reached the age of marriage.

34. Men., *Dys.* 842–844, cf. Men., *Mis.* 974–976; *Pk.* 1012–1015; *Sam.* 726–728; Soph., *Ant.* 569.
35. Lape 2009: 15–16. Demosthenes 46.18 attests that the *engye* was seen an act resulting in legitimate children. On the role and transmission of property in Greek marriages, see Leduc 1992.
36. Ferrari 2003; see also Redfield 2003: 40–46.
37. Plautus, *Poen.* 1155–9; *Trin.* 497–504.
38. Pliny, *HN* 33.12.
39. Pliny, *Ep.* 1.9; Suet., *Aug.* 53; Cic., *QF* 2.6.2.
40. Such documents might be created at the betrothal but only signed at the wedding. See Evans Grubbs 2010: 79.
41. The book-length studies of Oakley and Sinos (1993) and Vérilhac and Vial (1998) provide more extensive detail on the elements of the Greek ritual and their significance than is possible here.
42. Athens is chosen because of the wealth of evidence for life there; customs in other cities varied and are mentioned when relevant.
43. Aristotle, *Pol.* 7.1335a, recommends following tradition and marrying in winter.
44. Pollux 3.39, on *proaulia*.
45. Thuc. 2.15.4 says that the fountain known in his day as the Enneakrounos was used for premarital rites. Other cities would have similar regional traditions.
46. Schol. Eur. *Phoen* 347; Oakley and Sinos 1993: 15–16; and Vérilhac and Vial 1998: 294–295. The water-gathering is often depicted with torches, which suggests that the water might be brought at night for a bath on the following day.
47. Stafford 2013.
48. Women dedicated locks of hair and symbolic objects to Artemis, Hera, nymphs, or various youthful heroes. Each community would have its own local deities honored in this fashion. See, for example, Paus. 1.43.4, 2.32.1, 2.33.1, 2.34.12; Archilochus *AP* 6.133; *AP* 6.276; Eur., *Hipp.* 1423–1427. For a more detailed discussion of religious dedications as part of the wedding ritual, see Vérilhac and Vial 1998: 287–291; Redfield 2003: 111–118; and Dillon in this volume.
49. Paus. 9.3.7 even provides a *nympheutria* for the ritual wedding of Hera Daidala; in the *Acharnians* of Aristophanes, a *nympheutria* approaches Dikaiopolis with a request from the bride (1056). See also Pollux 3.41 and Hesychius, s.v. "nympheutria."
50. Pollux 3.36–39; Pherekydes fr. 2.13–19; Harpocration, s.v. "anakalypteria." See Llewellyn-Jones 2003: 227–248.
51. Hesychius, s.v. "epaulia"; Pollux 3.39.
52. Hague 1983. Lyghounis (1991) correlates extant songs with specific rituals.
53. Sappho fr. 116 and 117 V.; Theoc., *Id.* 18.49; Aristophanes, *Av.* 1743.
54. Hes. fr. 211.7 M-W.; Sappho fr. 112 V.; Eur., *Tro.* 311–312. See Hague 1983: 134–138; and Petropoulos 2003: 21–22.
55. Feeney 2013; Wasdin 2018.
56. The location for the feast was not set in stone, and it could occur at the house of either partner or even at a sanctuary. See Vérilhac and Vial 1998: 299–300. For the sesame cakes, see Schol. Aristophanes, *Pax* 869.
57. Eur., *IA.* 720–4; Evangelus, *Anakalyptomene* fr. 1.1 K.-A.
58. Redfield (2003: 69–71) reads the *anakalypteria* as a sign of the bride's consent.
59. Paus. Att. ε 87 Erbse and Zenobius 3.98.
60. Such readings of this rather poorly attested rite are especially popular in Structuralist scholarship. See Redfield 1982: 193. Parker (2005: 282–283) is slightly more agnostic about the symbolism of domestic implements in the ceremony.

61. The Evening Star (the planet Venus) would be visible in the evening during the winter months. Photius 1.246 Naber describes the cart-drawn procession.
62. Images of the procession elevate the status of the couple by showing them in a fancy chariot rather than the much more likely modes of transport like walking or donkey. See Oakley and Sinos (1993: 28–34) for a detailed analysis of the iconography of the procession, along with Sabetai (1997).
63. Hesychius, s.v. "hetairoi."
64. Eur., *Phoen.* 344; *IA* 732–34; *Tro.* 308–321. Many wedding vases prominently feature torches.
65. Sutton 1981: 181–182; Oakley and Sinos 1993: 32.
66. A mythical variant can be found in Demeter's distress at her daughter Persephone's abduction, for which see Foley 1994: 103–117.
67. For wedding laments, see Alexiou 2002: 120; Lardinois 2001: 83–88; and Levaniouk 2008.
68. Schol. Aristophanes, *Plut.* 768; Stesichoros fr. 187 PMG, with Deubner 1978.
69. On the bridal chamber, see Vatin 1970: 213–228. The eating of the quince is recorded by Plut., *Quaest. Rom.* 65 and *Con. Praec.* 138D, according to which the quince sweetens her mouth and voice.
70. According to Pollux 1.246 and 3.37, the bride carried house-goods like a sieve because of a decree of Solon.
71. It is tempting to claim that these songs deserve the title *epithalamia* (songs outside the door), in contrast to the *hymenaioi*, but the former term does not appear before the Hellenistic period and the two words are often used interchangeably. For more on wedding song terminology, see Muth 1954.
72. Later sources imply that the bride might call out for help from within the chamber, a plaintive reminder of her fearful virginity. See Schol. Theoc., *Id.* 18; Pollux 3.42.
73. Isaeus 3.79 and Demos. 57.43 show that grooms held a marriage feast for members of their *phratry*. Pollux 3.42 says that the *gamelia* was a sacrifice.
74. For changes in wedding iconography, see Stafford 2013.
75. More detailed accounts may be found in Caldwell 2015: 134–165; Hersch 2010a; and Treggiari 1991: 161–180. Evans Grubbs (2002: 81–135) provides the text of laws concerning betrothal and marriage and Boëls-Janssen (1993: 99–228) discusses the evidence for ceremonies in archaic Rome.
76. Pliny, *HN* 33.12.
77. For both, see Hersch 2010a: 23–27; Treggiari 1991: 17–28; and Dillon in this volume.
78. Gaius, *Inst.* 1.110–113 describes the legal processes of *manus*-marriages.
79. Romans avoided marrying on many days, especially holidays associated with festivals for the dead. See Plut., *Quaest. Rom* 86 and 105; Ovid, *Fasti* 2.555–562, 5.487–490. Late June weddings are recommended by Ovid *Fasti* 6.223–234. See Hersch 2010a: 44–51.
80. Persius 2.70 and Schol. ad Pers. 2.70 claim that girls offered dolls to Venus; Ps. Acro on Hor. *Sat.* 1.5.65.66 says the offering was to the Lares. Arnobius, *Ad Nat.* 2.67 says girls had previously offered little togas to *Fortuna Virginalis*.
81. Festus 282–3L and Serv. ad *Aen.* 4.166.
82. Festus 454L connects the style of the bride with that of the Vestal Virgins; Olson (2008: 22–23) argues that these were different hairstyles. Hersch (2010a: 80–84) asserts that we cannot know if the spear was used to create the bridal coiffure.
83. The spear is mentioned by Ovid, *Fasti* 2.559–60. Boëls-Janssen (1993: 112–126) argues that the spear was an actual weapon, not a smaller tool given that name, and notes that Arnobius, *ad nat.* 2.67 claims it was no longer used in his day.
84. For explanations of the *hasta*, see Plut., *Quaest. Rom.* 87 and Festus 55L.

85. LaFollette 1994 and Olson 2008: 21–25. Festus 364L says she slept in the tunic and a hairnet (*reticulum*) the night before the wedding.
86. It is emblematic of the wedding at, for example, Petr., *Sat.* 26.1; Lucan 2.360–361; Ovid, *Fasti* 3.690; Mart., *Ep.* 12.42 and 11.78.2; Suet., *Nero* 28. Festus 79L attributes its use to a similar garment worn by the Flaminica, a priestess of Jupiter.
87. Pliny, *HN* 21.46 says it is the color of an egg yolk.
88. The Roman wall painting called Aldobrandini wedding may represent a Greek tragedy, according to Müller 1994. Olson (2008) acknowledges the potential for mythical content while viewing the figures as representing Roman wedding iconography.
89. A bridal crown is described at Festus 56L; Plautus, *Cas.* 796–798 mentions a garlanded groom. For the associations of wedding crowns with parties, see Hersch 2010a: 90 and 138.
90. Cic., *de div* 1.16.28; Val. Max. 2.1.1. Linderski (1995) argues that Cicero is complaining about manipulation of the birds to ensure a favorable response.
91. D. 20.1.4. On marriage contracts, see Evans Grubbs 2010. The tablets may have specified that the marriage was "for the sake of obtaining children" (*pro liberorum quaerundorum causa*). See Suet., *Caes.* 52; Plautus, *Capt.* 889; Aul. Gell. 4.3.2.
92. Festus 364L. See Panoussi 2007: 279–280; and Hersch 2010a: 144–146.
93. Cat. 61 and 62; Plautus, *Cas.* 800–813. Romans may have held the procession during the daylight, according to Festus 282-3L and Serv. ad *Ecl.* 8.29.
94. The wedding cry *talasio/thalassio/talassio* is recorded by Livy 1.9.12; Plut., *Quaest. Rom.* 31, *Pomp.* 4, *Rom.* 15; Mart., *Ep.* 1.35.6–7, 3.93.25, 12.42.4. Some Roman evidence suggests that they used the Greek *hymen* refrain as well but these sources are all openly literary and Hellenizing and thus represent a mélange of Greek and Roman traditions. See Ter., *Ad.* 905, Plautus, *Cas.* 809, and Cat. 61 and 62 for Roman *hymenaioi*.
95. They were performed at other moments of potentially excessive praise, such as the triumph.
96. Verg., *E.* 8.30; Cat. 61.128–35; Pliny, *HN* 15.86; Festus 179L.
97. Cat. 61.114 mentions torches carried by boys. Many different woods are attested, including white thorn (Pliny, *HN* 16.75), but pine appears most commonly in texts of the first centuries BCE and CE (for example, at Ovid, *Fasti* 2.558; Sen., *Med.* 110–111; *Ciris* 439–441). Plut., *Quaest. Rom.* 2 describes five ritual torches.
98. D. 23.2.5–6.
99. Plut., *Quaest. Rom.* 30 and Auct. *de praen.* 10.7, with Quint. 1.7.28 on Gaius as the Roman version of John Doe.
100. Plut., *Quaest. Rom.* 30; Pliny, *HN* 8.194. On the importance of Tanaquil as a model for brides, see Hersch 2010b.
101. Serv. ad *Aen.* 4.458; Plut., *Quaest. Rom.* 31.
102. Plut., *Quaest. Rom.* 29; Serv. ad *Ecl.* 8.29; Lucan 2.359; Cat. 61.159–161.
103. Varro, *Ling. Lat.* 5.61; Ovid, *Fasti* 4.787–792; Plut., *Quaest. Rom.* 1; Serv. ad *Aen.* 4.103.
104. D. 24.1.66 with Hersch 2010a: 185.
105. Sometimes the feast appears to be at her father's house, as in Plaut., *Aul.*; it may be that the location of the dining was not standardized. Stat., *Silv.* 1.2 seems to have a celebration at the groom's house.
106. Hersch 2010a: 214–219. The Christian Arnobius (*ad. nat.* 2.67) refers to a couch spread with a toga and dedicated to the *Genius* of the husband as an outdated pagan tradition.
107. See Livy 1.9–13; Dion. Hal., *Ant. Rom.* 2.30–47; Ovid, *Fasti* 3.167–258; Plut., *Rom.* 14–20 with Miles 1995: 179–219.
108. Hersch 2010a: 200–205; Reinsberg 2006: 79–83.

109. Evans Grubbs (1989) shows that abduction marriage was a traditional part of Greek and Roman culture at all periods. See also Perry, this volume.
110. Lape (2009: 25–26) posits that marriages initiated by rape allowed for otherwise unusual unions between citizens of different economic classes in Athens. In Menander's *Georgos*, for example, a wealthy man marries the poor woman he has raped, making their child legitimate instead of a bastard. Caldwell (2015: 74–76) discusses Roman declamations on the punishment for rape as marriage or death; these contain fictional laws but do provide evidence for social norms.
111. Cartledge (1981: 99–102) and Pomeroy (2002: 39–45) discuss Spartan marriage as described by Plutarch, with some warnings as to his reliability.
112. Compare the report in Plut., *Mul. Virt.* 245f that the brides in Argos wore false beards.
113. Plut., *Lyc.* 15.
114. Reynolds (1994: 363–385) discusses the marital benediction and the role of the priest in Christian marriage, and Harper (2013: 166–170) discusses the continuation of non-Christian traditions.
115. See Hunter 2007: 590–592. A letter from the fourth-century CE Pope Siricius to a Spanish Archbishop (*Epist. ad Himerium PL* 13.1136–1137) mentions a wedding benediction and veil. Isidore, writing in the early seventh century CE, says that spouses were blessed by a priest, who joined them with a white and purple cord, and that veils were worn (*de eccl. officiis* 2.20.6–7).
116. Redfield (1982: 188) identifies the *engye* as a transaction and the *gamos* as a transformation.
117. Hersch 2010a: 2; Oakley and Sinos 1993: 3–4; and Vérilhac and Vial 1998: 282.
118. Much was also shared with the funeral. On tragic weddings, see Rehm 1994 and Ferrari 2003: 35–37.
119. Oakley and Sinos (1993: 46–47) recognize this tension; see also Sissa (2008: 89) and Hersch (2018), who argues that the Greek and Roman weddings highlight violence.
120. Treggiari (1991: 163) notes that, "Indeed, the verb used of the woman marrying, *nubo*, is related to *nubes*, a cloud, and means literally 'I veil myself.' From this come *nupta*, a married woman, *nova nupta*, a bride, and *nuptiae*, the wedding. The event turns on the bride and on her veiling." The Greek word for bride, *nymphe*, is also related to words for hiding, covering, and concealing.

CHAPTER 2

1. *Od.* 6.180–182, 280–281.
2. Hom. *Od.* 20.66–80, quote line 74.
3. Plato *Rep.* 458e, *Laws* 841b.
4. Diod. 5.73.2; Plut. *Mor.* 264b; cf. Diod. 5.73.3 on Zeus Teleios and Hera Teleia, to whom sacrifices are made first. For Hera Teleia, see Pollux 3.38.
5. Plut. *Mor.* 141 e-f.
6. Suppliants: Aeschyl. *Suppl.* 1034–1042, marriage: 1050, 1053; Seaford 1987: 114; Aeschyl. *Danaides* F44 (Radt).
7. Plut. *Mor.* 143d (*Advice to Bride and Groom* 38), paraphrasing Hom. *Il.* 14.205–209.
8. Plut. *Mor.* 140d (*Advice to Bride and Groom* 19).
9. Plut. *Mor.* 771d; Smith 2005: 4.
10. Alkibia: Archilochos F326, quoted in *Anth. Pal.* 6.133 [536–537 Page *FGE*]; Hippe: *Anth. Pal.* 6.276.

11. Hdt. 4.34.1; Paus. 1.43.4 (cf. 5.7.7); Callim. 4 *Hymn to Delos* 4.96–99. For dedications of hair by young women prior to their wedding: Hesych., s.v. "gamon ethe"; see Dillon 1999: 71–72, Dillon 2002: 215, 225–226, 235; Oakley and Sinos 1993: 14; Redfield 1982: 191.
12. Hom. *Od.* 6.100, 115.
13. Timarete: *Anth. Pal.* 6.280 (Oakley and Sinos 1993: 14); Hippe: *Anth. Pal.* 2.276.
14. Diod. 5.73.5–6.
15. *Anth. Pal.* 6.318.
16. Girdle dedicated before wedding: Apostolios 10.96; cf. *Anth. Pal.* 7.182; red-figure *lekythos*: Syracuse Museo Archeologico Regionale 21186 (ARV^2 1590; Lee 2015: 113, 4.7 [photo and line drawing; no comment on the possibility of dedication]; Oakley and Sinos 1993: 14–15, 56, fig. 9); Troizen: Paus. 2.33.1; dedicating the girdle: Suid., s.v. "lysizonos gyne"; Oakley and Sinos 1993: 14–15; Dillon 1997: 72.
17. For the *proteleia*, see Dillon 1999: 72–73.
18. Schol. Pin. *Pyth.* 4.104. The best discussion of the role of the nymphs in wedding ritual remains Ballentine (1904: 97–99).
19. Aeschylus *Semele* F220 (168) lines 16–21.
20. LSCG 115 (SEG 9.72 [see also most recently SEG 60.1834]), section 2.9–14; see Parker 1983: 345.
21. Eur. *Iph. Aul.* 433, 478–479; Seaford 1987: 108–109.
22. Plut. *Arist.* 20.6, noting that Eukleia was usually identified with Artemis.
23. Lucian: *Astrology* 23; spinster: Ar. *Lys.* 597; Plut. *Mor.* 772a; Theok. *Id.* 18.16–17.
24. *Enneakrounos*: Thuc. 2.15.5–6; EM, Harp., Suid. (Adler L694), s.v. "enneakrounos"; Poll. 3.43; Travlos 1971: 204–209; Larson 2001: 126–127. Ismenos: Eur. *Phoin.* 346–347. On the ritual bath, see Larson 2001: 111–112; Oakley and Sinos 1993: 15–16; and Reilly 1989: 420–423.
25. Karlsruhe Badisches Landesmuseum 69/78 (ARV^2 1102.2); Oakley and Sinos 1993: 16, 60 fig. 16; Sabetai 1998: 326; Smith 2005: 4–5.
26. Red-figure loutrophoros, Washing Painter, 450–400 BCE, Athens Nat. Mus. Arch. 1453 (ARV^2 1127.18); Oakley and Sinos 1993: 15–16, 58–59, figs 14–15.
27. NY MMA 1972.118.148; Reilly 1989: 62, pl. 78b; Oakley and Sinos 1993: 62, figs 20–21; Petersen 1997: 43, 43, fig. 5; Sutton 1997/1998: 41–42, 41, fig. 23 discusses this and other nude bridal scenes, as does Sabetai 1997: 319–321, 319 fig. 1.
28. Sabetai 1997: 320–321, 323, n.21; and Sutton 2009: 65–69, both noting that these naked women no longer need be interpreted as *hetairai* (prostitutes) but, rather, because of the wedding context, as brides at their toilette.
29. Boston MFA 03.802 (450–400 BCE; Oakley and Sinos 1993: 51, 109–111, figs 105–107; Petersen 1997: 42–43, 43, figs 6a-6b; Stafford 2013: 205, fig. 13). Eros is similarly shown on Martin-von-Wagner Museum 541 Würzburg (450–400 BCE; ARV^2 1133.196; Oakley and Sinos 1993: 65, fig. 24), which also shows a bridal attendant with the *loutrophoros*.
30. Ar. *Birds* 1737–1742; On Eros at weddings, see Stafford 2013: 201–206.
31. *Loutrophoros*: Karlsruhe Badisches Landesmuseum 69/78 (see above).
32. *Loutrophoros*: Harp., Phot., Suid., s.v. "loutrophoros, loutrophorein"; Hesych., s.v. "loutrophora ange, loutrophoros"; Poll. 8.66; Anec. Bekk., s.v. "loutrophoros" (Bekker i.276). On dedications, see Larson 2001: 228; and Travlos 1971: 361–363. On Artemis and Amynos, see Travlos 1971: 361.
33. Hom. *Od.* 1.275–278, cf. *Od.* 20.307.

NOTES

34. Dancing, see *Od*. 23.134; drinking, see Hom. *Od*. 1.225–26; Pin. *Olym*. 7.1–5; the centaurs—famously—became drunk at the wedding feast of Peirithoös and Deidameia, see Plut. *Thes*. 30.4. On libations and prayers, see Sappho 141. Plato: *Laws* 775c.
35. Hom. *Od*. 4.5–9.
36. Plut. *Mor*. 771d; Smith 2005: 4.
37. Pherekydes: 7 [B] 2 Diels; also of the gift Hades gave to Persephone at their wedding: Euphorion F107 (Powell; F56 [Loeb]). For the *anakalypteria*, see Oakley and Sinos 1993: 25; Redfield 1982: 192; Rehm 1994: 141–142; Smith 2005: 6–7.
38. Pandora, see Hes. *Works and Days* 70–76; Phrasikleia, see Stieber 2004: 167–170.
39. See Hallett et al. in this volume.
40. Pseudo-Hesiod *The Shield* 270–284. Weddings are mentioned in Homer's *Iliad*, but the references are largely to the "bride-price" that grooms paid to the daughter's father, and provide no details about wedding rituals. The *Odyssey* has several references to wedding feasts (see below).
41. Shield of Achilles, see Hom. *Il*. 18.490–495; Menelaos and Neoptolemos, see Hom. *Od*. 4.1–19; gods, see Hom. *Od*. 4.7; celebrations misinterpreted as a wedding, see Hom. *Od*. 23.133–139; black-figure lekythos NY MMA 56.11.1 (575–525 BCE; also discussed below); Oakley and Sinos 1993: 82, fig. 59.
42. Sappho 44.13–34. Oakley and Sinos 1993: 26.
43. Stesichoros F187 (*PMG*).
44. Chariton *The Loves of Chaereas and Kallirhoe* 812.
45. For a detailed discussion of various vases showing the wedding procession, see Oakley and Sinos 1993: 26–34.
46. NY MMA 56.11.1; Oakley and Sinos 1993: 88, fig. 70; *ThesCRA* ii, pl. 69.111, v, pl. 54.919A.
47. Plut. *Mor*. 138d.
48. Hesych., s.v. "Korythalia"; *EM* 531.53 (s.v. "Korythale," citing one Chrysippos); Calame 1997: 170–171; Harrison 1912: 503.
49. Eros *amphithales*, see Ar. *Birds* 1737. *Pais amphithales* in proverb, see Zenobios 3.98 (*PMG* 855, and Suida, s.v. "ephugin kakon"); for a definition, see also Beaumont 2012: 162–165; Dillon 2017a; Dion. Hal. *Rom. Ant*. 2.22.1–2; Oakley and Sinos 1993: 20, 25, 37, 133n14; Redfield 1982: 192–193; Reilly 1989: 426–427. Vase, MMA NY 56.11.1, for which, see Oakley and Sinos 1993: 29–30, 88, fig. 69; and Golden 2015: 26–27, with figure [no number]. Yet NY MMA 56.111.1 (Oakley and Sinos 1993: 87 fig. 68) has two bearded men in the same position on a wedding cart.
50. Callim. *Aet*. F75.1–3.
51. Sung at procession, Pseudo-Hesiod *The Shield* 274; Hom. *Il*. 18.491–493; at the wedding feast, Hom. *Od*. 4.15–19; at wedding announcement, Eur. *Troj*. 308–341, also Eur. *Hel*. 1433–1435; bridal chamber, Plut. *Mor*. 138b, see further below on this, for the epithalamia.
52. Pindar: *Threnoi* F 128c; Kassandra: Eur. *Troj*. 308–40; Theokritos: *Idyll* 18.58.
53. Wedding hymn, Ar. *Birds* 1731–1742; "Hymen Hymenaios": 1736, 1742; Eros *amphithales*, 1738; cf. Stafford 2013: 176. Note that the marriage of the goddess Harmonia was celebrated with a hymn, Pindar *Hymns* 29.6–7. For Greek wedding hymns, see Hague 1983.
54. Eur. *Iph. Aul*. 1036–1045. See also, for the invocation of Hymenaeus at weddings at Rome, Plut. *Rom. Quest*. 31 (*Mor*. 271f–272a) discussed in the *talassio* section below.
55. Sappho *Epithalamia* F116, cf. F113, F117a; F41. For *epithalamia*, see Calame 1997: 83–85.
56. Catullus 62 (see also his epithalamia 61, invoking Hymenaeus, and 64, on the marriage of Peleus and Thetis); Hague 1983: 142, n.12 argues against a Sapphic model for 62.

57. Theok. *Id.* 18; Pin. *Pyth.* 3.17–19; Aeschyl. *Prom.* 555–560 (the chorus of Oceanids, daughters of Ocean, sang at the "bath and bed" for their sister's wedding to Prometheus); Callim. *Aet.* 75.42–43 (cf. 44–45).
58. Luc. *Dial. Het.* 2.3.
59. Aeschyl. *Danaides* F43 (Radt); Theok. *Id.* 18.56–57, with schol.; Bachvarova 2009: 304.
60. Eur. *Troj.* 308–313, 319–320; see Calame 1997: 83–84. Cf. *Troj.* 343, where Hekabe refers to "Hephaistos, bearing the torch in the weddings of mortals."
61. Eur. *Phoin.* 344–345.
62. Athenian *pyxis*, see BM D11 (*ARV*² 899.146; 475–425 BCE) and Oakley and Sinos 1993: 105, fig. 98. Boiotian *pyxis*, see Sabetai 1998: pl. 63a-b; at 326, she interprets the lines on the altar as a round object, but the intention of the artist must be to show a lit altar as a sign of sacrifice.
63. Dillon 2017b: 239–241, figs 6.6–6.7.
64. Plut. *Mor.* 141f (*Advice to Bride and Groom* 27); Plut. F157 preface and 2; Sandbach; Eusebios *Praeparatio Evangelii* [*Preparation for the Gospel*] iii, Preface.
65. Plut. *Mor.* 753d (with Keuls 1993: 271); Suid., s.v. "katachysmata" (Theopompos *PCG* 7.716); Hesych., s.v. "katachysmata"; Oakley and Sinos 1993: 34–35; Smith 2005: 6.
66. Vase: Boston MFA 10.223 (*ARV*² 1017.44); Reilly 1989: 418; Oakley and Sinos 25, 34, 83 fig. 60; Smith 2005: 6, 28 fig. 7.
67. So Sabetai (1998: 328, pl. 64a-b), interprets Thebes Museum inv. 31923; 475–450 BCE.
68. Boston MFA 03.802.
69. Himerios *Oration* 9.19.
70. For the *epaulia*, see esp. Eustathios *Commentary on the Iliad* 24.29, quoting Pausanias, the second-century AD lexicographer (as do Suida and *EM*, s.v. "epaulia"), discussed by Oakley and Sinos 1993: 38–42; see also Topper 2012: 143–144. Vases, see Oakley and Sinos 1993: figs 115–119.
71. Red-figure Athenian *pyxis*, c. 350 BCE, Berlin 3373 (no *ARV*²); Reilly 1989: 29, n. 105; Oakley and Sinos 1993: 38, figs 116, 119.
72. Isaios 3.76, 79 (where that the *gamelia* had not been held is employed as proof that no wedding had taken place), similar is: 6.64 and 8.18; note Dem. 57.43, 69, where its celebration is an argument for the occurrence of a marriage and hence the legitimacy of the resultant children. See also *FGrH* 325 F 17; Pollux 8.107; Harp., Hesych., Suida, s.v. "gamelia"; *EM*, s.v. "gamelia"; Golden 1985: esp. 9.
73. Demeter's priestess: Plut. *Mor.* 138b (*Advice to Bride and Groom*, prologue). See Stafford (1999: 168), comparing this to a passage in the same treatise dealing with the sacred ploughings in Attica in Demeter's honor to promote the fertility of the fields: *Mor.* 144b (*Advice* 42). A reference to the marriage bed as being the province of Demeter is restored at Hesiod *Catalogue of Women* 177 (MW): "he who once [to much-bearing Demeter's marriage-bed] came." Menelaos and Helen: Theok. *Id.* 18.50–53.
74. See Hallett in this volume.
75. For the various rituals involved in a Roman wedding, and the involvement of the gods, see esp. Hersch 2010a: *passim* (the standard treatment), 2010b: 122–124; Benincasa 2012: 15–18; O'Bryhim 2008: 190–192. There is a brief treatment at Glazebrook and Olson 2013: 77.
76. See Hersch (2010a), who argues for caution in accepting a role for Juno Pronuba in cult and the *dextrarum iunctio* as a significant part of the Roman wedding.
77. Luc. *Bell. Civ.* 2.352–71; cf. App. *BC* 2.99. For the scarf, *supparus*, see also Fest., s.v. "supparus," 406, 407 (Paulus), 458.14L (Paulus 407L cites Afranius); Olson 2008: 15–16.

NOTES

78. See Hersch (2010a: 207–212), with bibliography.
79. Serv. *Aen*. 4.16; Fest. 92L, s.v. "Iugarius" (Paulus).
80. For the *dextrarum iunctio* in Roman art, see Hersch 2010a: 205–206.
81. The *dextrarum iunctio*, see Ter. *Andr*. 297; Tib. *El*. 1.6.59–60; Claud. *Carm. Min.* 25.28–29; Isid. *Etym*. 9.28; Plac. *Gloss. Lat*. 5.38.1; cf. Fest. 65L (Paulus; s.v. "dextera auspicium: prospera"); Rose 1924: 102; Williams 1958: 21–22. See also, generally, Ricks 2014.
82. Kampen 1981: 56, pl. 11, fig. 20 (drawing attention to the presence of Venus); Mantle 2002: 201.
83. Hersch 2010a: 192–199, 206.
84. Virg. *Aen*. 4.166, with Serv. *Aen*. 4.166; Phillips 1977: 30–31; Caldwell 2008: 423–424.
85. Aus. *Nupt*. 83–84.
86. For the mortal *pronuba*, see Tert. *Exhort*. 13.1 (but incorrect that the pronuba had never been married); Fest. 282L; Serv. *Aen*. 4.166; Isid. *Etym*. 9.7.8: "A bride's-woman (*pronuba*) is so called because she presides over a bride (*praeesse*, with *nubens*) and she is the one who joins the bride to her husband" (but not their hands); Plac. *Gloss. Lat*. 5.38.1; cf. Arn. *Nat*. 2.67; Treggiari 1994: 314–315, 321–322; Hersch 2010a: 205–208.
87. Bed, see Cic. *Cluen*. 14. See also Sen. *Med*. 37–38, *Troj*. 1132–33; Luc. *Bell. Civ*. 8.88–90 (the Fury, Erinys, as the *pronuba*). Prayer and undressing, see Sen. *Med*. 37–38; Claud. *Rap*. 2.361–364 (cf. 1.131); *Epithalamium Laurenti* 67–80; see Treggiari 1994: 321, n. 31.
88. Dion. Hal. *Rom. Ant*. 4.15.5; see also Aug. *Civ*. 4.11.
89. Macrob. *Sat*. 1.12.11.
90. Virg. *Aen*. 4.59: Juno patron of marriage, see also Macrob. *Sat*. 3.12.13, and Serv. *Aen*. 4.59.
91. Fest. 55L (Paulus); Arnob. *Nat*. 3.25; cf. Aug. *Civ*. 4.11; Hersch 2010a: 109–112.
92. Sen. *Med*. 1.
93. Tert. *Ad Nat*. 2.11.11–12; Arn. *Nat*. 4.11.1; Aug. *Civ*. 4.11, 6.9. For these minor deities of weddings, see esp. Hersch 2010a: 269–273; Caldwell 2015: 137.
94. Arnob. *Ad. Nat*. 4.7; Aug. *Civ*. 4.11, 6.9, 7.24; Lact. *Div. Inst*. 1.20.36; Tert. *Apol*. 25.3, *Ad. Nat*. 2.11.12; Treggiari 1991: 168; Hersch 2010a: 26–71.
95. Fest. 142.20-30L, 143L (Paulus); Richardson 1992: 264.
96. Clothing, see Prop. *El*. 4.11.3; toys, see Lact. *Div. Inst*. 2.3.14; Harlow and Laurence 2001: 61.
97. Arn. *Nat*. 2.67; Aug. *Civ*. 4.11 (Juno Virginensis); Hersch 2010a: 267–269; i.e., the temple of Fortuna Virgo, see Richardson 1992: 158.
98. Plin. *Nat. Hist*. 8.194; Fest. 364.21–25L, for *recta*: 342.30–33L; Harlow and Laurence 2001: 61; Hersch 2010a: 71, 106–109; Gallia 2014: 228–229.
99. Plin. *Nat. Hist*. 28.64; Fest. 55L, s.vv. "Cingillo," "Cinxiae Iunonis" (Paulus); Hersch 2010a: 109–112; Gallia 2014: 226.
100. Fest. 454L; Gallia 2014: 225. For the similarities (and dissimilarities) of the hair and dress of brides and Vestal Virgins, in particular the *seni crines* and *nodus Herculaneus*, see Gallia 2014: 223–230.
101. Plut. *Rom. Quest*. 87 (285b–d), *Rom*. 15.5; Arn. *Nat*. 2.67; Harlow and Laurence 2001: 61; Hersch 2010a: 80–84.
102. Crown:, see Hersch 2010a: 71, cf. 92–94. *Flammeum*, see Catull. 61.114–115, and numerous sources (Hersch 2010a: 53 and 95 notes that the flammeum is the article of a bride's clothing most mentioned by the ancient authors in the context of a marriage); Fest.

79L, s.v. "flammeo" (Paulus), cf. 82L, s.v. "flammeo" (Paulus); see also Hersch 2010a: 75, 94–106; Gallia 2014: 227–228.
103. For wedding divination, see Linderski 1995: 560–574; Hersch 2010a: 115–119.
104. Macrobius, see Macrob. *Sat.* 1.15.21–22; Parentalia, see Ov. *Fast.* 2.557–558; May, see Plut. *Rom. Quest.* 86 (*Mor.* 284f–285b); Ovid *Fast.* 5.488.
105. Tac. *Ann.* 11.27; cf. Juv. *Sat.* 10.336; Suet. *Claud.* 26.2; Dio 61.31.3–4. For the *auspices* at this wedding, see further below.
106. Cic. *Div.* 1.104; Val. Max. 1.5.4 ("sure omen"); Prescendi 2010: 80.
107. Sacrifices, see Plin. *Nat. Hist.* 2.22; eagle, see *Nat. Hist.* 10.11.
108. Myrrha, see Ov. *Met.* 10.452–456; O'Bryhim 2008: 192–194; Procne and Tereus, see *Met.* 6.428–434; O'Bryhim 2008: 192; for the bad omens, see esp. Gildenhard and Zissos 2007: 11–13.
109. Phyllis, see Ov. *Her.* 2.115–120; Hersch 2010: 194, 243, n.52; Hypsipyle, see Ov. *Her.* 6.41–46.
110. Pliny *Nat. Hist.* 16.75. For its apotropaic qualities, see Ov. *Fast.* 6.129, 165.
111. Virg. *Aen.* 4.166; Serv. *Aen.* 4.166.
112. Statius, see *Silv.* 1.2.229–230; Octavian: Vell. Pat. 2.79.2.
113. Catull. 45.17–18. Theokritos, as noted above, wrote that sneezes boded well for Menelaus's wedding.
114. Juv. *Sat.* 2.121 (here a *haruspex*). The *pronuba* (see above) could be an *auspex*, see Varro as cited by Serv. *Aen.* 4.66, with Treggiari 1994: 315.
115. Cic. *Cluent.* 14 (see above). Though we cannot always be sure of the *auspices'* role (Cic. *Div.* 1.28.8).
116. Messalina and Silius, see Tac. *Ann.* 11.27; Hersch 2010a: 38. Cato and Marcia, see Luc. *Bell. Civ.* 2.352–371; Sassia and Melinus, see Cic. *Cluent.* 14 (see above); Nero and Pythagoras, see Tac. *Ann.* 15.37.9. For Brutus as *auspex* at Cato and Marcia's wedding, see Hersch 2010a: 115.
117. See Harlow and Laurence 2001: 63–64; Hersch 2010a: 140–144.
118. *Codex Justinianus* 5.3.6; *Digest* 23.2.5, 22.2.6, cf. 24.1.61; Paul. *Sent.* 2.19.8; Frier and McGinn 2004: 56–58; Hersch 2010a: 56–57, 140.
119. Greek authors associate *patrimi et matrimi* with *amphithaleis* (see Greek weddings section), see Dion. Hal. *Rom. Ant.* 2.22.1; Dio 59.7; Zos. 2.6.21.
120. Catull. 61.114; Fest. 282L; Serv. *Eclog.* 8.29; Rose 1924: 102; Mantle 2002: 99; Hersch 2010a: 24–27; Prescendi 2010: 83, 86. Serv. *Georg.* 1.31, is too narrow in stating that the term *patrimi et matrimi* refers to children born of *confarreatio* marriages. For the role of children in Roman weddings, see Mantle 2002: 99–100.
121. See Zeiner-Carmichael in this volume.
122. Plut. *Rom. Quest.* 31 (*Mor.* 271f–272a); see also his *Rom.* 14.7, 15.4, 17.5, *Pomp.* 4.7, 4.10; Serv. *Aen.* 1.651. Livy 1.9.12–13 and Aur. Vict. *vir. illust.* 2.1.2–3, have the same account of the kidnap for Talassius; Fest. 479L, s.v. "Talassionem" (Paulus). For the *talassio*, see esp. Lázaro 2006; Hersch 2010a: 148–150.
123. Catull. 61.124–127 (see Hersch 2010a: 156; Caldwell 2015: 143); see Mart. 1.35.6–7, 3.93.25, 12.42.4, 12.95.5 (using *thalassio* and *Thalassus*).
124. Hersch 2010a: 236–261.
125. Catull. 61.119–120. See for these, Mantle 2002: 99; Hersch 2010a: 151–156; Caldwell 2015: 145–150.
126. Luc. *Bell. Civ.* 2.368–69; Sen. *Med.* 110–115; Aus. *Nupt.* 104.
127. Varro *Sat. Men.* (Riese, 95). See also Fest. 76.6–8L (Paulus); Serv. *Aen.* 7.695.
128. Livy 7.2.1–7.

129. Catull. 61.121–128; Hor. *Sat.* 2.3.171; Plin. *Nat. Hist.* 15.86; Aus. *Nupt.* 73; Fest., s.v. "Nuces: flagitantur nuptis et iaciuntur pueris, ut novae nuptae intranti domum novi mariti secundum fiat auspicium" (179L Paulus); Serv. *Eclog.* 8.29; Caldwell 2015: 157–158; Hersch 2010: 156–158; Mantle 2002: 99–100.
130. Plut. *Rom. Quest.* 30; Hersch 2010: 187–190; temple, see note in Richardson 1992.
131. Fat, see Plin. *Nat. Hist.* 28.142; vittae, see Serv. *Aen.* 4.458; wedding pig, see Varro *Rust.* 2.4.9. See Hersch 2010a: 177–180. The *vittae* for weddings dangled from *infulae* (similar to ribbons), see Luc. *Bell. Civ.* 2.355; Plin. *Nat. Hist.* 29.30.
132. Nonn., s.v. "nubentes"; Schulz 2006: 127; Hersch 2010a: 176–177; Johansson 2010: 138, 140, 143; Flower 2017: 76–86.
133. Catull. 61.159–161; Serv. *Eclog.* 8.29 (citing Varro); Plut. *Rom. Quest.* 29 (*Mor.* 271d), *Rom.* 15.5; Plaut. *Cas.* 815–816; Luc. *Bell. Civ.* 2.359 (quoted above); also Isid. *Etym.* 9.7.12; cf. Aus. *Nupt.* 67; Rose 1924: 106 (to avoid "evil spirits"); Williams 1958: 16–18; Hersch 2010a: 180–182; Benincasa 2012: 17, n.15.
134. Caldwell 2015: 143–156, on *deductio in domum mariti* in Catullus 61 and 62, and Petronius *Satyrica* 25.
135. Plut. *Rom. Quest.* 1; *Digest* (Scaevola) 24.1.66.1; Varro *Lat. Ling.* 5.61; Ovid *Fast.* 4.787–792; Fest. 3L (Paulus, s.v. "aqua et igni") 77L (Paulus, s.v. "facem"); Serv. *Aen.* 4.166–167: the lightning and storm at Dido and Aeneas's cave "wedding" could symbolize the water and fire of the traditional Roman wedding, but he also suggests that they signify bad omens, which seems more plausible (Hersch 2010a: 218); see Hersch 2010a: 182–186; Benincasa 2012: 17, 19–20. Cf. Isid. *Etym.* 13.12.2 (fire and water are the most potent elements).
136. Genius: Arnob. *Nat.* 2.67.3; Johansson 2010: 140.
137. For *confarreatio*, see Baldson 1962: 180; Treggiari 1991: 21–24; cf. Hersch "Confarreatio" in Wiley-Blackwell's *Encyclopedia of Ancient History* (2010).
138. Gaius *Institutes* 1.112; see 1.109–113 as a whole, defining *manus* in *usus, confarreatio*, and *coemptio* marriages, translated in Evans Grubbs 2002: 21–22.
139. Gaius *Inst.* 1.112; Dion. Hal. *Rom. Ant.* 2.25.2; Ulpian 9.1; also Fest., s.v. "farreum" (78L Paulus). Spelt is technically *triticum spelta*. For spelt, see Pliny *Nat. Hist.* 18.10.
140. Gaius *Inst.* 1.112: solemn words; Ulpian 9.1.
141. Serv. *Aen.* 4.374.
142. Fest., s.v. "In pelle lanata" (L102 Paulus).
143. Plut. *Rom. Quest.* 31 (*Mor.* 271f; this is his *Roman Question* about *Talassio*).
144. Veiled: Serv. *Aen.* 4.374.
145. Gaius 1.112; also Serv. *Aen.* 4.103, 4.374.
146. Plut. *Rom. Quest.* 50 (*Mor.* 276e). Not dissolved, see Aul. Gell. 10.15; Fest., s.v. "Diffarreatio" 65L (Paulus: *Dicta diffarreatio, quia fiebat farreo libo adhibito*) (he does not define *confarreatio* itself).
147. Pliny *Nat. Hist.* 18.3.10–11.
148. Tac. *Ann.* 4.16.

CHAPTER 3

1. The text is preserved in Stobaeus 4.507.6–512.7. Translation from Deming 2004: 223 (emphasis mine).
2. *Discourses* 14. Translation from Lutz 1947: 93 (emphasis mine).
3. Scheidel offers an excellent summary on the academic efforts to identify and define "state" (2013: 5–9).

4. For the significance of the household, see Saller 2007: 87–88.
5. For example, see Cox 1998: 3–37; Dixon 1985; Morris 1986: 113.
6. Robins 1993: 30–36; Snell 1997: 53–54, 69.
7. Robins 1993: 32.
8. Schwartz 2013: 181.
9. For the development of citizenship in Greece, see Blok 2013.
10. For the relationship between Athenian citizens and their *polis*, see Hansen 1998: 117–123; Manville 1990: 6–7.
11. Treggiari 1991: 84; Patterson 1998: 108.
12. Aul. Gel., *NA* 1.6.6.
13. Patterson 1998: 108.
14. On defining the state, see Scheidel 2013: 5–9.
15. Roth 1997: 4–5.
16. Questions about a religious or ethnic bar on intermarriage between certain groups begin to appear in Jewish texts in the sixth century BCE (Westbrook 2003: 45).
17. Ibid., 44.
18. Ibid., 45.
19. Most men living in cultures where polygamy was legal would have had only one wife; polygamy usually was used by the elite as a means of maintaining their political and economic power through family alliances.
20. Greengus 1969: 512–513; Westbrook 2003: 48.
21. Westbrook 2003: 45–46. As Westbrook notes, "bride-price" is the most common English translation for this payment, but modern scholars have debated the accuracy of this term.
22. Westbrook 2003: 65 on *HL* 28–29.
23. Robins suggests that individuals seeking to dissolve a marriage may have used courts as "witnesses" to the act (1993: 64).
24. Westbrook 2003: 45.
25. *LH* 128, translation from Roth 1997: 105.
26. *TCL* 1 61, translation from Harris 1974: 364.
27. BM 65169, translation from Roth 1988: 189.
28. Westbrook 2003: 47.
29. Westbrook notes that examples of women's independent financial action tend to be confined to widows, divorced individuals, or members of "female" professions, such as prostitute or tavern-keeper (2003: 39).
30. *MAL* A15, translation from Roth 1997: 158.
31. Roth 1988.
32. Gagarin 2005.
33. The two primary exceptions are a fifth-century Law Code from Gortyn and second-hand details about rules from Sparta.
34. After the year 403 BCE, all laws passed by the Assembly also had to be approved by another committee of citizens (*nomothetai*).
35. Scheidel 2011: 108. Scheidel notes that Archaic Greece is the earliest world culture for which there is unequivocal evidence for strict monogamy.
36. Lape 2002/2003: 119–120; 2011: 17–19; Scheidel 2011, esp. 110.
37. The circumstances by which a woman might receive this status of *alokhos* could vary greatly. As Gaca stresses, the somewhat innocuous language of bedmates and concubines can obfuscate and even normalize the coerccion and violence upon which many of these "relationships" are built (2015: 286–288).

38. Patterson 1998: 56–7.
39. Scheidel 2011: 110.
40. Lape 2002/2003.
41. Dem. 46.18 (*Against Stephanus*); cf. 44.49 (*Against Leochares*).
42. Todd 1993: 210–211.
43. Isaeus 10.10 (*On the Estate of Aristarchus*). For the property rights of women, see Sealey 1990: 36–40; Cantarella 2005a: 247–249.
44. Athenian men usually married in their late twenties, making it unlikely that a groom would still have a *kyrios*.
45. Harrison 1968: 1–60; Sealey 1990: 25–26. Both *engyē* and *ekdosis* were part of the legal language of property sale (Todd 1993: 213).
46. Limited sources make it difficult to ascertain the extent to which Athenian law treated a betrothal as a formal contract. It appears that *engyē* did not obligate the formation of a marriage, but there may have been a financial penalty. See Harrison 1968: 7–8; Just 1989: 49–50; Sealey 1990: 25–26.
47. 46.18 (*Against Stephanus*); cf. 44.49 (*Against Leochares*). Translation from Phillips 2013: 142.
48. There are no examples of marriages formed though *epidikasia* being dissolved by divorce, but it is unclear whether this represents Athenian law or a lack of surviving evidence (Todd 1993: 229).
49. Plut. *Sol.* 20.
50. Surviving laws from the city-state of Gortyn demonstrate comparable concern, outlining a similar procedure for a brother-less daughter (*patrōiōkos*). One noticeable difference is that a Gortynian patrōiōkos was allowed some (limited) choice in the selection of a husband, unlike the Athenian *epikleros*. See Sealey 1990: 63–69.
51. Her. 6.39.2.
52. Aristot. *Ath. Pol.* 26.4; cf. Aristoph. *Birds* 1661–1666; Plut. *Pericles*, 37.2. Pericles ostensibly promoted this measure in order to alleviate the financial burden that dowries had been placing upon Athenian fathers, who had been forced to offer higher and higher amounts in order to compete with foreigners seeking an Athenian husband for their daughters. A less-publicized impetus was to limit the power of the aristocracy by taking away their ability to conduct marriage alliances with powerful families from other states.
53. By "marry," the law seemingly meant undergoing *engyē* and *ekdosis* to form a union with the intent of producing legitimate children. See Just 1989: 62–64; Sealey 1990: 16–19.
54. [Dem.] 59.16–17, 51–53.
55. Plut. *Mor.* 493e; Dein. 1.71 (*Against Demosthenes*).
56. For concubinage, see Cox 1998: 170–189.
57. Dem. 23.53 (*Against Aristocrates*). This may have been a relic of the disparate polygynous relationships described in Homer.
58. Cox 1998: 173.
59. Isaeus 3.39 (*On the Estate of Pyrrhus*).
60. Patterson 1990.
61. Cox 1998: 186; cf. [Dem.] 59.122 (*Against Neaira*).
62. On *moicheia* please see Cantarella, this volume.
63. Lys. 1.32.33 (*On the Killing of Eratosthenes*). See Harrison 1968: 33.
64. Lys. 1.24–33 (*On the Killing of Eratosthenes*); Lys. 13.66 (*Against Agoratus*); Plut. *Sol.* 23.1–2. It seems likely that the charges for hubris (*graphê hybreôs*) and violence (*graphê biaiôn*) also would have been available, especially in cases of sexual assault (Philips 2013: 104–105).

65. Dem. 59.87 (*Against Neaira*). In this particular case, the woman was allegedly complicit in the adulterous liaison. It is not clear whether or not an exception could be made in cases where a woman was the victim of sexual assault.
66. Modrzejewski 2005: 344; Gagarin 2010: 225–228.
67. Modrzejewski 2005: 351–352.
68. Clarysse 1988; Modrzejewski 2005: 350.
69. Modrzejewski 2005: 349. The creation of written betrothal contracts continued to be a popular practice in the Hellenistic Near East (Yiftach-Firanko 2003).
70. Sealey 1990: 94.
71. Legislators and jurists treated *potestas* and *manus* as comparable, yet still distinct, forms of paternal authority (see Treggiari 1991: 30).
72. Looper-Friedman 1987. Please see Dillion and Wasdin, this volume.
73. For *conubium*, see Roselaar 2013.
74. Gardner 1986: 35; Treggiari 1991: 38.
75. *Digest*. 23.2.23, Celsus; *Digest* 23.2.44.pr, Paul; *Rules of Ulpian* 13.2; cf. McGinn 1998: 91–93.
76. Gardner 1986: 33–34; Phang 2001, esp. 132–133.
77. Bradley 1987: 47; Joshel 2010: 141–143.
78. Morabito 1981: 194–196.
79. *Digest* 21.1.35.
80. *Digest* 33.7.12.7.
81. Although it is difficult to discern if a *paterfamilias* actually could force a child to marry against his or her will.
82. Gardner 1986: 42; Treggiari 1991: 174–175.
83. See Hallett in this volume.
84. *Digest* 23.2.22, Celsus, translation from Treggiari 1991: 175.
85. Please see Dillon and Wasdin, this volume.
86. Treggiari 1991: 153–155. Eventually, seven became set as the minimum age for betrothal (*Digest* 21.1.14, Modestinus).
87. Gardner 1986: 45.
88. Treggiari 1991: 324–325.
89. Gaius *Institutes* 1.111.
90. If an independent woman entered into a marriage *cum manu*, all her property would transfer to her husband as a dowry (Cic. *Top.* 23).
91. *Digest* 24.1.1, translation from Watson 1985. See Cherry 2002.
92. The *lex Iulia de maritandis ordinibus* was passed in 18 BCE, followed by the *lex Papia Poppaea* of 9 CE, which revised and strengthened the provisions in the earlier law.
93. Treggiari 1991: 60–75.
94. *Digest* 48.5.12 (11).10; Papinian 48.5.27(26).pr, Ulpian.
95. McGinn 1998: 156–171.
96. *Pauli Sententiae* 2.20.1; *Digest* 45.1.121.1, Papinian.
97. Saller 1987: 71–76; Friedl 1996: 150–184.
98. McGinn 1991; Friedl 1996: 193–198.
99. Evans Grubbs 1995: 283–294.
100. Arjava 1996: 124.
101. Evans Grubbs 1995: 294–300.
102. Arjava 1996: 35.
103. Ibid., 124.

104. Ibid., 143–153.
105. *CT* 8.16.1.
106. *CT*. 2.25.1; cf. Evans Grubbs 1995: 307–309.
107. *CT* 11.36.1; cf. Amm. Mar. 28.1.
108. Please see Wasdin this volume.
109. *CT* 9.24.1. For the treatment of abduction marriage in later Roman law, see Arjava 1996: 37–41; Evans Grubbs 1989.
110. *CT* 9.24.2; Evans Grubbs 1989: 66.
111. Patterson 1998: 108–109.

CHAPTER 4

1. Scheidel 2011: 108–115; Friedl 1996: esp. 25–39, 214–228, 380–394; Ogden 1999; Manfredini 2017: 310–323, esp. 318–319. See, for example, Eur. *Andr.* 172.
2. For the purpose of the marriage, see, for example, Xen. *Mem.* 2.2.4; Men. *Dys.* 842–844. For the importance of the contracts, see the chapter "From Legendary Stories to Ordinary Families: Marriage Contracts."
3. See, for example, Vuolanto 2005: 121, 2015: 28–40.
4. Harlow and Laurence 2010: 56–77.
5. Ibid., 57.
6. Hersch 2010a: 39–43; on early betrothals in Jewish families, even before the child was born, see Sivan 2015: 299.
7. Mustakallio 2013: 24. For the preparations for the weddings, *engyesis*, etc., see Plato, *Leg.* 6. 774e; on betrothal and dowry, see, for example, Men. *Dys.* 842–46; see also Harlow and Laurence 2010: 56–58; for Roman rituals and habits, see Cic. *div.*1.28; Val. Max. 2.1, Serv. *Aen.* 3.136; on social ceremonies, see Plut. *QR* 29: Plut. *Romulus* 15.5.
8. See Wasdin and Perry in this volume.
9. Mustakallio 2013: 24–25.
10. For Greek customs, see Blundell 1995: 122–123. For Roman habits, see Evans Grubbs 2010: 78–79.
11. See, for example, Jolowicz and Nicholas 1972: 96.
12. But see Hersch (2010a) who claims that the marriage was formed by part of the wedding called the *domum deductio*.
13. Bernard 2011: 59. There is a discussion was this Roman vow a part of a *coemptio*-marriage or used in all marriages, see Hersch 2010a: 24.
14. See Dillon in this volume.
15. Gardner 1986: 31; Evans Grubbs 2010: 84; see Perry in this volume.
16. For the concept of marriage and its changes, see Cantarella 2005b: 29–30, where she points out that at least until the second century CE, the father could break off the marriage of his children, whether male or female. So, after that we may say that the spouses were more free to decide by themselves. Cantarella emphasizes that with the spread of consensual marriage, the dissolution of a marriage became extremely simple for both genders and made it easier to form a new couple.
17. Mustakallio 2013: 27.
18. For *Nummus*, see, for example, Berger 1968: 602.
19. See Gardner 1986: 5–22; see Wasdin in this volume.
20. Treggiari 1994: 21–23.
21. Gell. 10.15.23. Cf. Cantarella 1987: 117; and Treggiari 1994: 24, on *diffarreatio*.

22. Gaius 1.130; Ulpian, *Frag.* 10.5; Tac. *Ann.* 4.16.
23. See the discussion of C. Valerius Flaccus, in Liv. 27.8.
24. Gell. 10.15.1–32; Plut. *QR* 40 and 44; see DiLuzio 2019, 32.
25. Treggiari 1994: 21; see Perry in this volume.
26. Plut. *QR* 50, translated by Babbitt [1936] 1962: 83.
27. On identity and its construction, see Assmann 1992.
28. Plut. *QR* 50, cf. also 40; on complementary gender order, see, for example, Pintchman 1998: 257–282; on gender in history, see Scott 1986.
29. Di Luzio 2016: 33–34.
30. Ibid., 41; Serv. *Verg. Aen.* 8.664.
31. Fest. 79 L: Fest., s.v. "Tutulum, Rica"; Varro *L.L.* 7.44., see Boëls-Janssen 1989: 119–120. On *flammeum* in Roman weddings, see Sensi 1980/1981: 73–74; and Hersch 2010a: 94–106. Restrictions concerning both *Flaminica* and brides, see Hersch 2010a: 49; and DiLuzio 2016: 33.
32. Liv.1.1.9–10. On the Sabine abduction, see Dillon and Wasdin, this volume.
33. Liv.1.1.6–10; Dion. Hal. 1.64–12; Ogilvie 1965: 37–43.
34. For Lavinium, see Liv.1.1.11. Dion. Hal. 1.64. For *tutela muliebris*, see Liv.1.3.1; see also Torelli 1984: 31.
35. See, for example, Wiseman 2004: 160–168, including the versions by various authors describing the birth legend of Rome.
36. Beard 1999: 1–10; Mustakallio 1999: 5–57.
37. Liv.1.9.5–10.1; Dion. Hal. 2.30–44; Plut. *Romulus* 18–19.
38. Liv.1.9.4: *illas tamen in matrimonio, in societate fortunarum omnium civitatisque, et quo nihil carius humano generi sit, liberum fore.*
39. Liv. 1.11.5; Dion. Hal. 2.45.
40. Liv. 1.13.4 and 1.13.6–8; Dion. Hal. 2.47.4; Plut. *Romulus* 19.7.
41. Evans Grubbs (2002) on marriage contracts from Egypt and Near East, from Cave of Letters 122–130, from *Dura Europos* 133–135. See Perry this volume.
42. Evans Grubbs 2010: 83, who cites Yiftach-Firanko 2003: 41–54. On marriage contracts in general, see Hersch 2010a: 123–131. On contracts, see Perry this volume; on *ekdosis*, see Dillon, Perry and Wasdin this volume.
43. Evans Grubbs 2010: 84.
44. On these documents, see, for example, Evans Grubbs 2002: 131.
45. Evans Grubbs 2010: 85, note 33 (P.DURA 30). On other contacts, see Evans Grubbs 2010: 84. On soldiers and marriage, see Le Bohec 1993: 294–295.
46. Evans Grubbs 2010: 85; *P.Oxy* 10.1273.
47. Schmitt Pantel 2010: 147–168.
48. Plut. *Coniug.* 43 (Mor. 2.12).
49. Cic. *ep Fam.* 14.2 ; 14.4 ; Plin. *ep.* 6.4; 6.7; 6.24; 7.5.
50. Plin. *ep.* 7.5.
51. Val. Max. 6.7.2 and Appian *Bell. civ.* 4. 44; more about Turia, see Osgood 2014: 124.
52. *Laudatio Turiae*, see Wistrand 1976. Paulina's elogium for Vettius Agorius Praetextatus, *CIL* 4,1779. Hemelrijk 2004: 185–197.
53. See the analysis of Hemelrijk 2004: 194.
54. *ILS* 8393, 31–40.
55. Apuleius, *Apologia* 69; Haase and Steinacher 2017: 225–227, see also Mustakallio 2013: 29.
56. *CIL* 4. 1779, on the left side of the altar of the tombstone, translation: *Diotima* database.
57. Kahlos 1994: 13–25, and 2002: 2.3 *Cults*.

58. Plut. *Coniug.* 19.
59. Whittaker 2010: 45.
60. See Brown 1991: 72–73.
61. *Epistula ad Marcellam*, see Whittaker 2010: 43–54.
62. See, for example, Vuolanto 2010: 97–113.
63. See, for example, Brown 1991: 30–32.
64. *Conf.* 6.15; Haase and Steinacher 2017: 228. See Cantarella in this volume.
65. See Brown 1991: 49–60; Vuolanto 2010: 106; Wood 1997: 111–127.
66. Older women were considered responsible for getting the young widows remarried, see LaFosse 2017: 212.
67. Giardina 1993: 190–207. On the education of Melania the Younger, see Pentti 2015: 123.
68. Pentti 2015: 122; Vuolanto 2005: 119–132.
69. Bradley 1994: 50–51; Laes and Vuolanto 2017: 272–274.
70. John Chrysostom, *Hom. in Ephes.* 22.2 (PG 62, 158); Brooten 2015: 115–116; on household codes, see 124–125.
71. Brooten 2015: 116.
72. Mustakallio 2013: 29.
73. Although Plutarch said that when a Roman man had sufficient number of children to rear, another, who lacked children, could persuade him to give the wife to another. See Plut. *vitae Lyc.* et *Numa*, 3.1, and also Cantarella 2002: 220–232, Mustakallio 2013: 30.
74. See Hallett in this volume.
75. See Treggiari 1993: 229–261.
76. Plut. *Coniug.* 43 (Mor. 2.12).
77. Plut. *Coniug.* 19.
78. *Ep. ad Marcellam*, see Whittaker 2010: 43–54.
79. However, even if the Christian marriage of slaves was approved in principle, the facts of slavery were not changed: slavery still meant that these families were owned.

CHAPTER 5

1. *The American Heritage Dictionary of the English Language* (2011) 391. The *Oxford Latin Dictionary* (Glare 1982: 412) has entries for the Latin nouns *consensio* and *consensus*, defining both as "agreement in opinion or sentiment," and the latter as in addition "concord, unanimity." But the *OLD* does not include any attestations where either is used to describe the mutual willingness of two partners to enter a marriage. Treggiari (1991: 16, ch. 2 *passim*, esp. 54–57, 83, 147, 170–180) frequently uses the English noun "consent" in the context of Roman legal agreements to marry: for example, "Consent was initially signified when the marriage began" (54), citing here, in n. 68, a 1946 book by the Italian scholar P. Rasi, *Consensus facit nuptias*, and seeming to imply that the noun *consensus* refers to the agreement by the marital couple alone. Yet on p. 170 she also quotes Latin passages (*Digest* 23.2.2, Paul xxxv *ad edictum*, *Tituli Ulpiani*) where the verb *consentio* refers to the agreement by both the bridal couple (*qui coeunt*) and their parents under whose power they are (*quorum in potestate sunt*), indicating the equal importance of parental and particularly paternal consent to the union in Roman times. My discussion, which focuses on the mutual consent and consensuality of marital partners, seeks to avoid the confusion caused by the application of the noun *consensus* to the permission to marry granted by their (male) parents as well. Treggiari herself acknowledges the complications of employing this phrase for the marital couple, stating, "Whether the consent of the bride and even of the bridegroom was legally required may be academic if the pressure exerted by the family or by society

was strong" (83); she thereby supports my claim that partners may not in fact have freely consented to parental wishes or engaged consensually in marital sexual relations.
2. See, for example, State-by-State Marriage, "Age of Consent Law." Curiously, the fifth edition of the *AHD* does not include this phrase in its entry for "consent."
3. To be sure, Wildfell (2015) is not a scholarly study. But the book's title—and the author's concern with mutually respectful partnerships of an erotic nature—testify to the growing acceptability of "consensuality" as a noun that defines mutually agreed upon sexual acts and partnerships.
4. See the text of Question 6 Referendum Petition (General Election Ballot Question Language 2012: ch. 2 of the 2012 Legislative Session. Civil Marriage Protection Act; and Tavernise [2012]).
5. For *suasor*, see the OLD (Glare 1982: 1833): the "Socratic dialogue" I have here reconstructed with my interlocutor may perhaps be viewed as a *suasoria* of sorts.
6. For women's lack of property rights in fifth-century BCE Athens, see, for example, Foxhall 1989; and Just 1989: 76–104; for women's limited control of property in republican and early imperial Rome, see Gardner 1986: 74–77, 83, 259–260. For the *Lex Voconia*, see Astin 1978: 113–121; for Augustus's moral and marital legislation, see Treggiari 1991: 60–80 and Severy 2003: 52–56.
7. See Perry this volume.
8. For the Athenian epiclerate, see the discussions of Just 1989: 44–45 and 95–104; Foxhall 2005; Levick 2012; and Glazebrook and Olson 2013: 74. Just (1989: 98) concludes with the observation, "The *epikleros* stands in, as it were, for her non-existent brother until she has produced a son capable of carrying on her father's *oikos*. Her father's next of kin provides the seed and receives the benefit of control of the property until such time as this end is achieved."
9. Such as Just (1989) and Glazebrook and Olson (2013). Foxhall (2005) takes pains to point out the inaccuracy of this translation; Levick (2012: 100) translates *epikleroi*, correctly, as "those who went with the inheritance, through whom property passed from a man to his heirs."
10. I recognize that, as one of the anonymous referees has observed, my assertion about governmental intervention into ancient Greek and particularly Roman marriage contradicts much current scholarship; studies underscore that dotal or marriage tablets were not required to prove the existence of a Roman marriage, nor was state religion involved in the formation of a marital union. While scholars make much of Augustus's moral and marriage legislation, it is not clear how many Romans actually complied with these laws, or for how long this legislation was enforced. Marriages between former slaves and other non-elites, such as that between Trimalchio and his wife Fortunata in Petronius's *Satyricon*, however comic and exaggerated its description, merit attention for that reason.
11. See the discussion of Just 1989: 91–92 and 97–98.
12. For Spartan marriage, see Glazebrook and Olson 2013: 71; Levick 2012: 101; Pomeroy 2002: 33–50. As noted by one of the anonymous referees, too, the involvement of governmental officials in Spartan marital arrangements warrants attention here, too, since many scholars insist on the sacral nature of Greco-Roman marriage, with Hera/Juno and other lesser divinities presiding over marital unions, because the state, in addition to (or rather than) religious authority, is a guiding force.
13. See Severy (2003: 55–56), concluding with the observation: "In a variety of ways, the Julian laws on the marrying of the orders and adultery actually cut across the boundaries between

public and private they were trying to enforce, and inserted the state or Augustus into private families."

14. See State-by-State Marriage, "Age of Consent Law," which provides a state-by-state summary of the "age of consent" for marriage and other pertinent marriage information of the fifty US states, the District of Columbia, and Puerto Rico. In most states the age of consent is eighteen: exceptions are Mississippi (where the age of consent is twenty-one, though with parental consent and/or the consent of the judge males can marry at age seventeen and females at fifteen), Nebraska (where the age of consent is nineteen, though with parental consent, parties can marry at seventeen), and Puerto Rico (where the age of consent is twenty-one for both males and female, though women may apply for and receive a license by reason of pregnancy or the birth of a child).

15. See Obasogie (2017), on the fiftieth anniversary of the Supreme Court's landmark decision "Loving vs. Virginia." Loving was the last name of the white male plaintiff; he and his black wife had been sentenced to a year in prison in Virginia for marrying each other in violation of the state's anti-miscegenation statute. The Supreme Court decided unanimously that this prohibition was unconstitutional, thereby ending all race-based restrictions on marriage in the United States.

16. Glazebrook and Olson (2013: 70–71), citing studies by Helen King ([1983] 2002) and Lesley Dean-Jones (1991); see also King (1998).

17. Glazebrook and Olson (2013: 75), citing Treggiari (1991: 134–160) and Hersch (2010a: 39–43).

18. For the Maryland vote, see Wagner, Schwartzman, and Martel (2012), noting not only that "Voters in Maryland narrowly upheld the state's same-sex marriage law" but also that it was joined by the state of Maine in approving gay marriage.

19. For the US Supreme Court decision on June 26, 2015, legalizing same-sex marriage nationwide, see Liptak 2015.

20. The fifth edition of the *AHD* (1623) contains a brief entry for the noun "shotgun marriage," defining the term as "a marriage that is forced or necessitated because of pregnancy. Also called "shotgun wedding."

    The *AHD* entry on 843 for the adjective "honest" does not include the idiom "make an honest woman of." Used to describe a man's marriage to a woman with whom he has an existing sexual relationship, this expression has no male equivalent in the form of "make an honest man of." The expression implies that women who engage in premarital sex lack honor and truthfulness, whereas their male partners do not; needless to say, this idiom is also not employed to describe same-sex couples in an existing sexual relationship who later marry.

21. Here, again, the experiences of non-elites, such as the former slaves Trimalchio and Fortunata humorously depicted in Petronius's *Satyricon* as having chosen one another as marital partners, may have differed. It also warrants scrutiny that female fertility may not have mattered as much owing to the possibility of adult male adoption by elite couples.

22. See Hallett (2008), which raises the possibility that Tiberius may be the Augustan elegist who calls himself by the slave name Lygdamus. Suetonius testifies to the pain suffered by the former as a result of his forced divorce from his first wife Vipsania; "Lygdamus" attests to his own suffering at being parted from a woman he refers to as "Neaera," and describes in language that suggests she was once his wife. "Lygdamus" represents himself has having been born in 43–42 BCE, at approximately the same time as Tiberius. What is more, Suetonius documents Tiberius's close relationship with Marcus Valerius Messalla: Messalla's poetic protégés included Tibullus (whose third book of elegies contains the six

elegies of Lygdamus), Ovid (who uses the same words to describe his birth year of 43–42 BCE that Lygdamus does), and Messalla's niece Sulpicia. Hallett argues that Lygdamus is most likely to have been Sulpicia's aristocratic and politically prominent brother, writing under a pseudonym.

23. Hersch 2018. The scenario of Catullus 62, an epithalamium, wedding poem, merits note in this connection. It features a singing contest between a chorus of marriageable young men and a chorus of marriageable young women; Catullus poignantly represents the young women, in line 24, as likening the tearing of brides from their mothers' embrace to the cruel destruction in wartime of a city by its enemies: *quid faciunt hostes capta crudelius urbe?* (what more cruel thing do enemies do after a city has been captured?); he thereby has them associate marital defloration with violent battle, the bride with war's female victims, and her first intercourse with rape.

24. Consider, for example, the measures adopted to encourage procreative sexual activity on the part of an Athenian male married to an *epikleros*, discussed by Just (1989: 91). Or Catullus's hortatory address to the bridegroom in another epithalamium (61.189–198), reminding the young man that the sexual energy supplied by the erotic goddess Venus does not abandon him (*neque te Venus neglegit*) but nonetheless asking for Venus's help in consummating his marriage (*bona te Venus iuverit*).

25. As Richlin (2015) attests, even trying to understand what "consent" means in a slave-owning society is particularly difficult.

26. As pointed out by an anonymous referee, the authors of our extant Greek and Roman *epithalamia* may extol marriage but largely focus on the couple's erotic activities and end with wishes for eternal happiness, sentiments not generally associated with marriage elsewhere. Indeed, praise of marriage itself generally foregrounds the wife's fidelity and the ideal of a wife's status as a *univira*, a woman married to only one man in the course of her lifetime; a *univira* is not expected to be happy but faithful.

27. On Augustan Roman love poetry as "countercultural expression," see Hallett 1984; for the women portrayed as sexually desirable partners for more than a one-night stand, particularly in lyric and elegy, see Hallett 2013.

28. At *Satires* 1.2.57–59, in fact, the poet Horace lists several categories of sexually desirable women with whom actual men of his acquaintance as well as fictionalized male characters in such literary genres as comedy, satire, lyric poetry, and elegy enjoyed long-term relationships: other men's wives (*cum uxoribus ... alienis*); comic mime actresses (*verum est cum mimis*); and *meretrices* (*est cum meretricibus*).

29. What accounts, at least in part, for the representation of elegiac *dominae* as combining the characteristics of an adulterous married woman and a paid *meretrix* is that the elegists simultaneously looked to both Catullus and Cornelius Gallus as their literary models—and Catullus's female beloved, called by the literary pseudonym Lesbia, was portrayed and recognized as an adulterous matron, Clodia Metelli, whereas Gallus's mistress, referred to as Lycoris, was depicted and acknowledged to be the freedwoman and mime actress Volumnia Cytheris.

30. See, for example, the discussion by Wiseman (1985: 146) on Catullus's portrayal of Lesbia: "there is one thing about her that comes through clearly enough—her dominance. She acted, he reacted. His contribution was the concept of a love unparalleled (8.5), more than sexual, involving both the responsibilities of the marriage bond and the vulnerability of a virgin bride."

31. I recognize that my essay, unlike the others in this volume, shares salient details of a memorable personal experience: an incident that prompted renewed reflection upon how

and why "traditional Greek and Roman marriage" differs from its contemporary Western counterparts, and motivated me to explore the contemporary political context of this thought-provoking experience. It is far from my only scholarly essay in this vein. For over two decades I have adopted the personal voice in much of my writing and championed its adoption by others: initially justifying this decision in a 1997 volume, co-edited with Thomas Van Nortwick, entitled *Compromising Traditions: The Personal Voice in Classical Scholarship* (1997), for which I also wrote the introduction, and contributed an essay, "Doing What Comes Nationally: Writing as an American in Classical Scholarship." This autobiographical mode of scholarly communication allows me to acknowledge the role played by my own personal experiences in choosing research topics and formulating questions of my evidence, and to share with my readers my reasons for according importance to these topics and these questions.

CHAPTER 6

1. For an interpretation of the primordial Eros see Vernant 1990b: 465–478.
2. Nyx also gives birth alone to children that become responsible for both vital and destructive processes in the mental life of humans (Hes. *Th.* 211–225).
3. On the bed as an object that stands for the institution of marriage see Zeitlin's insightful essay "Figuring Fidelity in Homer's *Odyssey*," in Zeitlin 1996: 19–52.
4. Cf. Ares's violation of Hephaestus's bed symbolizes the violation of Hephaestus's wedlock with Aphrodite in Hom. *Od.* 8. 269.
5. In referring to the bed of Odysseus and Penelope, Zeitlin writes: "The fixity of the marriage bed may enact the principle of fidelity itself" (1996: 31, see also 42).
6. For a discussion of the architecture of the marital bed, see Bergren 2008: 229–233.
7. For the notion of remarriage in Greek mythology see "The (Re)Marriage of Penelope and Odysseus," in Bergren 2008: 215–241; and "Symbolic Remarriage," in Foley 2003a: 324–327.
8. Penelope's chamber in the women's quarters should be distinguished from the nuptial *thalamos*.
9. Cf. Catullus 1991: 64.
10. Only one loyal handmaid, *amphipolos mia moune*, is let into the secret room. Her main responsibility is to sit outside at the room's closed doors to keep away intruders.
11. The sacred space of the nuptial room is evoked in literary descriptions of its violations in adultery tales (for example, Ares and Aphrodite's in Hephaestus's and Aphrodite's nuptial bed, Gyges's in Herodotus and Apuleius's adultery tales).
12. Hes. *Th.* 133–153.
13. Hesiod uses *paides* (children) referring to the children of Gaia and Ouranos in Hes. *Th.* 138, 148, 155 and *tekna* (offspring) in Hes. *Th.* 149. For the Greek terminology, see Golden 1985b: 91–93 (91–104). Etymologically *teknon* connotes the ties between the offspring and the physical act of giving birth. In the *Theogony* the relationship between the term *tekna* is specifically connected to the term father *tokeus* (Hes. *Th.* 138, 155) Although the noun *tokeus* can refer generally to the parent, a father or a mother, its masculine form seems to attribute a more active responsibility in terms of the act of procreation to the male parent.
14. According to Athenaeus 600b 13 the identity of the speaker is Aphrodite. See Papadopoulou 2014: 2–21.
15. Froma Zeitlin translates *trosai* as "pierce" or "wound" (1996: 159).
16. Zeitlin 1996: 159.

17. Except for the virgin goddesses Athena, Artemis, and Hestia, whom Aphrodite cannot tame, cf. *Hymn to Aphrodite* 8–32.
18. In the *Hymn to Aphrodite* (68–74) the contagious force of Aphrodite is conspicuous in the description of mating animals.
19. "It is the similarity between the act performed and the result expected." For this reason Frazer describes this sort of magic as "imitative" or "homoeopathic" (Freud 2001b: 81).
20. Frazer 2011: 98.
21. Freud 2001b: 80.
22. For various conjectures about the trial and its significance for the trilogy see Gravie 1969: 205–207.
23. Zeitlin 1996: 167.
24. The association of the Danaids with the Thesmophoria is also made by Herodotus 2.171.
25. Zeitlin 1996: 167.
26. Ibid., 164–169; see also Papadopoulou 2014: 21–22.
27. Zeitlin translates "cereals to sustain life" literally as "life-giving wheat of Demeter" (1996: 159, 164).
28. Zeitlin 1996: 167.
29. For a discussion on the Thesmophoria as a civic festival, see Loraux 1984: 118. See also Detienne 1977: 78.
30. Zeitlin 1996: 168.
31. Her analysis of gender struggle in the *Theogony* leads Ann Bergren to argue that "the fundamental struggle of the *Theogony* is over the power of reproduction" (Bergren 2008: 18).
32. *ison eoute*, Hes. *Th*. 126.
33. Caldwell 1993: 145. Cf. Freud 2001a: 256.
34. Cf. the discussion of Apollonian strategies in Zeitlin 1996: 107–112.
35. *The Hymn to Aphrodite* 7–33.
36. *The Hymn to Aphrodite* 21–28.
37. The abundance of myths in which virgins resist marriage is a great source for many important studies. See Dowden 1989.
38. *illa velut crimen taedas exosa iugales* (Ovid, *Met*. 143).
39. Garvie 1969: 784–789.
40. *Homeric Hymn to Demeter* 19–30.
41. Cf. Catullus 62.20–25.
42. Plutarch, *Romulus* 15.5, trans. Bernadotte Perrin. On abductions see Dillon, Mustakallio, Perry, Wasdin this volume.
43. Hes. *Th*. 535–536.
44. On the Hesiodic golden age as a myth of sameness, see Lev Kenaan 2008: 48–75.
45. Jean-Pierre Vernant, "The Myth of Prometheus in Hesiod," in Vernant 1990a: 183–202.
46. Vernant 1990a: 199.
47. Loraux 1984: 77.
48. Vernant 1990a: 201. Cf. Vernant's 1973 piece "Marriage" republished in Vernant 1990a: 55–77.
49. Hes. *Th*. 600–612.

CHAPTER 7

1. In that sense see Cantarella 1976: 129–159.
2. Cohen 1984. In favor of his theory cf. Todd 1993: 277; and Hoffmann 1990: 12.

NOTES

3. More generally, on the personal paternal powers of the Greek fathers, see Cantarella 2015: 71–79.
4. The same law prohibited the husband who had surprised his wife with an adulterer to keep her as a wife and stated that if he did not repudiate her, he would be *atimos*, which meant that he would lose his civil rights.
5. Cf. Thomas 1986a; Thomas 1986b: 216 ff.; Cantarella 2002.
6. Xen. *Lac. Pol.* 1.2–10. See also Plut. *Lyc.* 15.6–8.
7. Lacey 1968: 199.
8. These documents are the Hammurabi Code written in Haccadic around 1750 BCE; the Ur-Nammu Code, coming from Ur, in Southern Mesopotamia, written in Sumeric around 2100; the Lipit-Ishtar Code, from Isin, in Southern Mesopotamia, written in Akkadic around 1770; The Medioassyrian Laws from Assur, in Akkadic, written in the fourteenth century BCE; the Hittite Laws, from Anatolia, written in Hittite in the thirteenth century BCE; the Neo-Babylonian laws, from Sippar, in central Mesopotamia.
9. Among the many cf. Westbrook 1985; Postgate 1992; Bottéro 1993; Roth 1995; Westbrook 2003.
10. Gagarin 2005.
11. Cf. Maffi 1991: 23.
12. Val. Max. 6.3.9.
13. On this episode, on the reasons of the above quoted law and more in general on women's status in the period of the kings, see Cantarella 1987: 113–122.
14. Val. Max., 6.3.9.
15. Established by two laws enacted in 18 BCE and 9 BCE, later united in a single law called *lex Iulia et Papia*.
16. As we read in Justinian's Digest: D. 48.5.6.1; still fundamental, on the point, Cohen 1991.
17. Further details on the *lex Iulia de adulteriis* in Cantarella 1991.
18. Cohen 1991: 124–125.
19. Tac. *Ann.* 3.25.2.
20. Suet. *Tib.* 35.2.
21. Tac. *Ann.* 2.85.1.
22. D. 48.5.11 (10). 2.
23. Daube 1972.
24. Tac. *Ann.* 2.85.1.
25. Suet. *Tib.* 35.
26. Juv. *Sat.* 2.37.
27. Cohen 1991: 125.
28. *CTh.* 11.36.4.
29. D. 48.5.39.8.
30. Coll. 4.3.6.
31. Paul. *Sent.* 2.26.1.
32. *Nov.* 117.5.
33. *Nov.* 134.10.
34. Dio. Hal. 3.67.39.
35. Dio Hal., 9.40.1–2.
36. Liv. 8.15.7.8.
37. Liv. *Per.* 14.
38. Macr. *Sat.* 1.10.5.

39. Suet. *Dom.* 8.
40. Dio Cass. 78.16.1–3.
41. In that case the execution was entrusted to an imperial officer, the *praefectus urbi*. For further information, see Cantarella 2011: 109–113.
42. Liv. 8.15.7; Plut. *Numa* 10.8–13; Dion. Hal. 2.67.4.

CHAPTER 8

1. As Wyke eloquently notes (2002: 208): "Our principal evidence for lives of ancient women is still on the level of representations, not realties. We encounter not real women but representatives shaped by convention of wall-paintings, tombstones, and most frequently, texts." Cf. Finley 2002.
2. Winkler 2002: 40.
3. Braithwaite and Orr 2016: 303.
4. Ibid., 304: "Representation is thus always referring to a struggle over the meaning of something or over meaning-making a process."
5. For example, "slidings of meaning," (Hall 1997: 32–33), or, the ways textual representations are "transportable" via different discourses and historical contexts.
6. The physical and symbolic exclusion of women from "public" spaces or the activities associated with them reinforced the patriarchal system; for example, Winkler 2002: 41–42.
7. On Greek betrothals, (especially in Athens), see Oakley and Sinos 1993: 2–3; for visual representations of the handshake, see Davies 1985.
8. Gardner 1986: 45–47; on Roman betrothal see also Treggiari 1991: 146–155. See also Wasdin and Hallett in this volume.
9. Blundell 1995: 176–180; Zeitlin 1990.
10. On class and social distinctions among Athenian women, see Cantarella 1987: 48–50.
11. Kallipides's betrothal of his daughter to Gorgias also specifically mentions the pragmatic purpose of producing "many legitimate children" (Menander, *Dyskolos*, 842); cf. Herodotus's description of Cleisthenes handing his daughter over to Megacles (6.130).
12. Blundell 1995: 119, 172–187.
13. Skinner 2014: 187–188.
14. This new context is also reflected in philosophical texts, education, and art: Pomeroy 1975: 131–147.
15. Konstan 1987: 139: "With the normalization of the *oikos* structure, Glykera's independence as concubine is dissolved into the silent role of wife." Cf. Lape 2010: 51–78; Scafuro 2014.
16. For example, Plautus *Poenulus* 1155–1157; cf. Treggiari 1991:138–145.
17. For example, Plautus's Selenium in *Cistellaria* and Palaestra in *Rudens*.
18. Edwards 1997: 82.
19. Ibid., 81.
20. Apollo was said to have been the first composer of the *epithalamium* in celebration of the marriage of Peleus and Thetis. Cf. Stesichoros, 187 PMG, Euripides's *Alcestis* 918–919; *Iphigenia in Aulis* 438–439; Lucan *Pharsalia* 2.350ff.
21. Hersch 2010a: 63–64.
22. Cf. Isaeus 3; Demosthenes 59.122 (and also 72–82, 85–86, 111). Marriage is a theme found in Roman courtroom speeches, as in the *Pro Caelio* (13–16) where Cicero's staged depiction of Clodia as a mistress who influenced Caelius's youthful poor choices, is the antithesis of the ideal wife and the humorous distraction for the defense case.

23. Treggiari 1991: 146–147; Digest 23.1.11; 23.2.2; Justinian, *Codex* 5.4.14.
24. On the *epithalamium* as a genre, see Keydell 1962; Wheeler 1930.
25. See Hersch (2010a: 17–18) for the "literary conceit" of the Roman *epithalamium* as an idealized version of reality. In discussing the bride's virginity, Oakley and Sinos (1993:14) point out that the groom was "past this stage." Although in reality the groom would have been in his late twenties or early thirties (and bearded) the Attic vase painting depicts him beardless, and thus youthful, "making him a less threatening and perhaps more romantic figure to a teenaged bride" (Foley 2003b: 126). See also Hes. *W&D* 698–699, discussed in Part 2, page 8.
26. Hersch 2010a: 135–136.
27. Cf. Sappho Fr. 94.
28. Rehm 1994.
29. Foxhall and Salmon 1998; Harlow and Laurence 2001: 76–78; Hersch 2010a: 135; Van Nortwick 2008.
30. For this theme as represented in the *epithalamia* of Catullus see Caldwell 2015: 145–150.
31. Treggiari 1991: 100–102.
32. Dover 2002: 21–22.
33. Glazebrook and Mellor 2013: 34–36.
34. King 2002: 92: "The Greeks saw 'woman' as a contrast between the undisciplined threat to social order and the controlled, reproductive *gynē*."
35. Mustakallio 2013: 25.
36. Leeds-Hurwitz 2002: 87; Oakley and Sinos 1993: 25–27.
37. Hersch 2010a: 162–167; Oakley and Sinos 1993: 26–27.
38. Feeney 2013; cf. Thomsen 2002.
39. Hersch 2007; Zeiner-Carmichael 2007.
40. Wyke 2002: 208: "The sexual domain of the elegiac *domina* contrasts with that traditionally prescribed for Roman wives, namely, keeping house and working wool."
41. See, for example, Pavlovskis 1965.
42. Wasdin 2014.
43. Chiappinello 2007:118–119.
44. Harlow and Laurence 2001: 24–33; Milnor 2013: 107–109.
45. Caldwell 2015: 138; Mustakallio 2013: 22–23.
46. Harlow and Laurence 2001: 95–99; Mustakallio 2013: 24–25. For biological perspectives on marriage and age, see Caldwell 2015: 94–100.
47. Harlow and Laurence 2001: 81–82.
48. On the topic of space and the overlap between public and private, see Foxhall 2013: 114–123; Glazebrook and Mellor 2013: 38–39; Milnor 2013: 105–124.
49. For example, Cantarella 1987: 24–37.
50. Dover 2002: 21–22; on the relationship among the marriage, community, and social order, especially as represented by philosophical sources, see Foxhall 2013: 24–32.
51. Skinner 1997: 9: "Whereas Greek custom discouraged women's presence in public space, elite Roman families of the late Republic exploited it as yet another occasion for competitive advertisement." Undoubtedly, participation in the public context offered women their own avenues for attaining status and securing their reputation as exemplary wives. On wives and their roles in public life for attaining status, see Pomeroy 1975: 176–189.
52. As quoted by Caldwell 2015: 97–98.
53. Ibid., 79; 105–133.
54. Ibid., 98.

55. On attempts to control the female body/sexuality, see Glazebrook and Mellor 2013: 34–38; King 2002: 78–81.
56. See also Lysias, *On the Murder of Eratosthenes* (6–9); Antiphon, *Prosecution of a Stepmother* (14–15).
57. As with most feminine ideals, however, binary contrasts emerge, and textile production might also be linked to a woman's cunning (e.g., Circe in *Odyssey* 24.138–151; Clytemnestra in the "carpet scene" (Aeschylus, *Agamemnon* 918–957). On the connection between textile production and drugs in Sappho's poetry, see Winkler 2002: 49–51. Textile production could also be symbolically connected to statecraft (e.g., Plato *Statesman* 297b; Aristophanes' *Lysistrata* 578); cf. Jenkins 1985; Karanika 2014; McNeil 2005.
58. For example, Semonides 7; cf. North 1977. The word could have multifaceted connotations depending on historical period and context, but in general delineates a woman's subordinate position in relation to men, either by her chastity, verbal silence, or moral restraint.
59. North 1977: 38–41.
60. Lattimore 1942.
61. Cf. Amymone (first century BCE, Dessau, ILS 8402); Murdia (first century BCE, CIL 6.10230); Allia Potestas (third-fourth century CE, CIL 6.37965).
62. Harlow and Laurence 2001: 133–134; 20–30.
63. Treggiari 1991: 60–80.
64. Larsson Lovén 2007.
65. Larsson Lovén 1998.
66. Joshel 2002: 163–187; cf. Phillipides 1983.
67. On the topos as played out in Greek tragedy see Pomeroy 1975: 109–112.
68. Cf, the story of Tiberius, the wife of Cornelia, who chooses to die in her stead, a decision partially based on his older age (Plutarch, *Life of Tiberius Gracchus*, 1.2–5).
69. Aelian, *Historical Miscellany* 14.45
70. Bremmer 2008: 205; cf. Euboulos, Fr. 77 PCG.
71. Martial *Epigram* 1.13; Tacitus *Annals* 6.29, 16.10; on women's deaths as represented by Tacitus, see Edwards 2007: 179–206.
72. Edwards (2007: 194) suggests additional reasons for why Pliny may have re-shifted focus away from Arria's suicide.
73. Cf. *Epistle* 7.19, which describes Fannia's courageous bout with an illness she contracted while nursing a sick Vestal Virgin; the letter celebrates Fannia's own marital fidelity by recalling her devotion to her exiled husband, also a philosopher.
74. For example, *Epistles* 4.19, 6.4, 6.7. For an extended study of how Pliny utilizes (his construction of) women for self-fashioning, see Carlon 2009.
75. Alston 2015.
76. Treggiari 1991: 484–485.
77. For death and funerals in relation to marriage and the life course of women, see Harlow and Laurence 2001: 132–143; Treggiari 1991: 489–498.
78. Scholars have attempted to connect the Turia of the *Laudatio* with the Turia described by Valerius Maximus: Horsfall 1983.
79. For example, *Letters to Atticus* 1.2, 2.2.
80. Harlow and Laurence 2001: 82–83.
81. For discussions about engendered, public vs. private space, see Milnor 2013: 103–124.
82. For this theme of distrust see Cantarella 1987; Hes. *Th.* 590–612, *W&D* 42–105; Semonides 7.
83. Cicero, *Letters to Atticus* 1.13.

84. *Epistle* 6.32.
85. Explicit expressions of achieved marital accord are found, for example, in Mart. *Epigram* 10.38; Statius *Silvae* 5.1.
86. *Silvae* 1.2.
87. Zeiner 2007.
88. Hersch 2010a: 231, 207–209; Hersch 2018.
89. Cf., the *Templum Faustinae*; CIL 6.1005; CIL 14.5236, which reproduced similar ideological messages.
90. Ando 2000: 157; Evans Grubbs 2005: 117; Noreña 2011: 133.
91. See Perry in this volume.
92. Blundell 1995: 66–71, 119–124; Finley 2002: 152–153; Gardner 1986: 47-9; Hersch 2010a: 9–10; Pomeroy 1975: 62–70.
93. For Greek wedding rites, see Oakley and Sinos 1993: 22–36; for Roman, see Treggiari 1991:161–169; Harlow and Laurence 2001: 60–64; Hersch 2010a.

BIBLIOGRAPHY

Aeschylus (2009), *Persians and Other Plays*, trans. Christopher Collard, Oxford: Oxford University Press.
Ager, Sheila L. (2005), "Familiarity Breeds: Incest and the Ptolemaic Dynasty," *Journal of Hellenic Studies*, 125: 1–34.
Alexiou, Margaret (2002), *Ritual Lament in Greek Tradition*, 2nd edn., Rev. edn. eds. Dimitrios Yatromanolakis and Pangiotis Roilos, Lanham, MD: Rowman & Littlefield.
Alston, Richard (2015), *Rome's Revolution: Death of the Republic and Birth of the Empire*, Oxford: Oxford University Press.
The American Heritage Dictionary of the English Language (2011), 5th edn., Boston, MA: Houghton Mifflin Harcourt.
Ando, Clifford (2000), *Imperial Ideology and Provincial Loyalty in the Roman Empire*, Berkeley: University of California Press.
Apuleius (2008), *The Golden Ass (Metamorphoses)*, trans. P. G. Walsh, Oxford: Oxford University Press.
Arjava, Antti (1996), *Women and Law in Late Antiquity*, Oxford: Oxford University Press.
Assmann, Jan (1992), *Das kulturelle Gedächtnis: Schrift, Erinnerung und politische Identität in frühen Hochkulturen*, Munich: C. H. Beck.
Astin, Alan E. (1978), *Cato the Censor*, Oxford: Clarendon Press.
Austen, Jane (2008), *Pride and Prejudice*, ed. James Kinsley, Oxford World's Classics, Oxford: Oxford University Press.
Bachvarova, Mary R. (2009), "Suppliant Danaids and Argive Nymphs in Aeschylus," *Classical Journal*, 104: 289–310.
Baldson, John P. V. D. (1962), *Roman Women: Their History and Habits*, London: The Bodley Head.
Ballentine, Floyd G. (1904), "Some Phases of the Cult of the Nymphs," *Transactions of the American Philological Association*, 104: 77–119.
Beard, Mary (1999), "The Erotics of Rape: Livy, Ovid and the Sabine Women," in Päivi Setälä and Liisa Savunen (eds.), *Female Networks and Public Sphere in Roman Society*, 1–10, Rome: *Acta Instituti Romani Finlandiae 22*.
Beaumont, Lesley A. (2012), *Childhood in Ancient Athens: Iconography and Social History*, Abingdon: Routledge.
Benincasa, Zuzanna (2012), "*Deductio in domum mariti* and the Conclusion of a *iustum matrimonium*," *Miscellanea Historico-Iuridica*, 9: 13–26.
Berger, Adolf (1968), *Encyclopedic Dictionary of Roman Law*, Philadelphia, PA: American Philosophical Society.
Bergren, Ann (2008), *Weaving Truth: Essays on Language and the Female*, Washington, DC: Center for Hellenic Studies.
Bernard, Nadine (2011), *Donne e società nella grecia antica*, Rome: Carocci.
Blok, Josine (2013), "Citizenship, the Citizen Body, and its Assemblies," in Hans Beck (ed.), *A Companion to Ancient Greek Government*, 161–175, Malden, MA: Wiley-Blackwell.

Blundell, Sue (1995), *Women in Ancient Greece*, Cambridge MA: Harvard University Press.

Boatwright, Mary (2010), "Antonine Rome: Security in the Homeland," in Björn Ewald and Carlos Noreña (eds.), *The Emperor and Rome: Space, Representation, and Ritual*, 169–197, Yale Classical Studies, 35, Cambridge: Cambridge University Press.

Boëls-Janssen, Nicole (1989), "La prêtesse aux trois voiles," *Revue des Etudes Latines*, 67: 117–133.

Boëls-Janssen, Nicole (1993), *La vie religieuse des matrons dans la Rome archaïque*, Rome: L'"Erma" di Bretschneider.

Boëls-Janssen, Nicole (2005), "De Gaia Caecilia aux fées-marraines: la survie mythique du *lanificium* initiatique," in H. Duchêne (ed.), *Survivances et métamorphoses*, Journée d'études de l'Equipe d'accueil, 1865 (Dijon): 73–93.

Bottéro, Jean (1993), "The Code of Hammurabi," in *Mesopotamia: Writing, Reasoning and the Gods*, 156–184, Chicago: University of Chicago Press.

Bradley, Keith (1987), *Slaves and Masters in the Roman Empire: A Study in Social Control*, Oxford: Oxford University Press.

Bradley, Keith (1994), *Slavery and Society at Rome*, New York: Cambridge University Press.

Braithwaite, Ann and Catherine M. Orr (2016), *Everyday Women's and Gender Studies*, New York: Routledge.

Bremmer, Jan N. (2008), *Greek Religion and Culture: The Bible and the Near East*. Jerusalem Studies in Religion and Culture, 8, Leiden: Brill.

Brooten, Bernadette J. (2015), "Early Christian Enslaved Families," in Christian Laes, Katariina Mustakallio, and Ville Vuolanto (eds.), *Children and Family in the Late Antiquity: Life, Death and Interaction*, 111–134, Leuven: Peeters.

Brown, Peter (1991), *The World of Late Antiquity*, London: Thames & Hudson.

Burkert, Walter (1992), *The Orientalizing Revolution: The Near Eastern Influence on Greek Culture in the Early Archaic Age*, Cambridge, MA: Harvard University Press.

Calame, Claude (1997), *Choruses of Young Women in Ancient Greece: Their Morphology, Religious Role, and Social Function*, trans. Derek Collins and Jane Orion, Lanham, MD: Rowman & Littlefield.

Caldwell, Lauren (2008), "Dido's Deductio: *Aeneid* 4.127–65," *Classical Philology*, 103 (4): 423–435.

Caldwell, Lauren (2015), *Roman Girlhood and the Fashioning of Femininity*, Cambridge: Cambridge University Press.

Caldwell, Richard (1993), *The Origin of the Gods: A Psychoanalytic Study of Greek Theogonic Myth*, Oxford: Oxford University Press.

Campanile, Domitilla, Filippo Carlà-Uhink, and Margherita Facella, eds. (2017), *TransAntiquity: Cross-dressing and Transgender Dynamics in the Ancient World*, London: Routledge, Taylor & Francis.

Cantarella, Eva (1976), *Studi sull'omicidio in diritto greco e romano*, Milan: A. Giuffrè.

Cantarella, Eva (1987), *Pandora's Daughters: The Role and Status of Women in Greek and Roman Antiquity*, Baltimore: Johns Hopkins University Press.

Cantarella, Eva (1991a), "*Moicheia*. Reconsidering a Problem," in Michael Gagarin (ed.), *Symposion 1990. Vorträge zur griechischen und hellenistischen Rechtsgeschichte*, 289–296, Vienna: Bohlau.

Cantarella, Eva (1991b), "Homicides of Honor: The Development of Italian Adultery Law," in David I. Kertzer and Richard P. Saller (eds.), *The Family in Italy from Antiquity to Present*, 229–246, New Haven, CT: Yale University Press.

Cantarella, Eva (2002), "Marriage and Sexuality in Republican Rome: A Roman Conjugal Love Story," in Martha C. Nussbaum and Juha Sihvola (eds.), *The Sleep of Reason*, 269–282, Chicago: University of Chicago Press.

Cantarella, Eva (2005a), "Gender, Sexuality, and Law," in Michael Gagarin and David Cohen (eds.), *The Cambridge Companion to Ancient Greek Law*, 236–253, New York: Cambridge University Press.

Cantarella, Eva (2005b), "Roman Marriage: Social, Economic and Legal Aspects," in Katariina Mustakallio, Jussi Hanska, Hanna-Leena Sainio, and Ville Vuolanto (eds.), *Hoping for Continuity: Childhood, Education and Death in Antiquity and the Middle Ages*, 25–32, Rome: Acta Instituti Romani Finlandiae 33.

Cantarella, Eva (2011), *I supplizi capitali. Origine e funzione della pena di morte in Grecia e a Roma*, Milan: Feltrinelli.

Cantarella, Eva (2015), *Non sei più mio padre. Il conflitto tra genitori e figli nel mondo antico*, Milan: Feltrinelli.

Carey, Christopher (1995), "Rape and Adultery in Athenian Law," *Classical Quarterly*, 45: 407–417.

Carlon, Jacqueline M. (2009), *Pliny's Women: Constructing Virtue and Creating Identity in the Roman World*, New York: Cambridge University Press.

Cartledge, Paul (1981), "Spartan Wives: Liberation or Licence?," *Classical Quarterly*, 31 (1): 84–105.

Catullus (1991), *The Poems of Catullus*, trans. Guy Lee, Oxford: Oxford University Press.

Cavalier, Odile, ed. (1996), *Silence et fureur: la femme et le mariage en Grèce*, Avignon: Les antiquités grecques du Musée Calvet.

Cherry, David (2002), "Gifts between Husband and Wife: The Social Origins of Roman Law," in Jean-Jacques Aubert and Boudewijn Sirks (eds.), *Speculum Iuris: Roman Law as Reflection of Social and Economic Life in Antiquity*, 34–45, Ann Arbor: University of Michigan Press.

Chiappinelli, Roberto (2007), "The *Carmen ad Uxorem* and the Genre of the Epithalamium," in Willemien Otten and Karla Pollmann (eds.), *Poetry and Exegesis in Premodern Latin Christianity*, 115–138, Leiden: Brill.

Clarysse, Willy (1988), "Une famille alexandrine dans la chora," *Chronique d'Égypte*, 63: 137–140.

Cohen, David (1984), "The Athenian Law of Adultery," *Review d'Histoire des Droits de l'Antiquité*, 31: 147–165.

Cohen, David (1991), "The Augustan Law on Adultery," in David I. Kertzer and Richard P. Saller (eds.), *The Family in Italy from Antiquity to Present*, 109–126, New Haven, CT: Yale University Press.

Corbeill, Anthony (2014), *Nature Embodied: Gesture in Ancient Rome*, Princeton, NJ: Princeton University Press.

Cornish, Francis W. (1912), *Catullus, Tibullus and Pervigilium Veneris*, Loeb Classical Library, London: William Heinemann.

Cox, Cheryl Ann (1998), *Household Interests: Property, Marriage Strategies, and Family Dynamics in Ancient Athens*, Princeton, NJ: Princeton University Press.

Daube, David (1972), *Civil Disobedience in Antiquity*, Edinburgh: Edinburgh University Press.

Davies, G. (1985), "The Significance of the Handshake Motif in Classical Funerary Art," *American Journal of Archaeology*, 89: 627–640.

Dean-Jones, Lesley (1991), "The Cultural Construct of the Female Body in Classical Greece," in Sarah B. Pomeroy (ed.), *Women's History and Ancient History*, 111–137, Chapel Hill: University of North Carolina Press.

Deming, Will (2004), *Paul on Marriage and Celibacy: The Hellenistic Background of 1 Corinthians 7*, 2nd edn., Grand Rapids, MI: William B. Eerdmans.
Dessau, H. ed. (1892–1916), *Inscriptiones Latinae Selectae* (= ILS), Berlin.
Detienne, Marcel (1977), *The Garden of Adonis: Spices in Greek Mythology*, Princeton, NJ: Princeton University Press.
Deubner, Ludwig (1978), "ΚΑΤΑΧΥΣΜΑΤΑ und Münzzauber," *Rheinisches Museum*, 121 (3/4): 240–254.
Dillon, Matthew (1997), *Pilgrims and Pilgrimage*, London: Routledge.
Dillon, Matthew (1999), "Post-nuptial Sacrifices on Kos (Segre, *ED* 178) and Ancient Greek Marriage Rites," *Zeitschrift für Papyrologie und Epigraphik*, 124: 63–80.
Dillon, Matthew (2002), *Girls and Women in Classical Greek Religion*, London: Routledge.
Dillon, Matthew (2017a), "Children in Archaic and Classical Greek Religion: Non-Adult Active and Passive Ritual Agency," in Lesley Beaumont, Matthew Dillon, and Nicola Harrington (eds.), *Children in Antiquity: Perspectives and Experiences of Childhood in the Ancient Mediterranean*, Oxford: Routledge.
Dillon, Matthew (2017b), *Omens and Oracles: Divination in Ancient Greece*, Oxford: Routledge.
DiLuzio, Meghan, J. (2016), *A Place at the Altar: Priestesses in Republican Rome*, Princeton, NJ: Princeton University Press.
Dixon, M. D. (2005), "Menander's *Perikeiromene* and Demetrios Poliorketes," *Classical Bulletin*, 81: 131–143.
Dixon, Suzanne (1985), "The Marriage Alliance in the Roman Elite," *Journal of Family History*, 10 (4): 353–378.
Dover, Kenneth J. (2002), "Classical Greek Attitudes to Sexual Behavior," in Laura McClure (ed.), *Sexuality and Gender in the Classical World*, 19–33, Malden, MA: Wiley-Blackwell.
Dowden, Ken (1989), *Death and the Maiden: Girls' Initiation Rites in Greek Mythology*, London: Routledge.
Edwards, Catherine (1997), "Unspeakable Professions: Public Performance and Prostitution in Ancient Rome," in Judith P. Hallett and Marilyn B. Skinner (eds.), *Roman Sexualities*, 66–95, Princeton, NJ: Princeton University Press.
Edwards, Catherine (2007), *Death in Ancient Rome*, New Haven, CT: Yale University Press.
Evans Grubbs, Judith (1989), "Abduction Marriage in Antiquity: A Law of Constantine (CTh IX. 24. I) and its Social Context," *Journal of Roman Studies*, 79: 59–83.
Evans Grubbs, Judith (1995), *Law and Family in Late Antiquity: The Emperor Constantine's Marriage Legislation*, Oxford: Oxford University Press.
Evans Grubbs, Judith (2002), *Women and the Law in the Roman Empire: A Sourcebook on Marriage, Divorce and Widowhood*, London: Routledge.
Evans Grubbs, Judith (2005), "Parent-Child Conflict in the Roman Family," in Michele George (ed.), *The Roman Family in the Empire: Rome, Italy, and Beyond*, 93–128, Oxford: Oxford University Press.
Evans Grubbs, Judith (2010), "Marriage Contracts in the Roman Empire," in Lena Larsson Lovén and Agneta Strömberg (eds.), *Ancient Marriage in Myth and Reality*, 78–101, Newcastle-upon-Tyne: Cambridge Scholars Publishing.
Friedl, Raimund (1996), *Der Konkubinat im kaiserzeitlichen Rom*, Stuttgart: Franz Steiner.
Feeney, Denis (2013), "Catullus 61: Epithalamium and Comparison," *Cambridge Classical Journal*, 59: 70–97.
Felson-Rubin, Nancy (1994), *Regarding Penelope: From Character to Poetics*, Princeton, NJ: Princeton University Press.

Ferrari, Gloria P. (2003), "What Kind of Rite of Passage was the Ancient Greek Wedding?," in David B. Dodd and Christopher A. Faraone (eds.), *Initiation in Ancient Greek Rituals and Narratives: New Critical Perspectives*, 27–42, London: Routledge.

Finley, Moses I. (2002), "The Silent Women of Rome," in Laura McClure (ed.), *Sexuality and Gender in the Classical World*, 147–160, Malden, MA: Wiley-Blackwell.

Flory, Marleen B. (1984), "Sic Exempla Parantur: Livia's Shrine to Concord and the Porticus Liviae," *Historia: Zeitschrift für Alte Geschichte*, bd. 33, H. 3 (3rd quarter, 1984): 309–330.

Flower, Harriet I. (2017), *The Dancing Lares and the Serpent in the Garden: Religion at the Roman Street Corner*, Princeton, NJ: Princeton University Press.

Foley, Helene P. (1994), *The Homeric Hymn to Demeter: Translation, Commentary, and Interpretive Essays*, Princeton, NJ: Princeton University Press.

Foley, Helene P. (2003a), *Female Acts in Greek Tragedy*, Princeton, NJ: Princeton University Press.

Foley, Helene P. (2003b), "Greek Mothers and Daughters," in Jenifer Neils and John Oakley (eds.), *Coming of Age in Ancient Greece: Images of Childhood in the Classical Past*, 113–138, New Haven, CT: Yale University Press.

Fowler, Warde W. (1916), "*Confarreatio*: A Study of Patrician Usage," *Journal of Roman Studies*, 6: 185–195.

Foxhall, Lyn (1989), "Household, Gender and Property in Classical Athens," *Classical Quarterly*, 39 (1): 22–24.

Foxhall, Lyn (2005), "Female Inheritance in Athenian Law," in Deborah Lyons and Raymond Westbrook (eds.), *Women and Property in Ancient Near Eastern and Mediterranean Societies*, Washington, DC: Center for Hellenic Studies, Harvard University; Baltimore: Johns Hopkins University Press.

Foxhall, Lyn (2013), *Studying Gender in Classical Antiquity*, Cambridge: Cambridge University Press.

Foxhall, Lyn and John Salmon, eds. (1998), *When Men were Men: Masculinity, Power, and Identity in Classical Antiquity*. London: Routledge.

Frier, Bruce W. and Thomas A. G. McGinn (2004), *A Casebook on Roman Family Law*, Oxford: Oxford University Press.

Freud, Sigmund (2001a), *The Interpretation of Dreams*, London: Vintage.

Freud, Sigmund (2001b), *Totem and Taboo and Other Works (1912–13)*, London: Vintage.

Gaca, Kathy L. (2010), "The Andrapodizing of War Captives in Greek Historical Memory," *Transactions of the American Philological Association*, 140: 117–161.

Gaca, Kathy L. (2012), "Telling the Girls from the Boys and Children: Interpreting Παῖδες in the Sexual Violence of Populace-Ravaging Ancient Warfare," *Illinois Classical Studies*, 35–36: 85–109.

Gaca, Kathy L. (2014), "Martial Rape, Pulsating Fear, and the Sexual Maltreatment of Girls (παῖδες), Virgins (παρθένοι), and Women (γυναῖκες) in Antiquity," *American Journal of Philology*, 135: 303–357.

Gaca, Kathy L. (2015), "Ancient Warfare and the Ravaging Martial Rape of Girls and Women: Evidence from Homeric Epic and Greek Drama," in Mark Masterson, Nancy Rabinowitz, and James Robson (eds.), *Sex in Antiquity: Exploring Gender and Sexuality in the Ancient World*, 278–298, London: Routledge.

Gagarin, Michael (2005), "The Unity of Greek Law," in Michael Gagarin and David Cohen (eds.), *The Cambridge Companion to Ancient Greek Law*, 29–40, New York: Cambridge University Press.

Gagarin, Michael (2010), *Writing Greek Law*, Cambridge: Cambridge University Press.

Gagarin, Michael (), "Inscribing Laws in Greece and the Near East," in H. A. Rupprecht (ed.), *Symposion 2003. Vorträge zur griechischen und hellenistischen Rechtsgeschichte*, 9–20, Vienna: Bohlau.

Gallia, Andrew B. (2014), "The Vestal Habit," *Classical Philology*, 109: 222–240.

Gardner, Jane F. (1986), *Women in Roman Law and Society*, Bloomington: Indiana University Press.

Garvie, A. F. (1969), *Aeschylus' Supplices: Play and Trilogy*, Cambridge: Cambridge University Press.

General Election Ballot Question Language (2012), *Elections.state.md.us*. Maryland State Board of Elections: Question 6. Referendum Petition (ch. 2 of the 2012 Legislative Session). Civil Marriage Protection Act.

Giardina, Andrea (1993), "Melania the Saint," in Augusto Fraschetti (ed.), *Roman Women*, 190–207, Chicago: University of Chicago Press.

Gildenhard, Ingo and Andrew Zissos (2007), "Barbarian Variations: Tereus, Procne and Philomela in Ovid (*Met.* 6.412–674) and Beyond," *Dictynna. Revue de poétique latine*, 4: 1–42.

Glare, P. G. W. (1982), *Oxford Latin Dictionary*, Oxford: Clarendon Press.

Glazebrook, Allison and Nicola Mellor (2013), "Bodies and Sexuality," in Janet Tulloch (ed.), *A Cultural History of Women in Antiquity*, 33–55, New York: Bloomsbury Academic.

Glazebrook, Allison and Kelly Olson (2013), "Greek and Roman Marriage," in Thomas Hubbard (ed.), *A Companion to Greek and Roman Sexualities*, 69–82, Malden, MA: Wiley-Blackwell.

Golden, Mark (1985a), "'Donatus' and Athenian Phratries," *Classical Quarterly*, 35: 9–13.

Golden, Mark (1985b), "*Pais*, Child and Slave," *L'Antique Classique*, 54: 91–104.

Golden, Mark (2011), "Slavery and the Greek Family," in Keith Bradley and Paul Cartledge (eds.), *The Cambridge World History of Slavery*, vol. 1: *The Ancient Mediterranean World*, 134–152, Cambridge: Cambridge University Press.

Golden, Mark (2015), *Children and Childhood in Classical Athens*, 2nd edn., Baltimore: Johns Hopkins University Press.

Greengus, Samuel (1969), "The Old Babylonian Marriage Contract," *Journal of the American Oriental Society*, 89 (3): 505–532.

Haase, Kai and Roland Steinacher (2017), "Family Forms and Conflicts in Roman North Africa," in Sabine R. Huebner and Geoffrey Nathan (eds.), *Mediterranean Families in Antiquity: Households, Extended Families, and Domestic Space*, 221–240, Malden, MA: Wiley-Blackwell.

Hague, Rebecca H. (1983), "Ancient Greek Wedding Songs: The Tradition of Praise," *Journal of Folklore Research*, 20 (2/3): 131–143.

Hall, Stuart (1997), "Representation, Meaning and Language," in Stuart Hall (ed.), *Representation: Cultural Representations and Signifying Practices*, 15–64, London: Sage.

Hallett, Judith P. (1984), "The Role of Women in Roman Elegy: Counter-cultural Feminism," in John Peradotto and John P. Sullivan (eds.), *Women in the Ancient World: The Arethusa Papers*, 241–262, Albany: State University of New York Press. (First published in 1973, in *Arethusa* 6 (1): 103–124. Reprinted in 2002, in Paul Allen Miller (ed.), *Latin Erotic Elegy: An Anthology and Reader*, 329–347, London: Routledge.)

Hallett, Judith P. (2008), "Cinematic and Poetic Lenses on Ancient Imperial Emotions: The BBC-TV *I, Claudius*, Tibullus 3.1–6 and Forced Divorce in Julio-Claudian Rome," in Stacie Raucci (ed.), "Recreating the Classics: Hollywood and Ancient Empires," special issue of *Classical and Modern Literature*, 28 (1): 111–127.

Hallett, Judith P. (2013), "Sexualizing the Puella in Latin Comedy, Lyric and Elegy," *Eugesta: Journal on Gender Studies in Antiquity* 3: 195–208.

Hansen, Mogens Herman (1998), *Polis and City-State: An Ancient Concept and its Modern Equivalent*, Copenhagen: Munksgaard.

Harlow, Mary and Ray Laurence (2001), *Growing Up and Growing Old in Ancient Rome: A Life Course Approach*, London: Routledge.

Harlow, Mary and Ray Laurence (2010), "Betrothal, Mid-Late Childhood and the Life Course," in Lena Larsson Lovén and Agneta Strömberg (eds.), *Ancient Marriage in Myth and Reality*, 56–77, Newcastle-upon-Tyne: Cambridge Scholar Publishing.

Harper, Kyle (2013), *From Shame to Sin: The Christian Transformation of Sexual Morality in Late Antiquity*, Cambridge, MA: Harvard University Press.

Harris, Rivkah (1974), "The Case of Three Babylonian Marriage Contracts," *Journal of Near Eastern Studies*, 33 (4): 363–369.

Harrison, Alick R. W. (1968), *The Law of Athens*, vol. 1, Oxford: Oxford University Press.

Harrison, Jane E. (1912), *Themis: A Study of the Social Origins of Greek Religion*, Cambridge: Cambridge University Press.

Heitman, Richard (2001), *Taking Her Seriously: Penelope and the Plot of Homer's Odyssey*, Chicago: University of Chicago Press.

Hemelrijk, Emily A. (2004), "Masculinity and Femininity in the 'Laudatio Turiae'," *Classical Quarterly*, 2 (54): 185–197.

Herodotus (2008), *The Histories*, trans. Robin Waterfield, Oxford: Oxford University Press.

Hersch, Karen K. (2007), "Violentilla Victa," *Arethusa*, 40 (2): 197–205.

Hersch, Karen K. (2010a), *The Roman Wedding*, Cambridge: Cambridge University Press.

Hersch, Karen K. (2010b), "The Woolworker Bride," in Lena Larsson Lovén and Agneta Strömberg (eds.), *Ancient Marriage in Myth and Reality*, 122–135, Newcastle-upon-Tyne: Cambridge Scholars Publishing.

Hersch Karen K. (2014), "Introduction to the Roman Wedding: Two Case Studies," *Classical Journal*, 109: 223–232.

Hersch, Karen K. (2019), "Violence and Submission in Wedding Ritual: Greek and Roman Sources," in Jeffrey Beneker and Georgia Tsouvala (eds.), *The Discourse of Marriage in the 1st Century CE*, Madison: Wisconsin University Press.

Hesiod (2006), *Theogony; Works and Days; Testimonia*, ed. and trans. Glenn Most, Loeb Classical Library, Cambridge, MA: Harvard University Press.

Homer (1974), *The Iliad*, trans. Robert Fitzgerald, New York: Anchor Books.

Homer (1996), *The Odyssey*, trans. Robert Fagles, London: Penguin Books.

Homer (2003), *Homeric Hymns. Homeric Apocrypha. Lives of Homer*, trans. Martin L. West, Cambridge, MA: Harvard University Press.

Horsfall, Nicholas (1983), "Some Problems in the '*Laudatio Turiae*,'" BICS, 30: 85–98.

Hoffmann, Genevieve (1990), *Le Châtiment des amants dans la Grèce Classique*, Paris: De Boccard.

Hubbard, Thomas K., ed. ([1994] 2014), *A Companion to Greek and Roman Sexualities. Blackwell Companions to the Ancient World. Literature and Culture*, Malden, MA: Wiley-Blackwell.

Hunter, David G. (2007), "Sexuality, Marriage, and the Family," in Augustine Casiday and Frederick W. Norris (eds.), *The Cambridge History of Christianity*, vol. 2: *Constantine to c. 600*, 585–600, Cambridge: Cambridge University Press.

Jenkins, Ian D. (1985), "The Ambiguity of Greek Textiles," *Arethusa*, 18 (2): 109–133.

Jeppesen-Wigelsworth, Alison (2013), "Political Bedfellows: Tullia, Dolabella, and Caelius," *Arethusa*, 46 (1): 65–85.

Johansson, Linnéa (2010), "The Roman Wedding and the Household Gods: The Genius and the Lares and Their Different Roles in the Rituals of Marriage" in Lena Larsson Lovén and Agneta Strömberg (eds.), *Ancient Marriage in Myth and Reality*, 136–147, Newcastle-upon-Tyne: Cambridge Scholars Publishing.

Jolowicz, Herbert F. and Barry Nicholas (1972), *Historical Introduction to the Study of Roman Law*, Cambridge: Cambridge University Press.

Joshel, Sandra (2002), "The Body Female and the Body Politic: Livy's Lucretia and Verginia," in Laura McClure (ed.), *Sexuality and Gender in the Classical World*, 163–192, Malden, MA: Wiley-Blackwell.

Joshel, Sandra (2010), *Slavery in the Roman World*, New York: Cambridge University Press.

Just, Roger (1989), *Women in Athenian Law and Life*, London: Routledge.

Kahlos, Maijastina (1994), "Fabia Aconia Paulina and the death of Praetextatus – Rhetoric and Ideals in Late Antiquity," (*CIL* VI 1779), *Arctos*, 28: 13–25.

Kahlos, Maijastina (2002), *Vettius Agorius Praetextatus – Senatorial Life in Between*. Rome: Acta Instituti Romani Finlandiae 26.

Karanika, Andromache (2014), *Voices at Work: Women, Performance, and Labor in Ancient Greece*, Baltimore: Johns Hopkins University Press.

Keydell, Rudolph (1962), "Epithalamium," *RAC*, 5: 927–943.

Kampen, Natalie B. (1981), "Biographical Narration and Roman Funerary Art," *American Journal of Archaeology*, 85 (1): 47–58.

Keuls, Eva C. (1993), *The Reign of the Phallus: Sexual Politics in Ancient Athens*, Berkeley: University of California Press.

King, Helen ([1983] 2002), "Bound to Bleed: Artemis and Greek Women," in Laura McClure (ed.), *Sexuality and Gender in the Classical World*, 77–97, Malden, MA: Wiley-Blackwell. (Also in Averil Cameron and Amalie Kuhrt, eds., *Images of Women in Antiquity*, 109–127, Detroit: Wayne State University Press.)

King, Helen (1998), *Hippocrates' Woman: Reading the Female Body in Ancient Greece*, London: Routledge.

Konstan, David (1987), "Between Courtesan and Wife: Menander's '*Perikeiromene*,'" *Phoenix*, 41 (2): 122–139.

Lacey, Walter K. (1968), *The Family in Classical Greece*, Ithaca, NY: Cornell University Press.

Laes, Christian and Ville Vuolanto (2017), "Household and Family Dynamics in Late Antique Southern Gaul," in Sabine R. Huebner and Geoffrey Nathan (eds.), *Mediterranean Families in Antiquity: Households, Extended Families, and Domestic Space*, 258–282, Malden, MA: Wiley-Blackwell.

LaFollette, Laetitia (1994), "The Costume of the Roman Bride," in Judith Lynn Sebesta and Larissa Bonfante (eds.), *The World of Roman Costume*, 54–64, Madison: University of Wisconsin Press.

La Fosse, Mona Tokarek (2017), "Age Hierarchy and Social Networks among Urban Women in the Roman East," in Sabine R. Huebner and Geoffrey Nathan (eds.), *Mediterranean Families in Antiquity: Households, Extended Families, and Domestic Space*, 204–220, Malden, MA: Wiley-Blackwell.

Lape, Susan (2002/2003), "Solon and the Institution of the 'Democratic' Family Form," *Classical Journal*, 98 (2): 117–139.

Lape, Susan (2009), *Reproducing Athens: Menander's Comedy, Democratic Culture, and the Hellenistic City*, Princeton, NJ: Princeton University Press.

Lape, Susan (2010), "Gender in Menander's Comedy," in Antonis Petrides and Sophia Papaioannou (eds.), *New Perspectives on Postclassical Comedy*, 51–78, Newcastle-upon-Tyne: Cambridge Scholars Publishing.

Lape, Susan (2011), "Heterosexuality," in Mark Golden and Peter Toohey (eds.), *A Cultural History of Sexuality in the Classical World*, 17–36, London: Bloomsbury.

Lardinois, André (2001), "Keening Sappho: Female Speech Genres in Sappho's Poetry," in André Lardinois and Laura McClure (eds.), *Making Silence Speak: Women's Voices in Greek Literature and Society*, 75–92, Princeton, NJ: Princeton University Press.

Larson, Jennifer (2001), *Greek Nymphs: Myth, Cult, Lore*, Oxford: Oxford University Press.

Larsson Lovén, Lena (1998), "*Lanam Fecit*: Woolworking and Female Virtue," in Lena Larsson Lovén and Agneta Strömberg (eds.), *Aspects of Women in Antiquity: Proceedings of the First Nordic Symposium on Women's Lives in Antiquity*, 85–95, Jonsered: Paul Åströms Förlag.

Larsson Lovén, Lena (2007), "Wool-work as a Gender Symbol in Ancient Rome," in Carole Gillis and Marie-Louise Nosch (eds.), *Ancient Textiles: Production, Craft and Society. Proceedings of the First International Conference on Ancient Textiles*, 229–236, Sävedalen: Paul Åströms Förlag.

Larsson Lovén, Lena (2010), "*Coniugal Concordia*: Marriage and Marital Ideals on Roman Funerary Monuments," in Lena Larsson Lovén and Agneta Strömberg (eds.), *Ancient Marriage in Myth and Reality*, 204–220, Newcastle-upon-Tyne: Cambridge Scholars Publishing.

Larsson Lovén, Lena and Agneta Strömberg, eds. (2010), *Ancient Marriage in Myth and Reality*, Newcastle-upon-Tyne: Cambridge Scholars Publishing.

Laurence, Ray and Agneta Strömberg, eds. (2012), *Families in the Greco-Roman World*, London: Continuum.

Lattimore, Richmond (1942), *Themes in Greek and Latin Epitaphs*, Urbana: University of Illinois.

Lázaro, R. 2006, "Talassio," *Cuadernos de Filología Clásica. Estudios Latinos*, 26 (1): 25–34.

Leduc, Christian (1992), "Marriage in Ancient Greece," in Pauline Schmitt Pantel (ed.), *A History of Women in the West*, vol. 1: *From Ancient Goddesses to Christian Saints*, 233–295, Cambridge, MA: Belknap Press.

Le Bohec, Yann (1993), *L'esercito romano. Le armi imperiali da Augusto alla fine del terzo secolo*, Rome: La nuova Italia Scientifica.

Lee, Mireille M. (2015), *Body, Dress and Identity in Ancient Greece*, Cambridge: Cambridge University Press.

Leeds-Hurwitz, Wendy (2002), *Wedding as Text: Communicating Cultural Identities through Ritual*, Mahwah, NJ: Lawrence Erlbaum Associates.

Lefkowitz, Mary and Maureen Fant (1982), *Women's Life in Greece and Rome*, Baltimore: Johns Hopkins University Press.

Levaniouk, Olga (2008), "Lament and Hymenaios in Erinna's *Distaff*," in Ann Suter (ed.), *Lament: Studies in the Ancient Mediterranean and Beyond*, 200–232, Oxford: Oxford University Press.

Levick, Barbara (2012), "Women and Law," in Sharon L. James and Sheila Dillon (eds.), *A Companion to Women in the Ancient World*, 96–106, Malden, MA: Wiley-Blackwell.

Lev Kenaan, Vered (2008), *Pandora's Senses: The Feminine Character of the Ancient Text*, Madison: Wisconsin University Press.

Linderski, Jerzy (1995), "Review of *Roman Marriage: Iusti Coniuges from the Time of Cicero to the Time of Ulpian*," *American Journal of Philology*, 116 (1): 154–156.

Liptak, Adam (2015), "Supreme Court Ruling Makes Same-Sex Marriage a Right Nationwide," *New York Times*, June 26, 2015.

Llewellyn-Jones, Lloyd (2003), *Aphrodite's Tortoise: The Veiled Woman of Ancient Greece*, Swansea: Classical Press of Wales.

Lobel, Edgar and Denys Page (1955), *Poetarum Lesbiorum Fragmenta* (= LP), Oxford: Oxford University Press.

Looper-Friedman, Susan E. (1987), "The Decline of Manus-Marriage in Rome," *Tijdschrift voor Rechtsgeschiedenis/Legal History Review*, 55: 281–296.

Loraux, Nicole (1984), *The Children of Athena: Athenian Ideas about Citizenship and the Division between the Sexes*, trans. Caroline Levine, Princeton, NJ: Princeton University Press.

Loraux, Nicole (1995), *The Experience of Tiresias*, trans. Paul Wissing, Princeton, NJ: Princeton University Press.

Lutz, Cora (1947), "Musonius Rufus: 'The Roman Socrates'," *Yale Classical Studies*, 10: 32–147.

Lyghounis, Maria Gilda (1991), "Elementi tradizionali nella poesia nuziale greca," *Materiali e discussioni per l'analisi dei testi classici*, 27: 159–198.

MacLachlan, Bonnie (2012), *Women in Ancient Greece: A Source Book*, London: Continuum.

Maffi, Alberto (1991), *Il diritto di famiglia nel codice di Gortina*, Milan: Cuem.

Manfredini, Matteo (2017), "Family Forms in Later Periods of the Mediterranean," in Sabine R. Huebner and Geoffrey Nathan (eds.), *Mediterranean Families in Antiquity: Households, Extended Families, and Domestic Space*, 310–323, Malden, MA: Wiley-Blackwell.

Manville, Philip Brook (1990), *The Origins of Citizenship in Ancient Athens*, Princeton, NJ: Princeton University Press.

Mantle, Inga C. (2002), "The Roles of Children in Roman Religion," *Greece and Rome*, 49 (1): 85–106.

Masterson, Mark, Nancy Sorkin Rabinowitz, and James Robson, eds. (2015), *Sex in Antiquity: Exploring Gender and Sexuality in the Ancient World*, New York: Routledge.

McGinn, Thomas (1991), "Concubinage and the Lex Iulia on Adultery," *Transactions of the American Philological Association*, 121: 335–375.

McGinn, Thomas (1998), *Prostitution, Sexuality, and the Law in Ancient Rome*, Oxford: Oxford University Press.

McNeil, Lynda (2005), "Bridal Cloths, Cover-ups and *Kharis*: The 'Carpet Scene' in Aeschylus' Agamemnon," *Greece and Rome*, 52 (1): 1–17.

Miles, Gary B. (1995), *Livy: Reconstructing Early Rome*, Ithaca, NY: Cornell University Press.

Milnor, Kristina (2013), "Public and Private," in Janet Tulloch (ed.), *A Cultural History of Women in Antiquity*, 105–124, New York: Bloomsbury Academic.

Modrzejewski, Joseph Mélèze (2005), "Greek Law in the Hellenistic Period: Family and Marriage," in Michael Gagarin and David Cohen (eds.), *The Cambridge Companion to Ancient Greek Law*, 343–354, New York: Cambridge University Press.

Morabito, Marcel (1981), *Les réalités de l'esclavage d'après le Digeste*, Paris: Annales Littéraires de l'Université de Besançon.

Morales, Helen (2004), *Vision and Narrative in Achilles Tatius' Leucippe and Clitophon*, Cambridge: Cambridge University Press.

Morris, Ian (1986), "The Use and Abuse of Homer," *Classical Antiquity*, 5: 81–138.

Müller, Frank G. J. M. (1994), *The Aldobrandini Wedding*, Amsterdam: J. C. Gieben, 1994.

Mustakallio, Katariina (1999), "Legendary Women and Female Groups in Livy," in Päivi Setälä and Liisa Savunen (eds.), *Female Networks and Public Sphere in Roman Society*, 53–64, Rome: Acta Instituti Romani Finlandiae 22.

Mustakallio, Katariina (2013), "The Life Cycle: From Birth to Old Age," in Janet H. Tulloch (ed.), *A Cultural History of Women*, vol. 1: *In Antiquity*, 15–31, London: Bloomsbury Academic.

Muth, Robert (1954), "Hochzeitslieder der Griechen," *Anzeiger für die Altertumswissenschaft*, 7: 253–356.

Noreña, Carlos (2011), *Imperial Ideals in the Roman West: Representation, Circulation, Power*, Cambridge: Cambridge University Press.

North, Helen (1977), "The Mare, the Vixen, and the Bee: *Sophrosyne* as the Virtue of Women in Antiquity," *Illinois Classical Studies*, 2: 35–48.

Noy, David (1990), "Matchmakers and Marriage-markets in Antiquity," *Echos du Monde Classique*, 34 (9): 375–400.

Oakley, John H. and Rebecca H. Sinos (1993), *The Wedding in Ancient Athens*, Madison: University of Wisconsin Press.

Obasogie, Osagie K. (2017), "Was 'Loving vs. Virginia' Really about Love?," *The Atlantic*, June 12, 2017. Available online: https://www.google.com/amp/s/www.theatlantic.com/amp/article/52929/ (accessed).

O'Bryhim, Shawn (2008), "Myrrha's 'Wedding' (Ov. Met. 10. 446–70)," *Classical Quarterly*, 58 (1): 190–195.

Ogden, Daniel (1996), *Greek Bastardy in the Classic and Hellenistic Periods*, Oxford: Clarendon Press.

Ogden, Daniel (1997), "Rape, Adultery and the Protection of Bloodlines in Classical Athens," in Susan Deacy and Karen Pierce (eds.), *Rape in Antiquity: Sexual Violence in the Greek and Roman Worlds*, 25–41, London: Bloomsbury.

Ogden, Daniel (1999), *Polygamy, Prostitutes and Death: The Hellenistic Dynasties*, London: Duckworth, with the Classical Press of Wales.

Ogilvie, Robert M. (1965), *A Commentary on Livy: Books I–V*, Oxford: Oxford University Press.

Olson, Kelly (2008), *Dress and the Roman Woman: Self-presentation and Society*, New York: Routledge.

Orrells, Daniel (2015), *Sex: Antiquity and its Legacy. Ancients and Moderns*, Oxford: Oxford University Press.

Osgood, Josiah (2014), *Turia: A Roman Woman's Civil War*, Oxford: Oxford University Press.

Ovid (1916), *Metamorphoses*, vol. 1, trans. Frank Justus Miller, Cambridge, MA: Harvard University Press.

Panoussi, Vasikili (2007), "Sexuality and Ritual: Catullus' Wedding Poems," in Marilyn Skinner (ed.), *A Companion to Catullus*, 276–292, Malden, MA: Blackwell.

Papadopoulou, Thalia (2014), *Aeschylus: Suppliants*, London: Bloomsbury.

Parker, Robert (1983), *Miasma. Pollution and Purification in Early Greek Religion*, Oxford: Oxford University Press.

Parker, Robert (2005), *Polytheism and Society at Athens*, Oxford: Oxford University Press.

Patterson, Cynthia B. (1990), "Those Athenian Bastards," *Classical Antiquity*, 9: 40–73.

Patterson, Cynthia B. (1998), *The Family in Greek History*, Cambridge, MA: Harvard University Press.

Pavlovskis, Zoja (1965), "Statius and the Late Latin Epithalamia," *Classical Philology*, 60 (3): 164–177.

Pentti, Mikko (2015), "The Role of Servants in the Upbringing of the Roman Elite Girls," in Katariina Mustakallio and Jussi Hanska (eds.), *Agents and Objects: Children in Pre-Modern Europe*, 112–145, Rome: Acta Instituti Romani Finlandiae 42.

Petersen, Lauren H. (1997), "Divided Consciousness and Female Companionship: Reconstructing Female Subjectivity on Greek Vases," *Arethusa*, 30 (1): 35–74.

Petropoulos, J. C. B. (Ioannis) (2003), *Eroticism in Ancient and Medieval Greek Poetry*, London: Duckworth.

Phang, Sara Elise (2001), *The Marriage of Roman Soldiers (13 B.C. – A.D. 235): Law and Family in the Imperial Army*, Leiden: Brill.

Phillipides, Stamatis N. (1983), "Narrative Strategies and Ideology in Livy's 'Rape of Lucretia,'" *Helios*, 10: 113–119.

Phillips, David D. (2013), *The Law of Ancient Athens*, Ann Arbor: University of Michigan Press.

Phillips, Jane (1977), "Juno in *Aeneid* 4.693–705," *Vergilius*, 23: 30–33.

Pintchman, Tracy (1998), "Gender Complementarity and Gender Hierarchy in Puranic Accounts of Creation," *Journal of American Academy of Religion*, 66: 257–282.

Plautus (2011), *Amphitryon*, trans. Wolfgang de Melo, Cambridge, MA: Harvard University Press.

Plutarch (1914), *Lives*, vol. 1, trans. Bernadotte Perrin, Cambridge, MA: Harvard University Press.

Pomeroy, Sarah (1975), *Goddesses, Whores, Wives, and Slaves: Women in Classical Antiquity*, New York: Schocken Books.

Pomeroy, Sarah (2002), *Spartan Women*, Oxford: Oxford University Press.

Postgate, John N. (1992), "Laws and the Law," in *Early Mesopotamia: Society and Economy at the Dawn of History*, 275–298, London: Routledge.

Prescendi, F. (2010), "Children and the Transmission of Religious Knowledge," in V. Dasen and T. Späth (eds.), *Children, Memory, and Family Identity in Roman Culture*, 73–93, Oxford: Oxford University Press.

Rasi, Piero (1946), *Consensus facit nuptias*, Milan: Giuffrè.

Rawson, Beryl (1974), "Roman Concubinage and Other De Facto Marriages," *Transactions of the American Philological Association*, 104: 279–305.

Redfield, James (1982), "Notes on the Greek Wedding," *Arethusa*, 15: 181–201.

Redfield, James (2003), *The Locrian Maidens: Love and Death in Greek Italy*, Princeton, NJ: Princeton University Press.

Reekmans, Louis (1958), "La 'dextrarum iunctio' dans l'iconographie romaine et paléochrétienne," *Bulletin de l'Institut Historique Belge de Rome/Institut Historique Belge* 31, 23–95, Rome: l'Institut Historique Belge de Rome.

Rehm, Rush (1994), *Marriage to Death: The Conflation of Wedding and Funeral Rituals in Greek Tragedy*, Princeton, NJ: Princeton University Press.

Reilly, Joan (1989), "Many Brides: 'Mistress and Maid' on Athenian Lekythoi," *Hesperia*, 58: 411–444.

Reinsberg, Carola (2006), *Die Sarkophage mit Darstellungen aus dem Menschenleben. Dritter Teil: Vita Romana-Sarkophage*, Berlin: Gebr. Mann Verlag.

Reynolds, Philip Lyndon (1994), *Marriage in the Western Church: The Christianization of Marriage during the Patristic and Early Medieval Periods*, Leiden: Brill.

Richlin, Amy (2015), "Reading Boy-love and Child-love in the Greco-Roman World," in Mark Masterson, Nancy Sorkin Rabinowitz, and James Robson (eds.), *Sex in Antiquity: Exploring Gender and Sexuality in the Ancient World*, 352–373, New York: Routledge.

Ricks, Stephen D. (2014), "*Dexiosis* and *Dextrarum Iunctio*: The Sacred Handclasp in the Classical and Early Christian World," *FARMS Review*, 18 (1): 431–436.

Richardson, Lawrence (1992), *A New Topographical Dictionary of Ancient Rome*, Baltimore: Johns Hopkins University Press.

Robins, Gay (1993), *Women in Ancient Egypt*, Cambridge, MA: Harvard University Press.
Rose, Herbert J. (1924), *The Roman Questions of Plutarch: A New Translation, with Introductory Essays*, Oxford: Clarendon Press.
Roselaar, Saskia T. (2013), "The Concept of *Conubium* in the Roman Republic," in Paul J. du Plessis (ed.), *New Frontiers: Law and Society in the Roman World*, 102–122, Edinburgh: Edinburgh University Press.
Roth, Martha T. (1988), "'She Will Die by the Iron Dagger': Adultery and Neo-Babylonian Marriage," *Journal of the Economic and Social History of the Orient*, 31 (2): 186–206.
Roth, Martha T., ed. (1995), *Law Collections from Mesopotamia and Asia Minor*, Atlanta, GA: Scholars Press.
Roth, Martha T., ed. (1997), *Law Collections from Mesopotamia and Asia Minor*, 2nd edn., Atlanta, GA: Scholars Press.
Rudd, Niall (1981), "Romantic Love in Classical Times?," *Ramus*, 10: 140–158.
Sabetai, Victoria (1997), "Aspects of Nuptial and Genre Imagery in Fifth-Century Athens: Issues of Interpretation and Methodology," in John H. Oakley, William D. E. Coulson, and Olga Palagia (eds.), *Athenian Potters and Painters*, 319–355, Oxford: Oxbow.
Sabetai, Victoria (1998), "Marriage Boiotian Style," *Hesperia*, 67 (3): 323–334.
Saller, Richard (1987), "Slavery and the Roman Family," *Slavery and Abolition*, 8: 65–87.
Saller, Richard (2007), "Household and Gender," in Walter Scheidel, Ian Morris, and Richard Saller (eds.), *The Cambridge Economic History of the Greco-RomanWorld*, 87–112, Cambridge: Cambridge University Press.
Sappho (1992), *The Poetry of Sappho*, trans. Jim Powell, Oxford: Oxford University Press.
Scafuro, Adele (2014), "Menander," in Michael Fontaine and Adele Scafuro (eds.), *Oxford Handbook of Greek and Roman Comedy*, 218–238, Oxford: Oxford University Press.
Scheidel, Walter (2007), "Roman Funerary Commemoration and the Age at First Marriage," *Classical Philology*, 102 (4): 389–402.
Scheidel, Walter (2011), "Monogamy and Polygyny," in Beryl Rawson (ed.), *A Companion to Families in the Greek and Roman Worlds*, 108–115, Oxford: Wiley-Blackwell.
Scheidel, Walter (2013), "Studying the State," in Peter Fibiger Bang and Walter Scheidel (eds.), *The Oxford Handbook of the State in the Ancient Near East and Mediterranean*, 5–57, New York: Oxford University Press.
Schmitt Pantel, Pauline (2010), "Les Mariages des Hommes Politiques Athénians Vème siècle: Histoire des Moeurs et Histoire de Politique selon Plutarque," in Lena Larsson Lovén and Agneta Strömberg (eds.), *Ancient Marriage in Myth and Reality*, 25–42, Newcastle-upon-Tyne: Cambridge Scholars Publishing.
Schultz, Celia E. 2006, *Women's Religious Activity in the Roman Republic*, Chapel Hill: University of North Carolina Press.
Schwartz, Seth (2013), "Jewish States," in Peter Fibiger Bang and Walter Scheidel (eds.), *The Oxford Handbook of the State in the Ancient Near East and Mediterranean*, 180–198, New York: Oxford University Press.
Scott, Joan W. (1986), "Gender: A Useful Category of Historical Analysis," *American Historical Review*, 77 (5): 1053–1062.
Seaford, R. (1987), "The Tragic Wedding," *Journal of Hellenic Studies*, 107: 106–130.
Sealey, Raphael (1990), *Women and Law in Classical Greece*, Chapel Hill: University of North Carolina Press.
Sebesta, Judith Lynn (1994), "Symbolism in the Costume of the Roman Woman," In Judith Lynn Sebesta and Larissa Bonfante (eds.), *The World of Roman Costume*, 46–53, Madison: University of Wisconsin Press.

Sensi, Luigi (1980/1981), "Ornatus e status sociale delle donne romane," *Annali della facoltà di lettere e filosofia Università degli studi di Perugia*, 18: 53–102.
Severy, Beth (2003), *Augustus and the Family at the Birth of the Roman Empire*, New York: Routledge.
Shaw, Brent D. (1987), "The Age of Roman Girls at Marriage: Some Reconsiderations," *Journal of Roman Studies*, 77: 30–46.
Sissa, Giulia (2008), *Sex and Sensuality in the Ancient World*, New Haven: Yale University Press.
Sivan, Hagith (2015), "Daughters as Disasters? Daughters and Fathers in Ancient Judaism," in Christian Laes, Katariina Mustakallio, and Ville Vuolanto (eds.), *Children and Family in the Late Antiquity. Life, Death and Interaction*, 289–308, Leuven: Peeters.
Skinner, Marilyn B. (1997), "Introduction," in Judith P. Hallett and Marilyn B. Skinner (eds.), *Roman Sexualities*, 3–25, Princeton, NJ: Princeton University Press.
Skinner, Marilyn B. (2014), *Sexuality in Greek and Roman Culture*, 2nd edn., Malden, MA: Wiley-Blackwell Press.
Smith, Amy C. 2005, "The Politics of Weddings at Athens: An Iconographic Assessment," *Leeds International Classical Studies*, 4: 1–32.
Smith, Anthony D. (2002), *Myths and Memoirs of the Nation*, Oxford: Oxford University Press.
Snell, Daniel (1997), *Life in the Ancient Near East*, New Haven, CT: Yale University Press.
Stafford, Emma (1999), "Plutarch on Persuasion" in S. Pomeroy (ed.), *Plutarch's Advice to the Bride and Groom and A Consolation to His Wife*, 162–172, New York: Oxford University Press.
Stafford, Emma (2013), "From the Gymnasium to the Wedding: Erôs in Athenian Art and Cult," in Ed Sanders, Chiara Thumiger, Christopher Carey, and Nick Lowe (eds.), *Erôs in Ancient Greece*, 175–208, Oxford: Oxford University Press.
State-by-State Marriage (), "Age of Consent Law," family findlaw.com. (accessed August 11, 2017).
Stieber, Mary (2004), *The Poetics of Appearance in the Attic Korai*, Austin: University of Texas Press.
Strong, Anise K. (2005), "Incest Laws and Absent Taboos in Roman Egypt," *Ancient History Bulletin*, 19 (1–2): 31–41.
Sutton, Robert F. (1981), *The Interaction between Men and Women on Attic Red-Figure Pottery*, PhD diss., University of North Carolina.
Sutton, Robert F. (1997/1998), "Nuptial Eros: The Visual Discourse of Marriage in Classical Athens," *Journal of the Walters Art Gallery*, 55/56: 27–48.
Sutton, Robert F. (2009), "Female Bathers and the Emergence of the Female Nude in Greek Art," in Cynthia Kosso and Anne Scott (eds.), *The Nature and Function of Water, Baths, Bathing and Hygiene from Antiquity through the Renaissance*, 61–86, Leiden: Brill.
Tavernise, Sabrina (2012), "In Maryland, House Passes Bill to Let Gays Wed: Maryland House Passes Same-Sex Marriage Bill," *New York Times*, February 17, 2012.
Thomas, Yan (1986a), "Le 'ventre'. Corps maternel, droit paternel," *Le genre humain*, 14: 211–236.
Thomas, Yan (1986b), "A Rome, pèeres citoyens et cité des pèeres (II siècle avant J.C.- III siècle après J.C.," in Claude Levy Strauss, Georges Duby, and Jack Goody (eds.), *Histoire de la famille*, vol. 1, 195–229, Paris: Armand Colin.
Thomsen, Ole (2002), "An Introduction to the Study of Catullus' Wedding Poems: The Ritual Drama of Catullus 62," *Classica et Mediaevalia*, 53: 255–287.
Todd, Stephen (1993), *The Shape of Athenian Law*, Oxford: Clarendon Press.

Topper, Kathryn (2012), "Approaches to Reading Attic Vases," in Sheila Dillon and Sharon L. James (eds.), *A Companion to Women in the Ancient World*, 42–152, Oxford: Wiley-Blackwell.

Torelli, Mario (1984), *Lavinio e Roma: Riti iniziatici e matrimonio tra archeologia e storia*, Rome: Quasar.

Travlos, John (1971), *Pictorial Dictionary of Ancient Athens*, London: Thames & Hudson.

Treggiari, Susan (1981), "*Contubernales* in CIL 6," *Phoenix*, 35 (1): 42–69.

Treggiari, Susan (1991), *Roman Marriage: Iusti Coniuges from the Time of Cicero to the Time of Ulpian*, Oxford: Clarendon Press.

Treggiari, Susan (1994), "Putting the Bride to Bed," *Echos du Monde Classique* 38: 311–331.

Treggiari, Susan (2007), *Terentia, Tullia and Publilia: The Women of Cicero's Family*, London: Routledge.

Tulloch, Janet H., ed. (2013), *A Cultural History of Women in Antiquity*, vol. 1, London: Bloomsbury.

Van Nortwick, T. (2008), *Imagining Men: Ideals of Masculinity in Ancient Greek Culture*, Westport, CT: Praeger.

Vatin, Claude (1970), *Recherches sur le mariage et la condition de la femme mariée a l'époque Hellénistique*, Paris: Éditions E. de Boccard.

Vérilhac, Anne-Marie and Claude Vial (1998), *Le mariage grec du VIe siècle av. J.-C. à l'époque d'Auguste*, BCH Suppl. 32, Paris: Dépositaire, De Boccard Edition.

Vernant, Jean-Pierre (1990a), *Myth and Society in Ancient Greece*, New York: Zone Books.

Vernant, Jean-Pierre (1990b), "One ... Two ... Three Eros," in David M. Halperin, John J. Winkler, and Froma I. Zeitlin (eds.), *Before Sexuality: The Construction of Erotic Experience in the Ancient Greek World*, 465–478, Princeton, NJ: Princeton University Press.

Vuolanto, Ville (2005), "Children and Asceticism: Strategies of Continuity in the Late Fourth and Early Fifth Centuries," in Katariina Mustakallio, Jussi Hanska, Hanna-Leena Sainio, and Ville Vuolanto (eds.), *Hoping for Continuity. Childhood, Education and Death in Antiquity and the Middle Ages*, 119–132, Rome: Acta Instituti Romani Finlandiae 33.

Vuolanto, Ville (2010), "Early Christian Communities as Family Networks: Fertile Virgins and Celibate Fathers," in Katariina Mustakallio and Christian Krötzl (eds.), *De Amicitia. Friendship and Social Networks in Antiquity and the Middle Ages*, 97–113, Rome: Acta Instituti Romani Finlandiae, 36.

Vuolanto, Ville (2015), *Children and Asceticism in Late Antiquity: Continuity, Family Dynamics and the Rise of Christianity*, Farnham: Ashgate.

Wagner-Hasel, B. (2010), "The Veil and Other Textiles at Weddings in Ancient Greece," in Lena Larsson Lovén and Agneta Strömberg (eds.), *Ancient Marriage in Myth and Reality*, 102–121, Newcastle-upon-Tyne: Cambridge Scholars Publishing.

Wagner, John, Paul Schwartzman, and Ned Martel (2012), "Vote on Maryland Same-sex Marriage is Close," *Washington Post*, November 8, 2012.

Wasdin, Katherine (2014), "Honorius Triumphant: Poetry and Politics in Claudian's Wedding Poems," *Classical Philology*, 109 (1): 48–64.

Wasdin, Katherine (2018), *Eros at Dusk: Ancient Wedding and Love Poetry*, Oxford: Oxford University Press.

Watson, Alan, ed. (1985), *The Digest of Justinian*, Philadelphia: University of Pennsylvania Press.

Westbrook, Raymond (1985), "Biblical and Cuneiform Law Codes," *Revue Biblique*, 92: 247–265.

Westbrook, Raymond (2003), *A History of Ancient Near Eastern Law*, 2 vols., Leiden: Brill.

Wheeler, Arthur L. (1930), "Tradition in the Epithalamium," *American Journal of Philology*, 51: 204–223.
Whittaker, Helene (2010), "A Philosophical Marriage: Porphyry's Letter to Marcella," in Lena Larsson Lovén and Agneta Strömberg (eds.), *Ancient Marriage in Myth and Reality*, 43–54, Newcastle-upon-Tyne: Cambridge Scholar Publishing.
Wildfell, Helen (2015), *Consensuality: Navigating Feminism, Gender, and Boundaries towards Loving Relationships*, Portland, OR: Microcosm Publishing.
Williams, Gordon (1958), "Some Aspects of Roman Marriage Ceremonies and Ideals," *Journal of Roman Studies*, 48: 16–29.
Williams, R. Deryck (repr. 1996), *Virgil: Aeneid I–VI*, Bristol: Bristol Classical Press.
Winkler John J. (2002), "Double Consciousness in Sappho's Lyrics," in Laura McClure (ed.), *Sexuality and Gender in the Classical World*, 39–71, Malden, MA: Wiley-Blackwell.
Wiseman, Timothy P. (1985), *Catullus and His World: A Reappraisal*, Cambridge: Cambridge University Press.
Wiseman, Timothy P. (2004), *The Myths of Rome*, Exeter: University of Exeter Press.
Wistrand, Erik, ed. and trans. (1976), *The so-called Laudatio Turiae*, Lund: Acta Universitatis Gothoburgensis.
Wood, Ian (1997), "The Transmission of Ideas," in Leslie Webster and Michelle Brown (eds.), *The Transformation of the Roman World AD 400–900*, 111–126, London: British Museum Press.
Wyke, Maria (2002), "Mistress and Metaphor in Augustan Elegy," in Laura McClure (ed.), *Sexuality and Gender in the Classical World*, 193–219, Malden, MA: Wiley-Blackwell.
Yiftach-Firanko, Uri (2003), *Marriage and Marital Arrangements: A History of the Greek Marriage Document in Egypt. 4th century BCE–4th century CE, Münchener Beiträge zur Papyrusforschung und antiken Rechtsgeschichte*, 93, Munich: C. H. Beck.
Zeiner-Carmichael, Noelle K. (2007), "Perfecting the Ideal: Molding Roman Women in Statius' *Silvae*," *Arethusa*, 40 (2): 165–181.
Zeitlin, Froma I. (1990), "Playing the Other: Theater, Theatricality and the Feminine in Greek Drama," in John J. Winkler and Froma I. Zeitlin (eds.), *Nothing to Do with Dionysus: Athenian Drama in Its Social Context*, 63–96, Princeton, NJ: Princeton University Press.
Zeitlin, Froma I. (1996), *Playing the Other: Gender and Society in Classical Greek Literature*, Chicago: University of Chicago Press.
Zipes, Jack D. (2012), *The Irresistible Fairy Tale : The Cultural and Social History of a Genre*, Princeton, NJ: Princeton University Press.

INDEX

abduction marriage 75
Achilles 5, 9, 40, 42, 43, 44, 66
Achilles Tatius 23, 24, 34
actresses 127–8
adultery 16, 65, 68, 73, 96, 114, 116, 120, 121, 122–3 (*see also moicheia*)
Aeneas 10, 11, 12, 13, 14, 48, 49, 51, 81, 87, 148–9
Aeschines 115
Aeschylus 7, 38, 45, 101, 102, 143
Agamemnon 7, 9, 40, 44, 66, 148
Agrippina the Younger 18, 19
Alexander Severus 122
Alexander the Great 62, 69
Anacreon 44
Andromache 4, 5, 6, 11, 29, 43, 135, 137
Antipater of Tarsus 38, 59, 62
Antonine Constitution 74
Antoninus Pius 122
Appian 83, 141
Appius Claudius 119
Apuleius 84
aqua et igni 54
Archilochus 38
Aristophanes 10, 40, 41
Aristotle 114, 116
Arnobius 49, 50, 54
arranged marriages 95
Arria 20, 138–41
artistic representations *see* representations of marriage
asceticism 86
Aspasia of Miletus 68
Assyria 65
Athens
    Athenian law 66–8, 113, 114
    marriage requirements 78, 79
    wedding rituals 26–31
augur 32
Augustine 49, 85, 86
Augustus 16, 17, 24, 69, 70, 73, 87, 93, 119, 120–2, 137, 138
Ausonius 48, 53

auspices 32, 47, 50, 52
Austen, Jane 1

Babylonian law 63, 64, 65
bachelorhood 59
barbarians 20, 77
beauty 131, 132
betrothal 25–6, 67, 72, 77–8, 126–8
brides 3, 7, 24, 130, 131
    age at marriage 24–5, 66, 72, 78, 94, 130, 133, 134
    Athens 24, 26–31
    fertility 28, 36, 87, 120, 131
    hair dedication 37, 38–9
    hair plaiting 50
    physical health 134
    Rome 31–3, 50
    Sparta 35

Caligula 16, 18
Callimachus 44, 45
Calpurnia
    wife of Julius Caesar 16
    wife of Pliny the Younger 83, 134, 141
Castricius, Titus 62
Catholicism xiii
Cato 52, 53, 118, 143
Catullus 45, 53, 54, 96, 131, 132
celibacy 2, 9, 74
chastity 20, 25, 50, 84, 99, 100, 119, 122, 131, 132, 135
Christianity xii–xiii, 24, 35, 74, 75, 84, 85, 122, 132, 142
    Christian marriages 85–6, 87, 88
Cicero 25, 32, 48, 51, 83, 120, 143
Cimon 67
citizenship 61–2, 66, 70, 74, 79
civil ceremonies xiv
Claudian 132
Claudius 18, 19, 50, 70
Cleopatra 16
coemptio 31, 72, 73, 79
Cohen, David 114, 121

comedies 10, 126
Commodus 122
Concordia 21, 33
concordia 33, 34, 144
concubines 68, 74, 85, 113, 126
confarreatio 31, 54–6, 72, 73, 79, 80
consensuality 89–96
consent xii, 74, 87, 89–96, 129
Constantine 74, 75, 122
contracts 26, 64, 79, 82–3, 87
contubernium 71
conubium 70, 79
Cornelia 15, 16
cosmological narratives 97–105, 108–11
Council of Trent xiii
courtship 23–6
Crassus, Marcus 61
Crete 113
cultural values 15, 125, 127, 130, 131, 134

Danaids 102, 105
Daphne 105, 106
Daube, D. 122
death 141–2
Deinarkhos 68
deities *see* gods/goddesses
Demosthenes 113, 114
dextrarum iunctio 34, 48, 144, 145
Dido 11, 12, 13, 48, 49, 51
Dionysius of Halicarnassus 55, 81, 87, 118
diplomatic marriages 60
divination 40–1, 50–2
divorce xiii, 1, 15–16, 55–6, 68, 79
domina 96
Domitian 55
Doric cities 113–18
dowries 26, 64, 67, 78–9
Draco/Drakon 68, 114

ecclesiastical courts xiii
Egypt 25, 69, 82
ekdosis 26, 28, 42, 67, 69, 82
elites 1, 10, 24, 37, 60, 70, 72, 78, 79, 83–4, 137
endogamic unions 25
engagement *see* betrothal
engye 25, 26, 69, 78, 79, 126
Enlightenment ideals xiv
epaulia 26, 28, 31, 46
epidikasia 67
epikleros 67, 93

epithalamia 6–7, 44–5, 46, 48, 54, 96, 129–30, 131, 132
Erinna 130
Etruscan kings 14, 15, 123
Euripides 7–9, 30, 40, 135, 138
extramarital unions 3, 16, 96, 113–15 (*see also* adultery; *moicheia*)
    Doric cities 115–16
    pederastic love 114
    Rome 118–24

family economy 89–96
    household tasks 135–8
family interests xii, 77, 78, 83, 87
feminine ideals 14, 25, 52, 85, 120, 127, 130, 131, 132, 133, 135, 137–8
feminism xv, 89
Ferrari, Gloria 26
fertility 28, 36, 87, 120, 131
Fescennina iocatio 53
Festus 50, 53, 56, 80
fidelity 1, 113, 114, 118, 123, 133, 135, 138, 140–1, 144
Flamen Dialis 31, 55, 56, 80–1, 88
Flaminica Dialis 80–1, 88
flammeum 32, 33, 50
Frazer, James George 101
Freud, Sigmund 101
funeral monuments 20–2, 142, 144 (*see also* sarcophagi; tombstones)
Furies 40, 51

Gaius (jurist) 55, 56
Galba 16
gamelia 31, 46
Gamelion 38
gamos 26, 28, 126
gender norms 125, 126, 127, 131, 132, 146
    feminine ideals 14, 25, 52, 85, 120, 127, 130, 131, 132, 133, 135, 137–8
    male dominance 125, 131, 133, 134, 143, 146 (*see also* patriarchy)
    male perspectives 108–11
    women's roles xv, 3, 133, 134, 135–41
Genesis 97
Germans 20
Glazebrook, Alison 94
globalization xiv
gods/goddesses 1, 4, 37
    Aphrodite 9, 27, 35, 38, 39, 40, 41, 52, 98, 101, 102, 142
    Apollo 43, 105, 106, 138

Aries 130
Artemis 9, 27, 38, 39, 40, 42, 52, 105
Athena 40, 42, 98, 105
bedroom rituals 46
Ceres 84
Chthonie 42
Concordia 21, 33, 144
confarreatio 31, 54–6
cosmological narratives 97–105
Demeter 47, 105
Di coniugales/deities of marriage 49
Dionysus 9, 35
divination 40–1, 50–2
Eros/Erotes 27, 35, 41, 44, 46, 97, 98, 101
Eukleia 40
Greek weddings 37–8, 56–7
Harmonia 38
Hecate 84
Hera 3, 11, 27, 35, 37, 38, 41, 44, 45, 47, 52
Hestia 105
Hymen 44, 51, 53, 130, 131
Iphinoe 39
Juno 3, 48–9, 50, 51, 53
Jupiter 55, 56, 80, 87
Leto 47
loutrophoroi 26, 30, 41–2, 46
Mars 13, 130
Mutunus 49
Nike 40
Nymphe 42
Pan 42
Peitho 38, 52
phallic deities 49
polytheism 84
Pothos 38
pre-wedding dedications 38–40
Priapus 49
priestly personnel 47
procession to the groom's house 43–4
proteleia: pre-wedding sacrifices 37, 40
Roman weddings 47–57
Venus 11, 31, 35, 48, 49, 50, 81, 130
Vesta 54, 123, 124
wedding feast 42
wedding hymn 44–5
wedding sacrifice at the groom's house 45
Zeus 6, 37, 38, 40, 41, 42, 44, 47, 52, 98, 105, 109
Gortyn 113, 117–18
Greek city-states 65–6, 113
    Doric cities 113–18
    Ionic cities 113

Greek comedies 10, 126
Greek cultural norms 66
Greek marriages 4–10, 66–8, 78, 79, 93, 94
Greek myths *see* myths
Greek tragedies 7
grooms 3, 7, 24, 130
Grubbs, Judith Evans 82
guardians 79

hair dedication 37, 38–9
hair plaiting 50
Hammurabi's Law Code 63, 64
happiness 1
Harlow, Mary 78
Hasmonean dynasty 60
Hattusilis 60
Helen of Troy 4, 5, 41, 43, 44, 45, 47, 131, 135
Hellenic culture 66, 69
Hellenistic world 69
Herod, King of Judea 60
Herodotus 4, 39
Hersch, Karen Klaiber 95
Hesiod 6, 8, 42, 97–9, 101, 103, 108–9, 110, 133, 134, 135, 143
hetairai 113
heteronormative ideologies 126, 127, 140
hieros gamos 99, 101, 102, 103
Homer 66
    Iliad 4–5, 38, 43, 135
    Odyssey 5–6, 37, 39, 42, 99–101, 135 (*see also* Odysseus)
homicide 68, 75, 114
Honorius 132
households 60, 66, 70
    household tasks 135–8
hymenaios 44
Hyperborean maidens 39
Hyperides 129

idealized representations 6, 126, 127, 130, 131, 132, 133, 135, 137–8, 142–4
incest 25
inheritance 93
intermarriage 24, 33
Ionic cities 113
Isaeus 129

Jerome 86
John Chrysostom 86
Julia (daughter of Augustus) 16
Julian Law *see leges Iuliae*
Julius Caesar 16, 61, 143

Justinian 123
   Digest 120–1
Juvenal 122

Kahlos, Maijastina 85
katachysmata 30, 45
kinship groups xv
Klytemnestra 5, 7, 40

Lares 53–4
Laudatio Turiae 15, 83, 142
Laurence, Ray 78
Lavinia 11, 81, 87
Law Code of Gortyn 113, 117
legal formalities 54–6
legal marriage 62, 79
   Athens and Greece 65
   Hellenistic world 69
   late antiquity 74–5
   Near East 62–5
   Rome 69–74
leges Iuliae 16
   lex Iulia de adulteriis coercendis 73, 74, 119, 120, 121, 122
   lex Iulia de maritandis ordinibus 24, 70, 120
legitimate children 2, 10, 14, 16, 24, 26, 31, 49, 60, 62, 66, 68, 131, 146
lex Iulia see leges Iuliae
lex Minicia 70
lex Papia Poppea nuptialis 120
lex Romana Visigothorum 122
Lex Voconia 93
LGBTQ movements xv
literary representations *see* representations of marriage
Livia 16, 17, 19, 137
Livy 13, 14, 33, 53, 81, 87, 137, 138
Loraux, Nicole 109
loutrophoroi 26, 30, 41–2, 46
Lucan 47
Lucian 40, 45
Lucretia 14, 119, 137, 138
Lycurgus 116
Lygdamus 95, 96

Macrobius 50
Majorianus 123
male dominance 125, 131, 133, 134, 143, 146 (*see also* patriarchy)
manus 31, 55, 56, 70, 72, 74, 78, 79–80, 120, 126, 127
Marcella 85, 88

Marcia 52, 53
Marcus Aurelius 122
marital love 20
marriage
   age at marriage 24–5, 66, 72, 78, 94, 130, 133, 134
   as education 85, 133–5
   Christian marriage 85–6, 87, 88
   civic importance 59–60, 75, 81
   cosmic and human marriages 97–105, 108–11
   governmental intervention 93
   Greek marriages 4–10, 66–8,78, 79, 93, 94
   happiness and 1, 87
   law and *see* legal marriage
   longevity 143
   male perspective 108–11
   purpose of 24, 27, 87
   Roman marriages 10–22, 69–74, 78, 79–81, 93, 94, 127
   state institution 60–2, 75, 146
   value placed on 7
marriage bed 99–100
marriage chamber 100–1
marriage contracts 26, 64, 79, 82–3, 87
marriage rites xiii–xiv, 2–3 (*see also* wedding rituals)
married life 133–41
Melania (Elder and Younger) 86
Menander 24, 25, 26, 126, 127
meretrices 96, 127
Messalina 18, 50, 52
Miltiades 67
misogyny 133, 143
moicheia 114–15, 117–18
monogamy 16, 20, 66, 70, 77
moral values 60, 75, 90, 93, 120, 137
Musonius Rufus, Gaius 59, 62
myths 7, 107–8
   cosmological narratives 97–105, 108–11

Near Eastern Codes 62–5, 117
Neoplatonism 85
Nero 18, 19, 52
Numa 14, 15, 116

Odysseus 2, 5, 6, 37, 43, 99, 100, 101, 111, 148, 151, 171
Oedipus 7, 104
Olson, Kelly 94
Ovid 13, 16, 50, 51, 54, 105
Oxyrhynchus 82

Paetus 20, 138
Pandora 6, 9, 42, 109, 110
Pantel, Pauline Schmitt 83
Papinius 121
papyri 82
parental control xiii, xiv
paterfamilias 70, 72, 120
patriarchy xii, xv, 77, 125, 126, 130, 131
Paulina, Fabia Aconia 84–5
Paulinus of Nola 132
Pausanius 39
pederastic love 114
Peloponnesian War 10, 41, 67, 127
Penelope 2, 5, 6, 42, 43, 99, 100, 101, 111, 135, 137, 148, 151, 171
Pericles 24, 67, 68
Persephone 105, 107
Petronius 20
phallic deities 49
phratriai 31, 46
Pindar 44, 45
Plato 42, 120
Plautus 26, 54, 127, 132
Pliny the Elder 15, 51, 53, 56
Pliny the Younger 20, 25, 83, 134–5, 138–41, 144
Plotinus 85, 88
Plutarch 3, 10, 13, 35, 38, 41, 42, 44, 45, 47, 50, 52, 53, 54, 55, 56, 80, 83, 85, 87, 93, 106–7, 113, 116, 118
poetry 28
polygamy 77
polytheism 84
Pompeia 16
Pompeius Magnus, Gnaeus 61
Pontifex Maximus 31, 55, 80, 123
pornai 113
Porphyry of Tyre, Pomponius 85, 86
Praetextus, Publius Vettius Agorius 84, 85
presents 78–9
priests/priestesses 47
proaulia 26
processions 28, 29, 30, 31, 32, 33, 41, 43–4, 128
Prometheus 109
pronuba 31, 33, 47
property 60, 74, 80, 82, 87
prostitutes 24, 70, 74, 96, 113, 114, 121, 122, 127, 162
proteleia 37, 40
Protestantism xiii
Ptolemies 25, 69

Ramses II 60
rape 13–14, 103–8
  Sabine women 31, 33, 50, 51, 52, 81, 106–8
Reformation xiii
regina sacrorum 80
remarriage 16, 25, 77
representations of marriage 125–6
  betrothal 126–8
  idealized representations 6, 126, 127, 130, 131, 132, 133, 135, 137–8, 142–4
  married life 133–41
  weddings 128–32
rex sacrorum 55, 80
rings 26
ritual bathing 41–2
Roman marriages 10–22, 69–74, 78, 79–81, 93, 94, 127
romantic love 24, 25, 127
Rome
  Augustan Age 16
  early Empire 16–22
  extramarital unions 118–24
  First Triumvirate 61
  founding myths 11, 13, 14, 24, 81
  polytheism 84
  Regal period 14
  Republic 14, 15, 69, 72, 73, 120, 127, 138
  wedding rituals 31–4
Romulus 10, 13, 14, 15, 81, 118, 149
royal marriages 60
Rufus of Ephesus 134

Sabine women 31, 33, 50, 51, 52, 81, 106–8
sacraments xiii
sacrifice
  self-sacrifice 8–9, 138, 139, 141
  wedding rituals 37, 40, 45, 46, 53
same-sex unions
  marriage 2, 18, 52, 90, 92, 95
  pederastic love 114
Sappho 6–7, 28, 35, 43, 44, 45, 128, 130, 131
sarcophagi 20–1, 34, 48, 49, 53, 145
Scaevola 54
secularism xiii, xiv
self-control 134
Semonides 131
Seneca 53
Servius 54

sex workers 113
sexual freedom 113, 114
sexual impropriety 68, 73
sexual preferences 6
sexual relations xi, xiv
slaves 20, 24, 61, 70, 71, 75, 77, 86, 88, 117
social status xii, 2
soldiers 70, 71, 82
Solon 61, 66, 68
songs 28
Sophocles 7
sophrosyne 134, 135
Sparta 10, 35, 93, 113, 115–17
spinning 14, 52, 53, 135, 136
sponsalia 25, 26, 72, 78, 126, 127
state institutions 60–2
Statius 132, 144
Stesichorus 43, 44
stipulatio 126, 127
Stoic philosophers 59
Suetonius 95, 121, 137
suicide 13, 14, 20, 119, 137, 138, 139
symposia 113

tabulae nuptiales 77, 82, 87
Tacitus 20, 50, 52, 121, 122
"Talasio/Talassio" 47, 52–3
Tarquin family 14, 119, 123, 137
Tertullian 49
Theocritus/Theokritos 41, 45, 47, 131
Theodosius 74
Thesmophoria 102, 103
Thucydides 10, 41
Tiberius 16, 56, 95
tombstones 84
torches 51, 52
tragedies 7
Trophonios 41
Tullia 25
Turia 15, 83, 141, 142–3
Twelve Tables 69, 70

Ulpian 55, 56, 71, 73
univira 86
urns 22
US law 90, 94, 95
usus 72, 79

Valerius Maximus 16, 83, 118, 141
Valerius Pinianius 86
Varro 53, 54

Vernant, Jean-Pierre 109
Vestal Virgins 2, 50, 123–4
Virgil/Vergil (*Aeneid*) 11–13, 14, 49, 51
 (*see also* Aeneas)
virginity 1, 2, 39, 54, 105, 119, 130
Visigoths 122
Vuolanto, Ville 77

weaving 5, 135
wedding rituals 2, 3, 23
 aqua et igni 54
 bedroom rituals 46
 bridal preparations 38–40, 50
 confarreatio 31, 54–6
 deities *see* gods/goddesses
 divination 40–1, 50–2
 entering the house: thresholds 106–7, 133–5
 epithalamia 6–7, 44–5, 46, 48, 54, 96, 129–30, 131, 132
 Fescennina iocatio 53
 Greek weddings 26–31, 37–47, 56–7
 Juno Pronuba 21, 48–9
 katachysmata 30, 45
 Lares 53–4
 literary representations 128–32
 loutrophoroi 26, 30, 41–2, 46
 pre-wedding dedications 38–40
 priestly personnel 47
 procession to the groom's house 43–4, 128
 proteleia: pre-wedding sacrifices 37, 40
 public ceremony 129
 ritual bathing 41–2
 ritual variants 34–5
 Roman weddings 31–4, 47–57
 songs and poetry 28
 "Talasio/Talassio" 47, 52–3
 torches 51, 52
 transferral, transformation, seduction, and reproduction 35–6
 wedding feast 42
 wedding hymn 43, 44–5
 wedding sacrifice at the groom's house 45
Wildfell, Helen 89
Wolff, Hans Julius 115
women
 feminine ideals 14, 25, 52, 85, 120, 127, 130, 131, 132, 133, 135, 137–8
 fidelity expected of 113, 114, 118, 119, 123, 133, 135, 138, 140–1
 gender roles xv, 3, 133, 134, 135–41, 162

household tasks 135–8
status 65, 93, 132
wool-working 3, 10, 15, 52, 53, 83, 131, 135–7, 138
written evidence 2

Xenophon 3, 93, 113, 116, 134, 135, 137

Zeitlin, Froma 101, 102, 103
Zenobios 44